DEAD DROP

The True Story of Oleg Penkovsky
and the Cold War's Most Dangerous Operation

Jeremy Duns

**SIMON &
SCHUSTER**

London · New York · Sydney · Toronto · New Delhi

A CBS COMPANY

First published in Great Britain by Simon & Schuster UK Ltd, 2013
This paperback edition published by Simon & Schuster UK Ltd, 2014

A CBS company

1 3 5 7 9 10 8 6 4 2

Simon & Schuster UK Ltd
1st Floor
222 Gray's Inn Road
London WC1X 8HB

www.simonandschuster.co.uk

Simon & Schuster Australia,
Sydney

Simon & Schuster India,
New Delhi

A CIP catalogue record for this book is available from the British Library

Paperback ISBN: 978-1-84983-929-7
eBook ISBN: 978-1-84983-930-3

Typeset in the UK by Hewer Text UK Ltd, Edinburgh
Printed in the UK by CPI Group (UK) Ltd, Croydon CR0 4YY

For Johanna

CONTENTS

PART I

Spy of the Century

The Tallest Building in Moscow

22 October 1962.

As Oleg Penkovsky emerged from the basement cafeteria on to the chill of Gorky Street, he heard a voice calling out his name. He looked up to see Sergei Nasedkin on the other side of the road, waving at him through the traffic. Surprised, Penkovsky raised a hand in return, and Nasedkin strode towards him, briskly sidestepping a mud-smeared delivery truck and kicking up a cloud of startled pigeons in the process.

'Hello, Sergei!' Penkovsky said once Nasedkin had reached the pavement and they had embraced. 'Is your canteen closed today?'

Nasedkin was a KGB officer, and they rarely ventured out for lunch. Penkovsky was a colonel in the GRU – military intelligence – but despite the often bitter rivalry between the agencies the two men had remained friends since their schooldays and still went drinking together, although their last bout had not been for several months.

Nasedkin laughed at Penkovsky's gentle jibe. 'I'm actually here to see you, Oleg,' he said. 'I was just on my way to your office when I spotted you emerging from your hiding place.'

Penkovsky was suddenly conscious of the smell of cabbage soup and sweat clinging to his clothes. With his rank, he should really have been eating at the Baku or the Praga, but he had a fondness for greasy food

– and besides, at the moment he couldn't afford to dine out anywhere more expensive.

'It's about work, then?' he said, trying not to seem concerned.

'Not really,' said Nasedkin. 'It's that passport you applied for – it came through. Fedorchuk was going to send one of his messenger boys to deliver it, but I overheard him giving the order and asked to do the honours myself.' He gestured elaborately with his hands as though he were a magician reappearing after a vanishing act. 'And here I am.'

Penkovsky nodded, a little dazed at the news. He had applied for an external passport months ago and had heard nothing back despite repeated enquiries. As a result, he had become convinced that the KGB didn't trust him enough to grant him one. He was immensely relieved they had finally come round.

'It's wonderful to see you again, Sergei,' he said. 'Come back to my office and give me the passport there. I'd love to hear all your news, and you can watch Kennedy with us – we've set up a television on the top floor.' The American President was due to give a speech in the early hours of the morning about a 'grave international crisis', and everyone had been ordered to stay behind to watch it. Many were speculating that the speech would be about Cuba.

'I'd love to,' said Nasedkin, walking in step with him, 'though I'm not sure I can stay until the speech as I've got a lot of paperwork to catch up on – you know what it's like. How are you feeling, by the way? I heard you'd been ill.'

Penkovsky smiled wanly. 'Is there nothing you lot don't know about? Yes, I was in hospital last month with a skin problem. It was painful, but it cleared up in a few days.' In fact, it had taken three weeks and had been an excruciating experience, as he had developed blisters on his buttocks – but there was no need to tell Sergei that.

A sudden gust of wind blew up from the street, lifting leaves from the pavement until they swirled about the two men. Sergei turned the lapel of his overcoat to shield himself against it. It was a beautiful coat, Penkovsky noticed – it draped perfectly on his frame and looked brand new. Penkovsky prided himself on his appearance and had a collection of

Western-style suits and silk shirts, but his coat was four years old and the sleeves were shiny and starting to bobble around the cuffs. These KGB bastards are so well paid, he thought. Sergei's a year younger than me and several ranks lower in their system, but he's still able to afford flashy clothes, keep in shape – no doubt his apartment is bigger, too.

When the wind had subsided Penkovsky started to walk back down the street, with Sergei directly behind him. A car suddenly veered up to the pavement, a polished black Chaika, and a rear door sprang open. 'Oleg!' a voice called from the back seat.

What was this? Penkovsky peered into the car's interior and glimpsed an outstretched hand. He leaned forward and felt a sharp shove in his back, which sent him tumbling on to the rear seat. The door thudded shut behind him and the car jerked forward, the sound of the engine reverberating in his skull.

Penkovsky lifted his face from the cold vinyl seat and righted himself. The man who had lured him into the car was looking down at him. A felt hat obscured most of his face, and Penkovsky could only make out a thin mouth and the tip of a fleshy nose.

'What the hell's this?' he said. 'Don't you know who I am?'

The man's nostrils flared. 'Be quiet, traitor.'

On hearing the final word, Penkovsky slumped back against the upholstery. So this was it. The dreaded day had finally come. He felt the remains of the shashlik he had eaten for lunch gurgling in his stomach, but was surprised to find how calm he felt, as though nothing had changed. But everything had. Everything he had experienced before this moment was now meaningless, unreachable. He would never again have lunch in that cafeteria, or see his office, or walk down this street . . .

A second Chaika had now come up alongside them. Penkovsky caught a glimpse in the driver's rear-view mirror of Sergei brushing down his overcoat as he stepped into a third car that had pulled up just behind. What a fool he was to have fallen for the story about the passport. He should have seen through it, but they had chosen wisely in sending Sergei. He had trusted him unthinkingly.

Penkovsky closed his eyes and let the idea of death sink in. There was no question about it, of course: Popov had faced the firing squad, and he would, too. He thought of Vera. He had met her during the war, when she had been just fourteen years old and he'd been a young officer in the Red Army. Gapanovich had invited him to his home to meet his wife and daughter and there she had been, smiling with her flashing eyes, promising so much. He had married her after the war, and had never been happier than on his wedding day, but their passion had dissolved soon after the birth of their first daughter, Galina, and he had turned to drinking and other women. If silence was broken between them now, it was mostly to fight. 'You've ruined my life!' she had yelled at him the night before last, after he had returned home at three o'clock in the morning smelling of another woman and waking baby Mariana.

Well, now he had definitely ruined it, and the guilt made him nauseous. She didn't deserve to be a traitor's widow: in a country where one's loyalty to the state affected every aspect of daily life, it was a fate worse than death. And his mother, his poor mother – how would she cope? He hoped Vera would be able to shield her from as much of what would be said about him as possible, for her sake. He thought, too, of their two daughters, and willed himself not to cry. He was a sentimental man and cried easily, but he would not cry now, not in the presence of another.

He also had a momentary pang of pity for the Englishman, Wynne. Perhaps the Queen could intervene and persuade them to let him go, he thought, and then dismissed the idea. No, the British would do nothing. They were scarcely any better than these fools. 'Oh don't worry, Oleg, we'll get you out in time, you and your family, we'll send a submarine, we'll pay you, handsomely . . .' Empty promises – he had just been left out to dry, waiting for the KGB to close in and pick him up.

He opened his eyes, catching sight of a bin outside one of the ministries as he did so. It reminded him of his idea, formulated over two years ago now, when he had first thought to contact the CIA. If you *whisked away twenty of those bins from the street in the middle of the night, you could reconstruct replicas of them with false bottoms, and inside you could place miniature nuclear weapons attached to timers. Put them back on the street, then take the first plane out of Sheremetyevo and wait for the explosion. Moscow knocked out in a single blow. Repeat the process in a few other cities and the Cold War could be ended in a matter of minutes. Penkovsky had worked out all the details, including which buildings to target, and had explained the plan to his handlers, but they had never acted on it. It was almost as if they didn't want to defeat the Soviet Union. Now, of course, there was no chance to carry it through.*

It was all over, but there was no point in wringing his hands about it. He'd had a good run, better than could be expected. He hadn't destroyed them all in a flash of blinding light, but he had damaged them irretrievably, of that there was no question – he'd told the Americans and the British everything he knew, about rockets, weapons, installations, agents; and photographed every document he could lay his hands on. There was nothing they could do about any of it now. Yes, and he had travelled, as he'd always wanted to. He smiled at the memory of the Moulin Rouge, and of the cabaret girl in London – what had her name been? Zeph, that was it. As the car turned into Dzerzhinsky Square and the familiar yellow façade came into view, Penkovsky closed his eyes again, and remembered Zeph . . .

*

Is this how it happened? I've imagined many details in the above scenario, but I think events much along these lines occurred. According to several Russian accounts, including a documentary made by the KGB for training purposes, Colonel Oleg Penkovsky was arrested on 22 October 1962 after being greeted on the street by a friend who told him his passport was ready. For eighteen months, Penkovsky had worked as an agent for MI6 and the CIA, who gave him the codename HERO. He photographed thousands of top-secret documents and met with his handlers for hours at a time, pouring out everything he knew about Soviet society, strategy, weapons systems and more.

But what happened after his arrest? A wealth of documents about Penkovsky have been declassified in recent years, but information is notably lacking from the Russian side. However, considering subsequent events, I imagine it went something like this . . .

★

In his wood-panelled office on the fourth floor of the Lubyanka, General Oleg Gribanov, head of the KGB's counter-intelligence directorate, peered at his chief investigator over rimless spectacles.

'I want more on Penkovsky,' he said. 'The General Secretary has decided to announce the trial soon, but we need something much more definite to present to him. Today.'

Alexander Zagvozdin didn't register any reaction: he was used to being given orders at impossibly short notice and knew there was nothing more likely to anger his boss than to question that they could be carried out. He glanced at the cache of enlarged photographs spread out across the baize field of Gribanov's desk, showing the microfilms, miniature cameras and radio transmitter they had found in the traitor's home.

'It's not enough,' said Gribanov, catching his look. 'This isn't about his guilt – we've known that for long enough – but who he was working for.'

Zagvozdin understood the point: unless they could prove that the CIA and MI6 had run Penkovsky, the trial would be a washout. The Americans and the British would simply deny all involvement, and probably claim that the Soviets had simply concocted the physical evidence to create a scandal – as indeed they could easily have done.

'What do you have in mind, General?' he asked. He knew he would not have been summoned here to ask for his own views.

Gribanov gave a sly smile. 'Let's restart the operation for them.'

'I don't follow,' said Zagvozdin. 'Send him out again, you mean?'

Gribanov shook his head. 'No, they'd smell that at once. But we can do it another way. They suspect we've arrested him, of course, but they don't know it for certain. So they'll be sitting at their desks, hoping he's simply been inconvenienced or is lying low, waiting for the control signal from him to make contact again. The question is: what form does that signal take? How is it activated, and what do they do when it is?'

Zagvozdin understood. If they could draw one or more of Penkovsky's handlers into the open, catching them directly in an act of espionage, all subsequent denials of involvement would be seen to be hollow – and they would have snatched a propaganda victory from the jaws of operational defeat. There was only one snag.

'We tried that before,' Zagvozdin said. 'But they didn't bite.'

Gribanov frowned. 'You're not your usual sharp self this morning, Alexander. The situation was different then. We knew the signal procedure, but we didn't know what their response would be, or the location of his dead drop. So if they did react to us, we might simply have missed it. But now we have Penkovsky in our hands and he has told us about his drop, nothing should be simpler than to discover the missing part of the puzzle.'

Zagvozdin gave a curt bow as he left the room. He'd show Gribanov how sharp he was – he gave himself twenty minutes to extract the intelligence and have it on the general's desk.

★

Penkovsky shivered involuntarily as the man in the felt hat entered the cell. It was partly from the cold, and partly from fear: something told him the investigator was about to do something very unpleasant. This was the first time he had visited him in his cell, instead of having guards bring him to his office, and he was alone.

Penkovsky, seated on the iron bed, tried to focus on the man's face to keep his mind off the pain in his stomach. He had lost a stone since his arrest ten days earlier, and felt both disgusted with and ashamed of his own body, skeletal beneath the dungarees and the thin blanket he had draped over himself. They had stopped allowing him to use the lavatory down the hall after the first day, and his own dried excrement was now smeared across the far corner of the cell's floor. He had become afraid to defecate, leading to constipation, and he felt weak, dizzy and nauseous – not only was he deprived of food and sleep, but also the cell was constantly lit by a bare bulb hanging above the bed, giving the eau-de-Nil walls a sickly sheen.

And yet, beneath the cold and the hunger, he had felt strangely exhilarated. Was this it? Was this all they were going to throw at him? When he had made the decision to contact Western intelligence he had known it was the point of no return, and had tried to imagine the worst that could happen if he were caught. Uppermost in his mind had been this place, the KGB's notorious headquarters. The Lubyanka was known as 'the tallest building in Moscow' on account of its floors of cellars, where executions were carried out by a single shot to the back of the head without warning. He had also heard of the tortures that went on in the cells, including a special room filled with transparent plastic pipes. Anyone who refused to break was placed in the centre of the room, and dozens of starved rats were funnelled through the pipes. If they still refused to talk, a valve would be unblocked and a single rat would be released into the room. Then another. Then another. When the prisoner finally broke – and they always did – high-pressure water hoses would be used to push the rats back into the pipes.

Penkovsky had had nightmares about this scenario for months, and in the first couple of days after his arrest had lived in constant dread of it happening. But they hadn't used the rats on him, or tortured him in any other way. The guards had spat 'Traitor' at him at every opportunity and he'd received a few kicks to the ribs, but the physical assaults had been minimal and had been conspicuous in their absence from his face. He had soon realised why: they were going to put him on public trial, and it wouldn't do if the world's press saw he had been mistreated.

Every few hours, he was awoken for interrogation. They had shown him the equipment they had found in his desk, as well as photographs of him using the transmitter in his living room, taken from a camera hidden in the ceiling. He remembered that the previous winter his upstairs neighbour, a steel trust executive, had announced he was taking a holiday to the Caucasus with his family. A young couple had moved in the following week, and had introduced themselves as the man's nephew and his wife. KGB officers, of course. That had been almost a year ago. They had been watching him all that time. No doubt listening, too, to his arguments with Vera . . . This in turn made him wonder if she had known – they could have taken her aside and asked for her cooperation or face the consequences. That might explain the coincidence of the holiday she had taken with the children just before he had been admitted to hospital. No doubt his blisters had not been a coincidence, either, and they had spiked his coffee at the office or something similar to bring them on. Perhaps Vera had drugged him. 'You've ruined my life,' she had spat out, and then a curious look had crossed her face, as though she had said something she shouldn't have done. At the time he had taken it that she had felt the remark had been too cruel, but perhaps not. Perhaps she had known he was a traitor and had simply been playing a part until he was arrested, 'assisting the authorities with their enquiries', as they put it in Pravda.

On being shown the evidence against him, Penkovsky had immediately signed a letter promising to cooperate and had even offered to turn triple agent, suggesting that as the Americans and British trusted him he could be sent back to them and pretend that nothing had happened. When that idea had been rejected, he had confessed – but not fully. He had realised that although they knew he was a traitor they had very little information about precisely what he had done, and had no way of knowing if he was telling them the complete story or not. As a result, he had pushed his luck as far as it could go. He had minimised just how much he had revealed, and the length of time he had been involved with the Americans and British, in the hope that he might be spared. He knew in his heart that there was no real chance of it, but he couldn't help trying for it nonetheless. And if they realised what he was up to, so what? They couldn't execute him twice . . .

'We need your signal.'

Penkovsky snapped out of his reverie.

'What signal?'

'The signal to contact your handlers, of course. How do you let them know you've filled the dead drop?'

Penkovsky hesitated.

'As you know, we want to put you on trial,' *said Zagvozdin,* 'but that will only be of any use if we can prove you were in contact with the British and the Americans. If not . . .' *He twitched his mouth.* 'There will be no trial.'

Penkovsky didn't react – it made little odds to him if he were tried before being shot. But Zagvozdin hadn't finished, and the deadness in his eyes was more terrifying than starved rats.

'Of course, a trial would wipe the slate clean. It would be unpleasant for your family, but justice would have been done and they could continue their lives relatively unaffected. After all, your actions are not their fault. We would give them new identities, and house them elsewhere. We were thinking of Leningrad. But if justice is not done, that could be very hard on them. The relocation would probably have to be to the countryside. So please tell me: what number do you call, and what procedure do you follow?'

If there had been any food in Penkovsky's stomach, he would have vomited it then. Rage clawed at him, clouding his mind, and he wanted to lash out at Zagvozdin, but didn't have the strength. He knew his mother would never survive a labour camp, and the thought of his daughters there, particularly the baby, made his mouth dry. It was unimaginable that Mariana would ever see such a place. But as Zagvozdin had talked he had imagined it anyway, for a fraction of a second he could never undo, had seen her crawling across a bare stone floor through a forest of emaciated legs.

He tried to shake his head of the image and focus. Zagvozdin had said something peculiar. He had presumed that Penkovsky's way of informing his handlers he had filled his dead drop was by telephone. But this wasn't the case, although one method did have something to do with telephones. There was a public phone in the foyer of a block of apartments in Kozitsky Pereulok. A line in red pencil marked on the phone's backboard signalled that the drop had been loaded. He also had standing appointments with his British contact, ANNE. They had worked out a routine whereby she would enter a block of apartments and he would follow her in a couple of minutes later. There, he could tell her the drop was filled and be gone within a matter of seconds.

He did have a way of contacting the CIA and MI6 by telephone, but that was to be used in the very gravest of emergencies – in the event that he knew of an imminent nuclear strike by the Soviet Union against the West. As he stared with utter loathing into Zagvozdin's vacant gaze, Penkovsky felt the seed of the idea forming in his mind. It was insane, of course, because if they took it seriously it could mean the end of everything . . . the deaths of all those he loved included – but what did life have in store for them otherwise? And it would mean he had not struggled, or died, for nothing. He would have achieved what he had originally set out to do, even if he was not there to see it. And it would remove the man with the dead eyes forever. He held the thought in his mind for a moment, the way he had once seen a pawn-broker hold a gem up to the light, and examined the idea again. For a moment he considered discarding it, but something kept it there, and he couldn't let it go. Why should he? What did he have to lose now?

'There are two telephone numbers,' he said, and Zagvozdin quickly removed a notebook and pen from his jacket. 'Forty-three, twenty-six, ninety-four. And forty-three, twenty-six, eighty-seven. I am to call either, and when someone picks up I breathe into the mouth-piece, three times, then replace the receiver. Exactly one minute later, the procedure is repeated.'

'And then they send someone to the drop?'

Penkovsky nodded. 'Yes. Then they send someone to the drop . . .'

★

I have long been fascinated by the Oleg Penkovsky case. It had the highest stakes of any espionage operation during the Cold War, taking place during two of the most dangerous episodes in recent history – the Berlin crisis in 1961 that led to the building of the Wall and the Cuban missile crisis of 1962. But it was also packed with human drama, as well as tradecraft familiar to millions from fiction: microfilmed documents, coded messages, assignations in safe houses in London and Paris and dead drops in Moscow. If it sounds like the plot of a John le Carré novel, that's no coincidence: it inspired one of his best-known books, *The Russia House*, and elements of it have seeped into many of his other works. And le Carré isn't alone: parts of the story feel familiar because so much spy fiction has been inspired by it, directly or indirectly.

But it was real. Penkovsky has been described as the most valuable agent in CIA history and 'the spy of the century', and his intelligence is widely believed to have been crucial in helping President Kennedy avert nuclear war during the missile crisis, as it revealed that Nikita Khrushchev was bluffing about the Soviet Union's military strength. An alternative theory about the operation, that the Russians deliberately sent Penkovsky to make contact with the West armed with faked intelligence, has been discredited, mainly because in the 1990s the CIA released over two thousand pages of material about the operation, including the transcripts of all their debriefings with him, and the sheer magnitude of high-level secrets he revealed can no longer be denied as a result.

Nevertheless, several key questions about the operation remain unanswered even today, most notably how and when the KGB realised Penkovsky was in contact with Western intelligence. The official version from the Russian side has always been that they detected him by a combination of pure chance and sloppy tradecraft by the CIA and MI6, around ten months before they arrested him. Over the years, this version of events has become the accepted history, both in Russia and in the West – but is it true?

I looked at the operation again a couple of years ago when I was writing a spy novel set in Moscow during the 1960s. I started noticing puzzling elements about it, and decided to research it in depth. This has mainly consisted of immersing myself in memoirs, newspaper archives and declassified documents, many of them newly released, as well as conducting interviews. Most of the key players are now dead, but two surviving participants of the operation spoke to me about it on the record. Felicity Stuart was the assistant to MI6's Head of Station in Moscow during the operation, while CIA officer Leonard McCoy played a major, though to date largely unheralded, role. Both were extremely forthcoming, and offered new insights into how the operation was run and what it felt like to be involved. I also interviewed Janie Chisholm, whose parents Janet and Ruari played a crucial part in the operation, as well as John Miller, a friend of the Chisholms in Moscow who worked for Reuters, and Tennent 'Pete' Bagley, a former CIA counter-intelligence officer, who both provided important new information.

The main protagonists of this book, though, are Oleg Penkovsky and his handlers: quiet, methodical Harry Shergold of MI6 – perhaps the closest real-life equivalent to George Smiley there has been – and the CIA's easy-going and immensely sympathetic George 'Teddy Bear' Kisevalter, who was largely responsible for coaxing the raw intelligence from this wildly unpredictable agent. Their invisible foe was General Gribanov, the mastermind behind dozens of KGB operations, and his team of investigators.

As I researched, I uncovered several pieces of evidence that the Russian story about when and how they detected Penkovsky is a lie. If I'm right, this might have a substantial knock-on effect on other events, particularly the Cuban missile crisis. Put simply, if the Russians were sure that Penkovsky was a traitor significantly before the crisis, why did they let him continue to pass dozens of top-secret documents about weapons, including nuclear missiles, to the West – and why have they never revealed that they did this?

In trying to answer these questions, I've looked more closely at incidents that have previously occupied the margins of the story – even a haphazard one night stand in London had unintended consequences, for example, and the way in which the KGB used their agent George Blake has not been fully explored in relation to this operation.

I hope I have built the case for an entirely new interpretation of this operation: that it was indeed the West's greatest intelligence coup during the Cold War, but that it was *also* part of a long-running Russian deception operation, the secret of which has remained hidden for half a century.

The Man on the Bridge

12 August 1960.

It was eleven o'clock on a Friday night in Moscow, and a light rain was falling on the city. Few people were on the streets apart from the *militsiya*: armed police. Eldon Ray Cox and Henry Lee Cobb, two Americans on a two-week study programme from Indiana University, trudged across Red Square towards their hotel after watching a film at a nearby cinema. As they approached Moskvoretsky Bridge a man suddenly appeared alongside them, and in heavily accented English asked them for a light for his cigarette. Wearing a suit and tie, he looked to be in his forties, was of medium height and build, and had swept-back reddish hair tinged with grey.

Neither of the students had a light, but instead of walking away the man hovered by them, apparently anxious to impart some sort of message. As they reached the bridge, which was guarded by four sentries standing with fixed bayonets, the man fell silent, but as soon as they had passed the sentries he suddenly became animated again, begging the students to help him. Speaking rapidly in Russian, with English phrases occasionally interspersed, he told them that he had seen them a few days earlier on a train from Kiev and had wanted to approach them then, but had held back as they had been accompanied by a minder whom he knew to be an agent assigned to watch them. The Russian said that he had once worked at the Soviet Embassy in Turkey, where he had been friends with an American diplomat, and that he was now trying to contact US authorities to give them a letter.

The students were, naturally, perturbed by this unexpected development in their evening. But they were both mature students, and had become friends while serving together in the Air Force. Cox asked the Russian if he was in the military, and if so what was his rank and number. The man replied that as soon as the embassy read his letter they would know who he was. What was his plan, the students wanted to know – was it to go to the West? Perhaps, he replied, in a couple of years. Cobb asked him if he was a Communist, to which he replied '*Byl*' – 'I was'.

Repeatedly looking around to check that nobody could hear their conversation, the man then told the students he had secret information about an event that had recently made headlines around the world. This was the downing of a U-2 over Sverdlovsk on 1 May. The US government had initially claimed the craft was a weather-observation plane flown by a civilian, until Khrushchev had revealed that the pilot, Gary Powers, was still alive and that surveillance equipment had been recovered from the plane. In a humiliating climb-down, the Eisenhower administration had been forced to admit publicly that the U-2 had indeed been conducting an espionage mission over Soviet airspace.

Now, in a still moment on a Moscow night, the strange Russian told the American students he had been given information about the U-2 incident by 'an officer friend' that contradicted the official Soviet version. Powers, he claimed, had not been shot down by a single direct hit at high altitude, as Khrushchev had stated. In fact, the Soviet Air Force had tracked the American plane from the frontier and had repeatedly tried to bring it down, firing fourteen rockets at it, using both ground-to-air and air-to-air missiles as well as MiG fighter jets. Finally, he said, one of the rockets had burst near the U-2, causing it to spin out of control and crash. 'In the process we destroyed one of our own MiG planes with ground-to-air missiles,' he said, 'killing the pilot.' Powers had ejected, he said, but had been unconscious by the time he had landed.

The Russian then thrust two sealed envelopes into Cox's hands, and implored the students to go to the embassy at once and deliver them either to one Edward Freers or to the military attaché, saying they contained very important information. He asked them to meet him on the bridge the following evening at the same time to confirm they had made the delivery. Then, as suddenly as he had appeared, he vanished into the night.

*

The two students had very different reactions to the encounter. Cobb was scared by it, and felt it was a trap designed to get them both kicked out of the country. But Cox was convinced the Russian was genuine. The young men argued, with Cobb imploring Cox not to act rashly. But he had made up his mind. As soon as they reached their hotel, Cox took a taxi to the American Embassy on Tchaikovsky Street, about a mile away. He paid the driver and approached the iron gates of the embassy.

Like all embassies in Moscow, it was guarded by KGB sentries – not to protect those inside, but to stop Soviet citizens from entering and defecting. Cox felt his heart pounding in his chest, and wondered if he shouldn't have listened to his friend after all. But when he showed his papers the sentries let him pass, and he walked through the archway into the embassy compound. He asked to see Edward Freers, but was told he was not there. Instead, he was greeted by security officer John

Abidian, who listened to his story – and was distinctly unimpressed by it. He took the envelopes, but told Cox he should not have accepted anything from a stranger on the street. Cox returned to his hotel, fuming at the scolding.

*

The next morning, John Abidian took the stairs to the ninth floor, where he nodded to a Marine guard standing outside a heavy door. The Marine stood to one side, and Abidian stepped into a curious windowless room. In the centre of it was a large transparent box of double-wall Plexiglas, which appeared to be floating. Inside the box was a small conference table and several chairs, and the entire structure was suspended by wires from the ceiling and floor.

Due to the acoustic barrier provided by the Plexiglas, this surreal room-within-a-room, nicknamed 'the Tank', was believed to be the only location in the Moscow Embassy that was secure from bugs. In 1952, an electronic sweep of the American ambassador's residence had revealed that a wooden replica of the Great Seal of the United States that had been a gift from a Soviet youth group at the end of the war contained a listening device. As a result, the Americans were convinced that microphones were hidden throughout the embassy, and some staff had taken to communicating with each other by writing on children's Magic Slate doodle pads, which they would wipe clean after each message so that no trace of sensitive conversations remained. It might seem like paranoia, but the KGB were in fact trying to listen in to the conversations in the embassy, from command posts stationed in neighbouring buildings.

Joining Abidian in the Tank were the Deputy Chief of Mission, Edward Freers, and the embassy's political officer, Vladimir Toumanoff, a fluent Russian-speaker. Together, they opened the two envelopes Abidian had taken from Cox the previous evening. Inside, they found several documents. One was a letter, typed in Cyrillic text, which read:

My dear Sir!

I request that you pass the following to the appropriate authorities of the United States of America.

It is your good friend who is turning to you, a friend who has already become your soldier-warrior for the cause of Truth, for the ideals of a truly free world and of Democracy for Mankind, to which ideals your (and now my) President, government and people are sacrificing so much effort.

I have consciously embarked upon this path of struggle. Many things have contributed to this. In my life, the last three years have been very critical, both in my way of thinking and in other things, about which I will report later.

I have thought long and hard. Now I have taken a mature and for me a correct final decision, which has impelled me to approach you.

I ask that you believe the sincerity of my thoughts and desires to be of service to you. I wish to make my contribution, perhaps a modest one but in my view an important one, to our mutual cause, and henceforth as your soldier to carry out everything which is entrusted to me.

You need not doubt that I will give all my strength, knowledge, and my life to this new obligation.

In presenting the above, I want to say that I am not beginning my work for my new cause with empty hands. I understand perfectly well and take into full consideration that to correct words and thoughts must be added concrete proof confirming these words. I have had, and do have now, a definite capability to do this.

At the present time I have at my disposal very important materials on many subjects of exceptionally great interest and importance to your government.

I wish to pass these materials to you immediately for study, analysis, and subsequent utilization. This must be done as quickly as possible. You will determine the manner of transmittal of this material yourself. It is desirable that the transfer be effected not through personal contact, but through a dead drop.

Again I request that you 'relieve' me as quickly as possible of this material which I have prepared; this should be done for many valid reasons.

Your reply: Please inform me (preferably in the Russian language) through my dead drop No. 1 (see its description and manner of use) concerning the manner, form, time, and place for passing of the indicated material.

If you designate your own dead drop for my passing the material, please take into consideration that your drop should be able to contain material equivalent in size to the book *Ven Klaybern* by S. Khentov, published in 1959.

After you receive the material from me, it would be desirable to arrange a personal meeting with your representative during the second half of August of this year. We must discuss many things in detail. I request four to six hours for this. Saturdays and Sundays are convenient for me. You decide upon the place and manner of setting this up.

I will wait for your orders regarding the questions raised above, through Drop Number 1 starting from 15 August 1960.

I ask that in working with me you observe all the rules of tradecraft and security, and not permit any slip-ups. Protect me.

May the justice of the ideas and goals to which I am devoting myself from this day forward aid us in our future collaboration.

Always your . . .

P.S. My best, best greetings to my first good friend, Colonel Charles MacLean Peeke and his wife. Mentally I send greetings to my friends: Cotter, Koehler, Ditta, Beckett, Daniel, Glassbrook and others. I remember with great pleasure the time I spent with them.

I had planned to meet your representative and pass him this letter before 9 August 1960, but it did not work out. Now this must be postponed to 15 August.

Having absorbed this – Toumanoff translating the letter aloud for the others – the men turned to the second envelope, which contained a detailed description of the location of the dead drop, as well as a diagram of it and instructions on how to use it. Also known as Dead Letter Boxes, or DLBs, dead drops are used to this day, pre-arranged locations in which messages or material can be left and picked up by someone else later. They are used to minimise the risk of an agent and his contact being spotted together. Ideally, a dead drop should be somewhere easily accessed without drawing any attention, and unlikely to be investigated: the hollow of a tree, say, or a cistern in a public lavatory.

Spies spend a lot of time looking for such spots, and good ones are prized. The man on the bridge had found what he felt was an ideal location in the city: the foyer of a quiet block of flats in Pushkinskaya Street, between two shops. 'The main entrance is open twenty-four hours a day,' he wrote. 'The entrance is not guarded, and there is no elevator.' On entering the foyer, there was a telephone to the left. Opposite, in an unlit corner, was a radiator, painted dark green, fastened to the wall by a single metal hook. 'If one stands facing the radiator, then the metal hook will be to the right, at the level of one's hand hanging from the arm. Between the wall, to which the hook is attached, and the radiator, there is a space of two to three centimetres.'

This tiny space in Moscow was the Russian's choice for a dead drop with American intelligence. Written material could be placed here, he wrote, in a matchbox, camouflaged by being wrapped in green wire that matched the colour of the radiator, with the end of the wire acting as a hook, allowing the box to hang from the radiator's bracket.

The writer also left detailed instructions about a telephone booth in a different apartment foyer, at 2 Kozitsky Pereulok, the location of which was indicated on the diagram. The telephone there was fastened to a wooden backboard, the veneer of which had broken off in the bottom right-hand corner, leaving a lighter spot exposed – a stroke with a red pencil on this part of the board would indicate that the drop had been loaded.

In addition, there was a list of around sixty Russian names. 'I know that you have no sound basis for completely trusting everything that I have said to you, so I must prove myself,' read an accompanying note. 'In order to do so, I am enclosing a list of incoming Military Diplomatic Academy students and their future assignments. Many of these facts I am giving to you can be checked by you, because a number of these people have already been abroad before and were previously exposed to you. In addition, I want instructions from you as to how I might safely deliver to you some top secret nuclear information. I don't know how to do this securely. I need your guidance and help.'

The significance of this list was probably lost on the men in the Tank, none of whom were intelligence officers. The Military Diplomatic Academy sounded relatively innocuous, but it was in fact run by Glavnoye Razvedyvatel'noye Upravleniye (GRU): the Soviets' highly secretive military intelligence agency. The academy was the GRU's elite espionage school in Moscow, and was so called because its students were drawn from the armed forces and most practised intelligence roles under diplomatic cover abroad, often as military attachés. Most, but not all – some were 'illegals', spies who work outside the protection of diplomatic immunity, usually under a false identity. The Russian had placed asterisks next to eighteen students who had been earmarked for such work, including details of their backgrounds, languages and where they were expected to be sent after graduation.

There was one final item in the package: a photograph of three men at what looked to be a social occasion, perhaps a diplomatic cocktail party. The tall man on the left of the photo was wearing the uniform of an American colonel. The man on the right, his face away from the camera, also seemed to be in a uniform, but it was not possible to make out what it was. And the man in the centre of the picture was invisible, everything but the top of his forehead having been cut out with scissors or a razor. Above his forehead were the words 'I am'. It seemed that, fearing the package could be intercepted, this was as far as the Russian was prepared to go in identifying himself.

What to make of this strange letter and its accompanying documents? The men in the Tank were intrigued, but cautious. On the one hand, the man was offering access to material 'of exceptionally great interest and importance' to the United States' government, including 'top secret nuclear information'. On the other, what if it were a provocation or some other form of trap?

*

It was raining again, and the Moskvoretsky Bridge had a sinister look it hadn't possessed the previous evening. Eldon Cox and Henry Cobb approached slowly, both resisting the temptation to glance over their shoulders to see if they were being followed. As they reached the bridge, a man in an overcoat emerged from beneath a streetlight. It was the Russian from the night before.

'Good evening, my friends,' he whispered. 'Did you deliver my package?'

Cox nodded. 'They took it, but they didn't seem very interested. In fact, they were angry with me for taking it from you.'

The Russian's face dropped at the news.

'You followed my instructions?' he asked. 'Did you give it to Freers?'

'Freers wasn't there, so I gave it to another security official. He said he would look into it, but the way he reacted I'm not sure he will.'

The Russian cursed. 'They must!' he said. 'Khrushchev is a madman, and someone must stop him!' Conscious that he had raised his voice in his excitement, he lowered it to a whisper again. 'Thank you for trying to help me,' he said. 'You are both good men.' Then he turned and once again walked off into the night.

*

Unknown to the Russian or the students, the documents were now making their way through the American government's red tape, and would soon reach CIA headquarters, where they were scrutinised again. One CIA officer later described the reaction to the letter in Washington as 'near-paralysis', although this is perhaps understandable given the context of the time. Soviet intelligence specialised in provocation and aggressive actions. All KGB officers were given annual quotas for the number of agents they were expected to run, and their careers depended on meeting these requirements. As a result, attempts to recruit foreigners were rife, often by use of extortion. The technique was usually very simple: a pretty woman, or man, seduced you, and before you knew it you were being shown photographs or film of your dalliance and being pressured to provide secrets or face exposure. The CIA had discovered this to their cost in 1956, when the first officer they had sent to Moscow, Edward Ellis Smith, had been seduced by his maid, who he had boasted made wonderful Martinis. The maid, of course, was a 'swallow', and Smith had fallen into a classic 'honey trap'. The KGB used the relationship to force one meeting with Smith, but he then confessed all to his superiors and was fired.

The KGB also pursued disinformation campaigns against Western targets. A typical strategy was to forge damaging documents and post them to foreign embassies. In 1959, the KGB had created 'Department D', a section in its First Chief Directorate dedicated to running *dezinformatsiya* operations: from its inception, the department had fifty officers.

Another weapon in the KGB's armoury was 'dangles', or false defectors. In the previous few years, several Russians had simply approached American authorities and volunteered either to defect or, as seemed to be the case here, hand over secrets while remaining in the Soviet Union. But some of these 'walk-ins', as they were known, had turned out not to be all they had seemed. They would hand over some information to establish their bona fides, but this would either be disinformation or what was known as 'chickenfeed': genuine intelligence that the KGB had already established was known to the other side, or that was insignificant enough to sacrifice. After the bait had been taken, the Russian would suddenly return to KGB headquarters, having retrieved some intelligence of his own: the layout of a CIA station, perhaps, or the identities of those who had interviewed him.

The Americans and the British had both been caught out by such ploys before, with disastrous consequences. In the 1920s, Soviet intelligence had created the appearance of an entire anti-Communist organisation: the fictitious Monarchist Association of Central Russia, also known as 'The Trust', ensnared among others the British agent Sidney Reilly, who was shot. Similarly, in the 1940s and 1950s, American and British intelligence had supported several anti-Communist organisations behind the Iron Curtain, only to discover that the Soviets had taken complete control of them: hundreds of agents were killed as a result.

Even when agents were genuine, they didn't always stay that way. If the Russians discovered one of their own was handing secrets to the West, they might arrest them – but they might also decide to 'turn' them, allowing them to continue their contact in order to feed disinformation or force an embarrassing diplomatic incident. This had happened with Lieutenant-Colonel Pyotr Popov, the most significant source the CIA had ever had inside the Soviet Union. In 1953, Popov approached the CIA and began to hand over top-secret material. Six years later, the KGB finally realised what he was doing. They arrested him, but decided to let him out of his cell every so often to continue his meetings with the CIA, only now provided with doctored information to give them. Finally, at a meeting in a Moscow restaurant, Popov managed to pass a message to his CIA handler that he had been acting under KGB control for months. The KGB later pounced on the CIA man as he carried out a brush contact, a very rapid exchange of material in person, with Popov on a bus. The American was 'PNGed' – made *persona non grata* by being asked to leave the country – while Popov was executed.

It was against this background that the CIA now tried to assess the documents that had been handed over by the man on the bridge in Moscow. Heading the investigation was Joe Bulik. A handsome, driven 44-year-old, Bulik typified the can-do spirit of the CIA, an organisation that had only been formed thirteen years earlier. From a family with Slovakian roots, he didn't speak fluent Russian but had valuable experience – he had been an agricultural attaché at the US Embassy in Moscow in the 1940s, in which role he had once been given the task of smuggling out of the country wheat and rye hybrid seeds developed by Russian scientists to counter bacterial warfare.

The CIA had been set up while Bulik was in the Soviet Union and, having determined from observing the country at close quarters that it would soon become the United States' 'mortal enemy', he had applied and been accepted into the agency. He now headed SR/9, a unit that had been established within the CIA's Soviet Russia division to run Pyotr Popov in Moscow. It oversaw all the agency's activity within the Soviet Union – such as it was. Following Popov's arrest and the expulsion of his handler, there was no longer any official CIA presence in Moscow at all.

Bulik commanded the respect of his colleagues, and was particularly admired for his strict adherence to the principle of 'compartmentalization', whereby the fewest number of people necessary are informed of a source's identity, position or intelligence. Joe Bulik, says one former colleague, 'knew how to keep a secret'.

He also knew how to investigate, and got to work doing so. Key parts of the information given by the Russian on the bridge – such as his version of how Gary Powers's U-2 had been downed – were compiled into a document. All clues as to the identity of the source were stripped out, and the document was then circulated among the intelligence community. The responses were unanimous: the information sounded genuine, or as one CIA officer commented: 'It looks like we've got a live son of a bitch here.'

The next step was to identify the man on the bridge. He had left a few clues: he had signed off his letter with greetings to several Americans, and there was the photograph – presumably he was the man whose head had been cut out. He had also listed those sixty Russian students at the Military Diplomatic Academy.

Bulik soon determined that Colonel Charles MacLean Peeke, the 'first good friend' mentioned in the letter, had been a US military attaché in Turkey between 1955 and 1956, and that he was the man on the left in the photograph. Scanning photographs of Soviet military attachés who had been in Turkey at that time, Bulik came to the preliminary conclusion that the man on the bridge was Colonel Oleg Vladimirovich Penkovsky. There were reports that while in Turkey Penkovsky had sold small items of jewellery to others in the foreign community, apparently because he had needed the money, and that he had also tried to sell a camera. Judging by his role as a military attaché and the list of students accompanying the letter, Penkovsky was also in the GRU.

Bulik assigned a crew of officers to analyse the list of sixty students. Working around the clock, they eventually identified around forty of the names on the list, and located photographs of around twenty-five of them. It was an extraordinary take: their anonymous benefactor had led them to forty Soviet agents. Bulik was particularly struck by the fact that one of the students was currently working in Japan and that the list claimed the GRU planned to send him as an illegal to South America – indeed, as Bulik could see from a photograph, he looked decidedly Latino.

With the bit now between his teeth, Bulik tracked down the two American students the Russian had approached. Interviewed in a Washington safe house, Henry Lee Cobb remembered the incident vividly. Bulik showed him around fifteen photographs of various Russians and Cobb picked out one of them: it was a snapshot of Oleg Penkovsky taken in 1955.

Bulik wanted to be sure, so he flew to Alaska, where Eldon Cox had moved to work. In a hotel in Anchorage, Cox told much the same story as Cobb, differing in only a few minor details. Bulik took out the snapshots. Cox looked through them, then punched his forefinger on the picture of Penkovsky and said: 'That's the man.' Bulik leaped out of his chair. 'I knew it!' he said.

Bulik was now sure that the man on the bridge was Colonel Oleg Penkovsky, who appeared to be a Soviet intelligence officer anxious to pass crucial intelligence to the CIA. It was still possible he was a plant or some form of provocation, but the signs were increasingly pointing to his being genuine: the identities of so many illegals didn't feel like chickenfeed, but rather more like intelligence gold. If they were very lucky, Penkovsky might even be able to offer greater access to Soviet secrets than Popov had done. But if he were genuine, he would also no doubt have been checking his dead drop since 15 August, as per his letter, and been perplexed that the Americans had not yet responded. Bulik knew Penkovsky could be discovered by his colleagues, or simply change his mind, at any moment. He had to be contacted in Moscow at once.

★

But Bulik faced two major hurdles, both from his own side. The first was the American ambassador in Moscow, Llewellyn Thompson. Following the Martini-making maid incident and the expulsion of Popov's handler, Thompson didn't want any further intelligence headaches, and so rejected the CIA's request to send someone into the embassy under cover. As a sop, he instead offered the position of a janitor in America House, a compound in the city that housed many of the Marine guards from the embassy. Bulik had no choice but to accept.

The second problem was a shortage of suitable candidates for the job. The KGB were so omnipresent in Moscow that risking a senior CIA officer having their cover blown was out of the question. The officer who was eventually chosen, COMPASS – he has never allowed his real name to be declassified – was young, inexperienced, barely spoke a word of Russian and had a serious drinking problem. He arrived in Moscow in October and was assigned a room in America House facing a cement factory. He immediately became convinced that the KGB were following him everywhere, so he hardly moved from the compound. As winter arrived, his reports became increasingly erratic. He proposed that Penkovsky walk past America House at a set time and throw a package of material over the wall, where he would be waiting to receive it in the yard. But there was a kennel in the yard containing a puppy, which he soon claimed had become 'an unmanageable beast'.

*

In the meantime, Penkovsky took matters into his own hands. He had been appointed to a cover role in the State Scientific Technical Committee, a Soviet organisation that arranged scientific visits overseas and supervised visiting foreign delegations, both of which offered ample opportunities for espionage. Penkovsky wasted no time in putting his new job to use. When a delegation of British steel companies visited Moscow in December, he followed one of the scientists, Arthur Merriman, to his hotel room under the pretext of cadging a cigarette. Penkovsky turned the radio up to drown out their voices in case there were microphones switched on, and pleaded with Merriman to call the American Embassy at once and ask them to send someone to pick up a package he had for them. Merriman suspected a provocation and refused to cooperate, but on returning to London he told the American Embassy there, who in turn informed the CIA.

CIA headquarters now instructed COMPASS to call Penkovsky at home, following a procedure he had described to Merriman in the hotel room. But COMPASS fluffed it: he rang the number an hour after the scheduled time and spoke in such garbled Russian that Penkovsky hung up, mystified. Worried that further errors might endanger Penkovsky, the CIA quietly withdrew their man from Moscow.

But Penkovsky kept trying. After his approach to Arthur Merriman failed, he persuaded a visiting Canadian geologist to introduce him to his trade attaché. It was no dice again – the attaché also smelled provocation, and a day after accepting a package from Penkovsky returned it to him unopened.

But now a new player entered the scene: MI6. After Arthur Merriman had informed the American Embassy in London, the CIA asked their British colleagues whether they could provide any information on Penkovsky. The British obliged, passing over a report from a former military attaché in Ankara. Penkovsky was 'pleasant and well-mannered, 5'9", slender; iron-grey hair; 160 lbs.; Western appearance'. The attaché had added, in a poetic touch, that he had noticed that Penkovsky's genial expression 'fades when one leaves him, and is replaced by a rather weak and frightened look'.

This may have been moderately useful to the CIA, but it had an unintended effect: MI6's interest had been piqued. Why were the Americans interested in this Penkovsky? The delegation Merriman had been part of in Moscow had been organised and chaperoned by Greville Wynne, a bluff British engineering consultant with a Terry-Thomas moustache, a sheepskin car-coat and offices in Chelsea. And Wynne was 'one of us'.

Wynne's precise relationship with MI6 has never been clear, but such relationships rarely are. In 1960, MI6 – the Secret Intelligence Service, known to insiders as 'the Firm', 'the Office' and other vague euphemisms – didn't even officially exist. Most members of the public had never heard of it, and if they did discuss intelligence matters tended to refer to 'the secret services' and didn't distinguish between MI6 and MI5, which was responsible for domestic threats. In this atmosphere, men and women were often recruited to 'a branch of the Foreign Office' without a clear idea of what the organisation they were entering did. Similarly, MI6 also often asked British businessmen who travelled behind the Iron Curtain to discuss on their return what they had seen and heard. Such contacts were almost always on an informal – and therefore deniable – footing. The line between talking with someone from the Foreign Office over dinner and being an intelligence asset was a deliberately fuzzy one.

Wynne had been recruited into this game by Dickie Franks, who ran MI6's department DP4, which oversaw such contacts. On realising that the Americans were interested in Penkovsky, Franks took Wynne for lunch at The Ivy in London and asked what he had made of the man. Wynne said he had liked him: he was easy-going for a Russian, as well as being amusing and enjoying a drink. Franks suggested to Wynne that he return to Moscow and set up another delegation with the State Committee, this time for their scientists to visit London, and to make sure that Penkovsky came along. If they could get him out of the Soviet Union, where surveillance was a fact of life, it would be much easier to talk to him.

*

Wynne arrived in Moscow in early April 1961 to discuss a delegation to London with the State Committee. Penkovsky quickly realised the opportunities such a trip offered, but he couldn't even wait until then. On 6 April, he visited Wynne in his hotel room and, after ushering him into the bathroom and turning on the taps, showed him a compartment in his trousers in which he had sewn documents – he had been so frightened of leaving them anywhere he carried them around with him at all times. Taking a razor, he slit open the secret pocket and handed the papers to Wynne, begging him to take them back to London.

Wynne was alarmed, but took two of the documents. In an echo of Penkovsky's own frustrated attempts to be taken seriously, the British Embassy turned Wynne away when he tried to give them to the ambassador so they could be flown out in the secure diplomatic bag. This meant that Wynne was forced to run the gauntlet of customs instead. Worse, Penkovsky accompanied him to the airport and, minutes before Wynne was due to board his plane, drew him to one side in one of the bathrooms and tried to persuade him to take even more documents. Wynne eventually accepted one additional sheet of paper. The two men then gave each other a bear hug and Wynne rushed off, secret Soviet documents tucked tightly under his coat as he walked across the tarmac and on to the plane that would take him back to London.

Spilling Secrets

The Mount Royal near Hyde Park had originally been a block of flats, but had since been converted into a slightly shabby maze of a hotel that mainly catered to the tourist trade. To an outside observer, the four men in dark suits pacing its carpets and chain-smoking cigarettes on the evening of 20 April 1961 would probably have looked like businessmen, perhaps anxiously awaiting news of a deal. In fact they were intelligence officers, and they were mentally preparing for what they hoped would be the operation of their lifetimes.

Two of the men were Americans, and two were British: after some negotiation, the CIA had agreed to join forces with MI6. The Brits had beaten them to the punch by making contact with Penkovsky through Greville Wynne, and had also managed to arrange for him to visit London as part of an official Soviet trade delegation, the members of which were staying in the Mount Royal. But the CIA had figured out who Penkovsky was in the first place, had done the legwork on his list of sixty agents and, perhaps most significantly, had the money to fund a full-scale operation if he turned out to be the real deal.

Still, it hadn't been an easy decision. The US and Britain were strong allies and the CIA and MI6 had a history of working together, but a joint operation increased the security risks, simply because people would need to know about it in both London and Washington. This was a particularly sensitive point, as several recent spy scandals had raised questions about the Brits' competence and reliability. In 1951, decoded Soviet intelligence messages from the Second World War had pointed to British diplomat Donald Maclean being a Soviet agent, but just before he had been brought in for questioning he had fled the country with another diplomat, Guy Burgess – the two men had later turned up in Moscow. As a result of Burgess and Maclean's flight, MI6's Head of Station in Washington at the time, Kim Philby, had also come under suspicion of being a Soviet spy: he had known that the net was closing in on Maclean and had been a friend of Burgess. But despite being named as 'the Third Man' in the House of Commons, Philby had never been apprehended and had even remained unofficially attached to MI6, to the horror of some CIA officers who remained convinced he was a traitor.

More troubling than Burgess, Maclean and Philby was a case that had only fully come to light a few weeks earlier. A Polish intelligence officer, Michael Goleniewski, had defected to the Americans and, among other things, revealed that the KGB had two further British agents. Goleniewski didn't know their identities, but some of the intelligence he had seen appeared to come from a Royal Navy research establishment, and some from MI6 documents. By early 1961, MI5 had identified the naval spy, Harry Houghton, and he had been arrested with three associates, all illegals: Konon Molody, a Russian operating in Britain as a Canadian businessman named Gordon Lonsdale, and Morris and Lona Cohen, two American Communists who had created cover identities as antiquarian booksellers Peter and Helen Kroger.

A major Soviet spy ring had been wrapped up, but Goleniewski's clues about a traitor in MI6 had been harder to crack. Frustrated at the lack of progress, the head of MI6, Dick

White – 'C' – had put senior officer Harry Shergold on the case. Before the war, Shergold had been a schoolmaster at Cheltenham Grammar School: shy and with thinning hair, he still would not have looked out of place in a senior common room, quietly marking papers in a corner. But despite his inconspicuousness, or perhaps partly because of it, 'Shergie' was already approaching legendary status within MI6. During the war he had worked with the Intelligence Corps in the Middle East and Italy, and in its aftermath had become a highly effective interrogator and agent-runner, heading MI6's operations from Bad Salzuflen in the British Zone of Germany. In the years since he had transferred his area of expertise to the new enemy, and was now MI6's 'best Soviet specialist'.

After an extensive investigation, Shergie had concluded that the only person who could have had access to all the documents Goleniewski had seen was George Blake. This was explosive, because Blake was a career MI6 officer, and so could have done untold damage. He had joined during the war, and in 1948 had been appointed Head of Station in Seoul. However, he and several others at the British Legation had been taken prisoner by the invading North Korean Army, and he had spent three years in captivity. On his release and return to England, Blake had been regarded by many colleagues as a hero – but unknown to them he was harbouring a dark secret. While in captivity he had become a committed Communist. In the autumn of 1951, he had slipped into the guardroom of his camp and handed the North Koreans a note addressed to the Soviet Embassy in Pyongyang. A few weeks later the KGB had sent an officer to meet him under the pretext of interviewing all the prisoners, and Blake's life as a traitor had begun.

Blake's greatest intelligence coup for his new masters had taken place shortly after his return from North Korea. In 1953, MI6 and the CIA had embarked on a major joint operation:

the building of a tunnel beneath the Soviet Zone of Berlin. In the 1940s, the two agencies had been able to intercept Soviet radio transcripts, but the Russians had got wind of this and switched to using one-time pads in 1948. These were tiny pads of paper, each page of which contained a fresh string of random letters. There were only two copies of the pads in the world, and each sheet of paper was only used once before being burned: unless you had one of the pads, messages coded using them were unbreakable. The new tunnel meant the British and Americans would be able to get around this, by listening in to communications running from the joint Soviet–East German intelligence base in Karlshorst before they were enciphered.

However, George Blake had attended an early CIA–MI6 meeting about the operation in London, and had immediately informed his Soviet controller, Sergei Kondrashev. Blake was codenamed DIOMID, meaning 'diamond', and was so highly valued by Moscow that Kondrashev was the only person in the KGB's London station (*rezidentura*) to know his name or position – even the Head of Station, the Rezident, was not informed.

Blake's information about the plans for the Berlin tunnel was a coup for the Russians, but it also placed them in a very difficult position. If the tunnel went ahead, the West would be able to gain an enormous amount of intelligence about their activities. But if they exposed the tunnel, the British and Americans would naturally try to figure out how they had known about it. As only a handful of people were aware of the operation, MI6 and the CIA might investigate and discover that Blake had been the source.

The KGB considered its options. One was to let the tunnel go ahead and feed disinformation through the tapped lines, but this was overruled: a single error could alert the British and Americans to the fact that they knew about the tunnel all along, and Blake would once again be in the frame. Planting disinformation would also have meant involving more people, increasing the risk of compromising Blake's security.

In the end, the KGB took just one measure to minimise the damage. They tapped the same lines as MI6 and the CIA were doing, and presented the resulting recordings of officers being overly talkative to the marshal responsible for the Karlshorst base: he immediately issued orders to his staff that discretion be observed on the telephone at all times.

But other than that, the Soviets left the tunnel completely alone, and MI6 and the CIA intercepted an enormous amount of classified material as a result. In terms of chess strategy, the KGB were losing a bishop, but Blake was the equivalent of a queen or even a king, and protecting him was worth the sacrifice of a lesser piece.

In the spring of 1956, the Soviets finally decided it was time to put a finger in the dyke. Khrushchev instructed the KGB to find a way to expose the tunnel that would provide them with a propaganda coup, and would not reveal how they had learned about it. Sergei Kondrashev discussed it with Blake, who felt that enough time had now gone by to remove him from suspicion. When heavy rains swept Berlin and disrupted phone lines, the Soviets seized the opportunity and sent soldiers in to carry out repair work. When they 'accidentally' came across the tunnel as a result they decried the operation at a press conference, while the Communist newspaper *Neues Deutschland* called it a 'gangster act'.

The ruse paid off, for a time. MI6 and the CIA were dismayed that the tunnel had been discovered, but believed the Soviets' story of accidentally discovering it, reasoning that the operation had been so successful for so long that the KGB would never have let it continue had they known about it. A CIA assessment concluded that the discovery had not been the result of 'a penetration of the UK or US agencies concerned, a security violation, or testing of the lines by the Soviets or East Germans', but had been 'purely fortuitous'.

Blake had escaped suspicion for a while longer, but events finally caught up with him. Thanks to the information from Goleniewski, by February 1961 Harry Shergold had deduced that he was a Soviet agent. However, Shergold didn't have enough evidence to be certain of a successful prosecution, so in early April he asked Blake to report to MI6's personnel department in London without specifying what it was about. Once Blake had arrived, he took him to an elegant conference room in the grand and sedate Carlton Gardens, overlooking St James's Park. MI6 had special interrogation centres, known as 'rubber rooms' because the walls were soundproofed, in the basements of several houses and hotels in London, but Shergold had decided that such an approach would be counterproductive in this case, as Blake might simply seize up and refuse to talk. Instead, he was going to smother him with politeness.

As soon as they had settled in the conference room, Shergold accused Blake of working for the KGB. Blake strenuously denied it, and continued to do so under intense questioning for two days. Exasperated, Shergold suggested he had been brainwashed by the North Koreans. Something in the accusation made Blake snap, and he suddenly burst out that Shergold was completely wrong. Yes, he said, it had happened when he was in the hands of the North Koreans, but he hadn't been brainwashed: he had known perfectly well what he was doing all along, and had chosen to serve Communism purely as a result of his own beliefs.

Shergold had swiftly tied up the loose ends. He had taken Blake off to his cottage in Richmond for three days, where his wife Bevis, a former Olympic shot-putter, had cooked pancakes and vegetarian meals for them. Once Shergold had secured a legally binding confession, a two-part ciphered telegram was sent to every MI6 station in the world. The first part stated: 'THE FOLLOWING NAME IS A TRAITOR'. The second spelled out Blake's name.

The message sent shockwaves through the agency. Burgess and Maclean had been diplomats, not intelligence officers: Blake was a colleague. He confessed to having betrayed the true identities of every MI6 officer and agent he had known; it has been claimed the figure was around forty (he was given a forty-two-year prison sentence, 'about one year for each agent'), but by his own estimation in later life it was 'more likely 400'. It's also likely that in many cases his betrayal would have resulted in their deaths.

Blake later engineered a spectacular escape from Wormwood Scrubs and defected to Moscow. But beyond all the agents, assets and operations he could have betrayed were some even more disturbing implications to his case. It was starting to look like Burgess and Maclean hadn't been isolated cases, but that the Soviets had recruited them as part of a wide-ranging effort to penetrate the British establishment. The idea was in stark contrast to MI6's own record: it didn't have a single agent-in-place in the KGB, and the only notable defector it had received since the end of the Second World War, Grigori Tokaev, had arrived in 1947 and so had no knowledge of recent organisational changes, personnel or operations.

MI6 had discovered Blake by chance: Harry Shergold cracked the case, but only because he had clues to follow in the first place. If Goleniewski hadn't decided to switch sides, Blake might have remained undetected for decades, and we might be none the wiser today that the KGB knew about the Berlin tunnel operation all along, and that their claim to have accidentally discovered it was a carefully constructed cover story designed to protect a valuable agent-in-place in the West.

Blake's confession, then, opened several cans of worms. Most importantly, it changed the nature of the Berlin tunnel. Both MI6 and the CIA had believed that operation to be one of their greatest triumphs: it had yielded recordings of nearly half a million conversations, using up some 50,000 reels of tape, and much of it had been highly secret material. But it was now clear that the Soviets had been prepared to let them have all of it because they had held a far greater asset.

*

All of this was in the background when MI6 and the CIA discussed working together on Penkovsky. But despite American reservations about British security, the deal had been struck for a joint operation. Shergold, fresh from having secured Blake's confession, led the MI6 contingent, supported by a junior officer, Mike Stokes.

Bulik had chosen for his deputy George 'Teddy Bear' Kisevalter, who would also act as the frontline handler for Penkovsky, as he was the team's best Russian speaker. Kisevalter was a large, gregarious 51-year-old, 'rumpled and roly-poly' as a colleague would later describe him. He was well liked within the CIA, with his nickname derived from his bear-like physique but also the fact that he had a lifelong affection for the animals – as a young man he had worked for the Parks Commission in New York, and had known the name of every bear in the city's zoo.

Beneath the cuddly exterior lay the mind of a very sharp and experienced intelligence officer. He had been born in 1910 in St Petersburg to a family of the *dvorianstvo*, Russia's hereditary nobility. His grandfather had served as a deputy finance minister under two tsars, while his father was an engineer who had married a French schoolteacher. At the age of six, Kisevalter had accompanied his parents to the United States when his father had led a contingent of Russian munitions experts who were looking to buy weapons for the war against the Central Powers. The family had stayed on in the United States, and after the Bolshevik Revolution became stranded there, because they supported the White Russians. Almost all the Kisevalters' extended family in Russia had been killed in the following years, with the result that George had grown up in the United States with great pride in his Russian roots – but a deep hatred of Communists.

Kisevalter had entered the espionage world in 1944, working in G-2, an Army intelligence unit. After the war he had joined the CIA, where his perceptiveness and fluent Russian had led to his running Pyotr Popov, his and perhaps the agency's finest hour to that point. An unpretentious man, Kisevalter was wary of the agency's urbane elite, perhaps sensing he would never rise higher in the ranks due to having been born in Russia, and there was tension between him and Bulik. Having run Popov, Kisevalter felt capable of running this operation himself. But no two operations are alike. Popov had been a rather uptight figure, and Kisevalter had bonded with him over long drinking sessions at safe houses in Vienna. Would Penkovsky be shy or talkative, distant or engaging, trustful or suspicious?

These questions circled the four men as they waited in the Mount Royal. Penkovsky had landed at Heathrow earlier that day, and had been met by Greville Wynne. Safely installed in Wynne's Humber Snipe saloon, he had handed over a package that included a letter, in a similar vein to his first, addressed to the Queen, Prime Minister Macmillan and President Kennedy among others. As well as reaffirming his desire to be a 'soldier' for the West, Penkovsky asked to be made a British or American citizen, and to be granted a rank in the US Army, both of which he wanted in preparation for a future life in the United States. The package also included material he had gathered over the previous year, and in the letter he asked that its significance be assessed, and that a decision on a 'fixed sum' of payment for it be reached and placed in an American bank, again with defection in mind.

Now Penkovsky was due at any moment. The plan was

for him to have dinner with his colleagues from the delegation and then make his excuses, saying he was heading to his room for the night. Instead, he would take a back stairway and meet the team in another room. But would he come? Despite all his attempts to contact them, now he was in London he might decide that it was too risky, or ask for too much in exchange, or simply clam up. And if he did go through with it, what would he be able to reveal? Penkovsky was entering the picture at a point in the Cold War when the Soviets seemed to have the upper hand. They were winning the space race – Yuri Gagarin had become the first man in space just over a week earlier – and also appeared to be winning the arms race: President Kennedy had repeatedly claimed in his election campaign that the Eisenhower administration had allowed the Soviets to gain a large lead on intercontinental range ballistic missiles (ICBMs), a lead he referred to as the 'missile gap'.

Finally, at around twenty to ten, there was a knock on the door. Joe Bulik opened it to see a man wearing a dark suit, white shirt and tie: Oleg Penkovsky.

*

The five men seated themselves around a small serving table, on which there was a bottle of white wine and several glasses.

'Would you prefer to speak Russian or English?' asked George Kisevalter.

'I would much rather speak Russian,' Penkovsky replied, explaining that he had used English for work when he had been stationed in Turkey but that it had since become rusty. He then looked at the expectant team. 'Well, gentlemen,' he said, 'let's get to work.'

With a recording device in Shergold's briefcase capturing everything for later translation, transcription and analysis, the meeting began in earnest. It started shakily: Penkovsky wanted to know why it had taken so long to arrange the meeting, pointing out that he had been trying to make contact since the previous August.

'If you knew how many grey hairs I have acquired since that time,' he said, 'if you had only marked the signal just so I would have known that the message got into the proper hands. I worried so much about this.'

Kisevalter tried to reassure him that the delay had been for his own protection, arguing that they had needed to establish a secure way to receive his material. 'This was done exclusively in consideration of your security,' he said.

'And, between friends,' Penkovsky added, sourly, 'admit that you did not trust me. That is the most unpleasant and painful to me.'

'No, it is quite the opposite,' Kisevalter insisted.

The moment passed, and the meeting settled down. The men removed their jackets and rolled up their sleeves – the window had been closed to prevent anyone overhearing the conversation from the street, and the room had rapidly become hot, stuffy and filled with cigarette smoke. Mike Stokes, much to Kisevalter's irritation, lay back on the bed.

As they sipped the Liebfraumilch, Penkovsky explained who he was and what had brought him to contact the West. He was clearly happy to talk, and had even brought along his own agenda. Bulik was enormously relieved. 'Here was a man who had held a secret in his heart for many months and was obviously waiting to unload,' he later recalled. 'I think we all knew it. This would probably be the case of the century.'

The team had agreed in advance that they would allow Penkovsky to steer the meeting as he saw fit, and so let him talk, prompted by occasional questions from Kisevalter. The primary objective was to obtain intelligence that would establish if he were the genuine article.

'I was born,' Penkovsky began, 'in 1919 in the Caucasus.'

His father had been a first lieutenant in the Tsar's Army, from Stavropol, while his grandfather had been a judge. But, there was a problem with his family history. 'Only recently,' he said, 'I have been accused and confronted with having come from a background of nobility.'

Descendants of the nobility, or anyone whose family had fought against Communism during the Revolution, were still highly suspect in the Soviet Union. A few months after Penkovsky's birth, his father had vanished without trace. 'Either he died of illness,' he said, 'or was shot during the Revolutionary days since there were very violent conflicts in that district of the Caucasus.'

Hearing this, Kisevalter may have had a pang of empathy, as most of his own family in Russia had been killed during this period. But Kisevalter, as a result of his father's fortuitous visit to the United States, had escaped life under Communism, whereas Penkovsky had had to try to survive within that system. To do so, he had hidden the secret of his father's disappearance all his life: to have stated that his whereabouts were unknown after he had served on the White side would have been impossible. 'One simply would be blocked for life from progressing in any speciality,' Penkovsky explained. 'They would not accept one in the Party and one would just about be a common labourer.'

To avoid that fate, he had concocted a story that his father had died in 1919. This had been believed, and his career had advanced. He had joined the Komsomol, the youth wing of the Communist Party, and then the Army. In 1939 he had graduated from artillery school in Kiev, and had immediately been sent to help, as he put it, 'liberate the Western Ukraine' – the Soviet Union and Germany had invaded Poland. Penkovsky served in several Army units, and had survived the purges by the NKVD, the precursor of the KGB, which executed hundreds of thousands of people at this time, many of them from the Army.

During the war, Penkovsky met two men who would have an enormous impact on his life. After fighting in Poland and Finland he returned to Moscow, where he served as a military instructor. There, Lieutenant-General Dmitri Gapanovich took the dashing young officer under his wing and introduced him to his 14-year-old daughter Vera. Penkovsky had been smitten at once, and four years later he married her.

But before then, there was a war to win. In 1943, Penkovsky had returned to the front. This had been at his own request, because he had realised it might prove useful for his career. 'At that time the recapture of Kiev was being celebrated,' he said, 'and I thought that the war would end very soon. Here I was with no distinctions or decorations. I received nothing for the Finnish campaign, only a commendation and a cigarette case.'

Penkovsky had been sent to the First Ukrainian Front, where he had been assigned to a subdivision of the headquarters of General Sergei Varentsov. Like Gapanovich, Varentsov had taken a liking to him, and appointed him commander of a training reception centre for anti-tank artillery regiments. But in the summer of 1944 Penkovsky had been injured, and had been sent back to Moscow for treatment. He had been about to return to the front when he heard that Varentsov had also been injured, and had been flown to hospital in Moscow. At Varentsov's request, Penkovsky acted as his liaison officer with the front. 'I knew that he would reward me tenfold for anything I did for him,' Penkovsky told the team. While Varentsov was in hospital his daughter committed suicide – Penkovsky arranged for the funeral, selling his watch to be able to afford it. Deeply grateful, Varentsov told Penkovsky he was like a son to him.

Penkovsky's loyalty to Marshal Varentsov, as he would become, paid off more than tenfold. He had received special protection in his career ever since, despite a few upsets along the way. Penkovsky revealed that he even had Varentsov to thank for his presence here in London, as he had asked him to intervene in a decision not to grant him permission to travel abroad. Varentsov knew that the Central Committee had requested that Penkovsky remain in Moscow, but was unaware that this was because the KGB had become suspicious about his father. Varentsov had hesitated, but at the last minute – just the day before – had supported his protégé, and had made sure the visa was granted.

This was doubly significant. On the one hand, it was clear that Penkovsky was mistrusted due to questions about his father, and that he was in a precarious position. He had only squeaked through on this trip thanks to Varentsov's patronage. On the other hand, what patronage to have! Penkovsky was very close to one of the most powerful men in the Soviet Union: Varentsov commanded the country's tactical missile forces.

Penkovsky continued to fill in his life story. After the war, he had married Vera and they had moved to Moscow, where he had studied at the Frunze Military Academy and then the prestigious Military Diplomatic Academy near the underground station Sokol. 'Is it not 13 Peschannaya Street?' asked Kisevalter, and Penkovsky confirmed the address.

This was a rare misstep by Kisevalter. He knew a great deal about the inner workings of the Soviet Union from having been Popov's handler, and was keen to show Penkovsky he was in the hands of professionals by referring to some of this knowledge. But on this and a few other occasions, Penkovsky was visibly unsettled at having his sentences finished in this way. After all, he was revealing Soviet state secrets – how could this man know such things? Harry Shergold was worried Kisevalter might overplay his hand.

In 1953, Penkovsky had graduated from the Military Diplomatic Academy, and joined the GRU. Two years later, he had been given his first and, it would turn out, only foreign posting, being sent to Turkey as the deputy Rezident.

Kisevalter asked what rank he had held at this time, prompting a clue about Penkovsky's motivation for switching sides. He said he had been appointed a full colonel in 1950, but that he would never be made a general. 'They have already said so and they have said I was unreliable.' And he added, jokingly: 'Maybe I will become a general in another army.'

The Soviet diplomatic community in Ankara was closely knit, even claustrophobic. Penkovsky had begun an affair with the wife of the KGB Rezident, but when the Rezident had propositioned Vera, Penkovsky had become enraged. But amid the cocktail parties and affairs, deeper intrigues were unfolding. In Ankara, Penkovsky had taken his first steps towards betraying the Soviet Union. It hadn't been for ideological or financial reasons, but out of petty vengeance: Penkovsky fell out of favour with his own boss, the GRU Rezident, and when a colleague had conspired with the Rezident to undermine him Penkovsky made an anonymous phone call from a public booth to Turkish counter-intelligence and told them where and when the officer met his agents. The Turks swooped, and the man was expelled from the country. Penkovsky then informed the KGB that the GRU Rezident was to blame for the incident, because he had allowed sloppy tradecraft. The tactic worked, and the Rezident was withdrawn from Turkey and discharged from the GRU, his career in tatters.

Penkovsky escaped unpunished, and went on to betray another colleague in Turkey in the same way. Turkish intelligence, which had strong links with the West, were interested – could Penkovsky perhaps become a full-time double agent? But he broke off contact: his career was now in the ascendant.

However, when his posting ended and he returned to Moscow, the picture suddenly appeared much less promising. Other GRU officers were angry at the way he had reported the Rezident in Turkey, and told him that no generals would work with him because he was a tattle-tale. Worried, Penkovsky turned to Varentsov. His mentor told him to wait until things had blown over, but the damage had already been done. Penkovsky had not been expelled from the GRU – perhaps because he had Varentsov's patronage – but he had been sidelined, placed in the agency's reserves. He was given intermittent assignments until in 1958 he had been sent to the Dzerzhinsky Military Academy, where he studied rocket artillery, graduating from three courses with distinction.

This led to a reconsidering of his abilities, and he was informed that he was being posted to India. However, just as he was about to leave he was told that the decision had been reversed and that he was to stay in Moscow after all, overseeing students at the academy. 'I was very disappointed about this and was very worried,' Penkovsky said. 'To be quite honest with you, my disaffection with the whole political system began quite a long time ago . . . the whole set-up was one of demagoguery, idle talk and deceit of the people.' Penkovsky was conveniently ignoring that he had been deceitful himself, and that there was a transparent connection between his supposed disaffection with the system and how far he had been able to advance in it.

In 1960, the KGB had discovered that his father had fought on the White side and that there was no record of his death. The GRU's chief of personnel had called Penkovsky in and asked for an explanation. Penkovsky replied that he had never met his father, or received any help from him, but could not explain why he had claimed he was dead, rather than missing.

He had not been called in again, but now felt as though he were no longer trusted. Fearful of being kicked out of the GRU, and resentful that he was still a colonel, Penkovsky had made the irreversible decision to switch allegiance. 'I was thinking of becoming a soldier in a new army,' he said, 'to adopt a new people, to struggle for a new ideal, and in some measure, to avenge my father and millions of other people who have perished in a terrible way – as well as for my close relatives . . .'

He had realised that there would be little point in approaching the West empty-handed: he needed something to bring with him. He had been appointed the master sergeant of a class of eighty students at the academy, and as a result had certain privileges. This included a pass allowing him to study books and lectures in the academy's classified library. He took to studying alone there, blocking the door by placing a chair under the knob as he laboriously copied out secret documents about guided rockets and launching equipment by hand. 'If anyone knocked I would slide everything into my briefcase, which was sealed, and I would simply say that I was studying.'

Penkovsky had copied out dozens of documents in this way, and hidden much of it in bundles wrapped in insulation tape in his uncle's *dacha* outside Moscow. He had sewn some documents into his clothing, had found a dead drop and had written a letter of introduction. After work, he had loitered outside the American Embassy and America House looking for a reliable-looking foreigner he could approach. But KGB sentries guarded both buildings, and he had never dared make a move. Finally he had become desperate, and had sidled up to the students on Moskvoretsky Bridge.

*

Having established whom Penkovsky was and why he had decided to make contact, Kisevalter now tried to discover what specific intelligence he could provide. This, too, poured out: Penkovsky described the GRU's structure in detail, explained the development of the Sputnik, discussed an accident that had killed a marshal that had been hushed up and gave some background to Yuri Gagarin's recent mission to orbit the earth.

It was juicy stuff, and Penkovsky was clearly knowledgeable about some highly technical subjects, particularly related to rockets. Kisevalter asked if he were aware of any Soviet plans to build launch sites for intercontinental ballistic missiles. Penkovsky said he didn't know, but that he had heard that bases and rocket troops for use against Britain were located north of Leningrad, in the region of Murmansk. 'The exact coordinates of their location are known to a very small group of people and the data lies in underground safes in the Arbat district,' he said, referring to the area in Moscow where his own office was located.

A map of Moscow was swiftly found, and Penkovsky pointed out the locations of key Ministry of Defence buildings, including the headquarters of the country's anti-aircraft forces, and the artillery, engineering, military training and chemical directorates. 'This should all be blown up with small, two kiloton bombs,' he said matter-of-factly. He added that in the event of a war, at two minutes after 'H-hour' – the GRU's term for the launch of an attack on the Soviet Union by the West – 'critical targets such as the General Staff, the KGB Headquarters on Dzerzhinsky Square, the Central Committee of the Party which organizes everything and similar targets must all be blown up by atomic prepositioned bombs, rather than by means of aircraft bombs or rockets which may or may not hit the vital targets'.

It was an astonishing suggestion, but it soon became clear it was not a casual one. As well as the documents sewn into his clothing, Penkovsky had also been carrying around a secret desire to wreak vengeance on the system that had denied him his rightful rank, and had channelled his professional energy into creating an extraordinary plan, which he now presented to the team.

'In our Soviet Army we have a five kiloton, a ten kiloton and higher weapons,' he said, 'but they have not been able to produce a one kiloton weapon yet. Our scientists are still working on it. I know this exactly. Such weapons would not need to be set within the buildings themselves, but there are many adjacent buildings where they can be concealed.' He gave as an example a branch of Gastronom, one of the 300 official food halls, next to the Lubyanka. Continuing with his plan, he said that a 'small group of saboteurs' should plant one- or two-kiloton nuclear bombs in specific locations that would simultaneously destroy all the buildings he had mentioned. He also proposed that attacks be carried out elsewhere, estimating that each major Soviet city would only need one man to destroy its military district head-quarters in the same way. If all the bombs were detonated at the same time, he said, it would send the Army into disarray and allow 'the execution of a military decision'.

He offered several variations of how this plan could be carried out. One was that the bombs, connected to timers, could be hidden inside small suitcases or satchels, which he volunteered to place himself. He also suggested disguising them as baskets of fruit and checking them into the baggage storage area of GRU's headquarters, where an old lady looked after packages during the day, and even that MI6 and the CIA could create replicas of the rubbish bins found in Moscow's streets and hide the bombs in specially prepared false bottoms: having been given these by dead drop, he could then put them in the boot of his car and drive around the city placing them next to the targets.

Penkovsky didn't just want to inform the West about Soviet intentions: he had devised his own action plan for how the USSR could be destroyed in a surprise attack, with himself helping to execute it. In one blow, he would defeat his enemies.

The plan was based on his knowledge that the Soviet Union

was vastly exaggerating its military might. He claimed that although Khrushchev was prioritising the arms race above everything else, the Soviet Union was still significantly behind the West. 'There simply is no monolithic Warsaw Pact,' he said. He claimed that the pumping of money into weapons development had led to the lowering of Army officers' pay and privileges, which in turn had caused a major slump in morale, with countless cases of ill-discipline. Penkovsky felt the West should exploit all these weaknesses. 'Of course, I am sorry for the people,' he said, 'but they have suffered so much already that if they suffer just once more for the sake of a really better future, it would be worthwhile having this war. But in that case, let me know when I should be in Moscow.'

The phrase 'this war' seems revealing of Penkovsky's thought processes. *He* had raised the idea of an imminent war, not the CIA–MI6 team, but he spoke as though it were accepted fact it would happen. He also presumed that the West would *want* a war with the Soviet Union, provided they could win it, and had already convinced himself of the merits of it taking place, and how he could play a part.

Casting himself as an armchair general, Penkovsky said that the West's leaders should ignore all the peace talk coming from the Kremlin, which was simply empty rhetoric. Instead, they should press their advantage. 'Back in 1956 when the Egyptian affair was going on,' he said, referring to the Suez crisis, 'the Soviet Union should have been sharply confronted, and even today this should be done. With Cuba, for example, I simply can't understand why Khrushchev should not be sharply rebuked. I do not know what answer Mr Kennedy will give him, but he certainly should be accused of arming Cuba with Soviet tanks and guns, right under the gates of America . . . Kennedy should be firm. Khrushchev is not going to fire any rockets. He is not ready for any war. I respect and love the United States and I certainly, in Kennedy's place, would be firm.' He asked why Kennedy shouldn't intervene to support 'patriotic elements' in Cuba, especially, he added, 'when you know what arms have been sent to Cuba from the USSR? This is my opinion and the opinion of many of our officers.'

The situation in Cuba was of intense interest to the United States – Fidel Castro's revolution of 1959 had established a Communist bulwark just ninety miles off the coast of the United States. Unknown to Penkovsky, as he was speaking the CIA was attempting to invade the island and overthrow Castro. The operation had begun at midnight on 17 April: 1,400 Cuban exiles, accompanied by CIA operational officers, had landed on beaches at Bahía de Cochinos – 'the Bay of Pigs' – on the southern coast of the island. They had immediately met with heavy fire from the Cuban Air Force, and dozens of exiles had been killed or captured. By 20 April, it had become clear in the White House that the operation was a 'real big mess'.

So for reasons Penkovsky could not know, his suggestion that Kennedy be firm with Khrushchev on Cuba was, at that moment, impractical: with the American backing of the failed invasion undeniable, Kennedy was now placed on the back foot. But Penkovsky's proposal that the United States accuse the Soviet Union of supplying Cuba with arms because Khrushchev would not retaliate was eerily prescient – that very issue would soon bring the two nations to the brink of an unimaginable catastrophe.

Penkovsky had mentioned that his view on Cuba was shared by other officers. This prompted Kisevalter to ask if he were acting as a representative for any group. 'No,' he said, 'I am all alone.' Nobody, including his wife, mother or teenage daughter, knew he was in contact with the West. However, he said that his views were widespread, and that many in the Soviet Union were disaffected, from the younger generation who were envious of the clothes they saw Western tourists wearing and who were turning to petty crime as a result, to senior members of the military who felt Khrushchev's reforms were a sham. Despite repeated promises that the country's situation would improve, it was instead worsening. He described the difficulty of finding decent food outside Moscow and Leningrad, saying he had heard that in some cities people had resorted to eating horse meat, and reported that poor roads and delays in the supply chain had led to rotting grain.

Khrushchev was ignoring all these problems, he said, and instead appeared to be looking for a chance to start a war with the West, claiming he wanted to bury imperialism under a 'rain of rockets'. But Penkovsky felt that, for the time being anyway, this was also a bluff. 'He will rant and rave and even send arms here and there just as he did to Cuba and possibly even send small-calibre rockets there. In fact, there was talk about this with Castro and possibly a few rockets are already there.'

This was the second time Penkovsky had mentioned that the Soviet Union were arming Cuba. The team didn't react to his claim that Khrushchev was considering sending rockets to the island, or may have already done so, nor did they ask what type they might be – everything he said would have to be analysed later, and followed up as seen fit.

Penkovsky had now explained who he was, why he had contacted them, and provided a wealth of intelligence. His cards on the table, he wanted to know what they thought of him so far, saying he was ready to carry out any missions they assigned him. All he asked in return, he said, was that they protected his life. He also said he was not prepared to defect if it meant leaving his family in Moscow. 'I would be happy now to go to England or America myself,' he said, 'but I cannot leave them behind.'

He also raised the question of payment, as he had done in the letter he had passed to Greville Wynne. Kisevalter replied warmly but cautiously, saying that they would give him what he needed in hand and deposit monthly payments in a bank for him. Penkovsky seemed satisfied with this, saying that he only wanted a nest-egg to secure his future. 'I see in your faces official, responsible high stature workers, my comrades,' he said, 'and also being an intelligence officer I know how to vet people. There is no need to keep things in the dark. No one needs this. I wish that your governments, and I consider them both my governments, trust me as their own soldier. It doesn't matter whether you confer the title of colonel on me or not.'

Considering his repeated references to having been denied promotion, and his written request to be given a military rank in the US Army, it seemed more likely that it was in fact very important to him that he be conferred such a title. Kisevalter had avoided mentioning figures, so Penkovsky now explained what he felt he deserved, pointing out that he was a man of substance: 'I have been a colonel now for eleven years. Previously I have received 5,000 rubles per month; now I receive 4,500. I have an apartment with quite a few personal items. I have been a regimental commander, and I have also been abroad.' In addition, he had married the daughter of a lieutenant-general, and had a good standard of living. 'But I would like to live even better,' he said, 'and to provide luxuries for my family.'

He explained that any additional income he received would not attract suspicion, because officers who travelled to the West often bought goods from their savings to bring back to Moscow. He also wanted some money in hand already, because he was considering buying a *dacha* outside Moscow. 'A modest *dacha* is entirely normal for someone of my age and status,' he said. 'This would cost about 10,000 rubles in new money. After returning from the Front, I had a Mercedes-Benz, but after riding around in it I sold it since I couldn't get parts and I was thinking about buying a Volga. All my comrades have cars. From my small savings and the money I have I usually spend quite a bit on my family and go out to restaurants. I am not an ascetic.'

In return, Penkovsky said he was prepared to sign an oath of allegiance to the West and to act as an agent-in-place in Moscow 'for at least a year or two'. He asked the team to prepare a way for them to be able to communicate once the delegation's visit had ended and he returned to Moscow, as he didn't want to risk meeting contacts personally, and to be given a miniature Minox camera so that he would be able to photograph documents.

Finally, at just after one o'clock in the morning, Colonel Oleg Penkovsky left Room 360 of the Mount Royal and made his way to his own room.

On Her Majesty's Secret Service

One thing was immediately obvious: Penkovsky was genuine. Both the quality and the amount of intelligence he had handed over in the meeting could not plausibly be chickenfeed: under close questioning by experienced and wary case officers he had given a detailed description of Soviet intelligence structures, and had also discussed many other institutions, giving names, addresses and precise details of the dynamics between departments and personalities, as well as a wealth of technical information. He had spoken vividly about the mood of the country: a first-person report from the front lines of the enemy camp. The team also examined the material he had passed to Greville Wynne at Heathrow, and found it included top-secret field manuals for intermediate- and medium-range ballistic missiles, including for the R-12, which carried a one-megaton nuclear warhead. This intelligence would later prove crucial.

Another key factor in determining whether an agent is genuine is their motivations. Penkovsky's were clear: deep resentment at having been passed over for promotion, and a desire for recognition, with remuneration to match. The KGB's accusation that he had concealed the fact that his father had fought with the White Army was also a clear psychological trigger behind his decision to approach the West, and he had returned to the topic obsessively.

Experience and common sense said that none of this could be part of a disinformation operation cooked up by the Soviets. Penkovsky's intelligence had tumbled out naturally, messily, and the way in which he had told his life story was far too humanly flawed to have been an act: he was eager to please and quick to sentimentalise, but also self-important, driven and, when discussing those who had crossed him, savage. By his own admission he could be vengeful, deceitful, petty and had been unfaithful to his wife – but, perversely, all these qualities pointed to his being genuine. It would have required the world's greatest and best-prepared actor to have created such a plausible impression of a man desperately seeking vengeance against those who had overlooked him and a better lifestyle for his family, while pretending to his listeners and himself that his decision to betray his country was solely the result of principle and geopolitical necessity.

Another clincher was his insane scheme to use nuclear weapons to attack key command and control centres in Moscow, which he repeatedly insisted should be carried out. It was hard to imagine any Soviet intelligence chief thinking it would be a good idea to inform the West of the most vulnerable points of his country's armed forces and suggest a way to blow them to smithereens in order to establish the bona fides of a plant.

History often alters course after widely publicised events: grand speeches, summits and treaties. But in this case it would be affected by what one man had said in a hotel room in London. It would take time to filter through to the decision-makers in Washington and London, but in less than four hours Oleg Penkovsky had presented a completely new picture of the state of the Cold War. By his reckoning, the Soviet Union was not leading the arms race but was in fact significantly *behind* the United States: it was a paper tiger, and Khrushchev was simply roaring as loudly as he could in the hope that the

Americans might continue to believe it to be a real one. A huge amount of money and resources were being poured into trying to rectify the situation, with the result that the whole society was suffering.

That Penkovsky was genuine was a cause for celebration within the team: they were now, finally, in contact with a major source within Soviet intelligence, who had as his personal mentor one of the most powerful men in the country, Marshal Varentsov. This level of access to Soviet strategic thinking was unprecedented – more significant than even Popov had been.

But while the greatest hurdle had been cleared, the excitement was tempered by the realisation that they now faced several new problems. Penkovsky's motivation rang true, and seemed powerful enough to drive him on to spy for some time yet, but might it also affect his work? Would he exaggerate snippets of intelligence he had heard in order to impress them with what they wanted to hear – or with what they didn't? Bulik had been deeply impressed by Penkovsky, but was bearing in mind an old spooks' proverb: 'Never fall in love with your agents.' Others were more unforgiving still. When Dick White read the transcript of the first meeting in his red-carpeted office on the fourth floor of MI6's headquarters, he was stunned by the intelligence haul but hard-nosed about what it revealed of Penkovsky's character: he felt the Russian was neurotic, vain and crazy.

That transcript had been prepared by female MI6 officers working in the basement of a large facility in Pall Mall that acted as the operation's command centre. They would occasionally surface to ask Kisevalter the meaning of certain Russian words, as the language had evolved from tsarist times and some military terms were in no existing dictionaries. Like many Russians, Penkovsky swore a fair amount, and swear words also tended to be absent from Russian dictionaries. To spare their blushes, Kisevalter would give them a sanitised translation.

Once the transcripts were completed, the team pored over them with another CIA officer, Leonard McCoy, who was an expert in rocketry and missiles. McCoy was the team's technical brain and his evaluation of Penkovsky's intelligence, and advice on which questions to ask to elicit more of it, would prove integral to the operation. He had another important job – he distributed the sherry in the command centre at four o'clock sharp every afternoon.

★

Having prepared follow-up questions with McCoy, the team met Penkovsky in Room 360 the following evening. Within minutes, he was discussing the inner workings of the GRU: how it monitored radio communications, its relationship with the KGB and even the location of secret compartments in its cars.

Some of his information was incomplete, but intriguing nevertheless. At one point he said that he hoped that the GRU might one day send him for training to work under cover in Britain, Canada or the United States. 'May God grant that this happens,' he said, 'because then I could play an important role. Everything would be in my hands, everything – ciphers, radio intelligence, people. This would be important to us. There is one agent – I don't know whether he is in England or America, but I'll swear by my life that there are agents.'

He doesn't seem to have been talking about Soviet intelligence officers here, many of whom worked out of embassies, but foreign agents working for the GRU. This passing remark was never followed up, but it suggests that there may have been at least one undiscovered Soviet agent working in the West.

In the first meeting, Penkovsky had explained that a lot of the material he had gathered he had hidden at his uncle's *dacha* outside Moscow. He said he would have no trouble retrieving it once he was back in the Soviet Union, but he needed a way to then pass it to them. He suggested they set up several more dead drops for him in Moscow, but Kisevalter felt this would be too risky.

'Remember that the servicing of a dead drop by one of our people who is possibly – probably – under heavy surveillance is a constant danger,' he said. 'For you to fill and clear a dead drop where there is no surveillance is no problem. But although you live in Moscow and although you are forty-two, I am sure that you can have no idea how heavy the surveillance of all our people in Moscow is.' Penkovsky said he understood. 'Then double this understanding,' said Kisevalter, 'and you will be closer to the actual facts.'

Perhaps aware that this had sounded a little harsh, he went on to explain that it was not their officer that they were primarily worried about. 'What can happen to him as a diplomat? A small scandal and he is thrown out. We will be alive and well, but . . .'

Penkovsky finished the sentence for him: '. . . I am gone.'

The other problem with using dead drops was timing – the longer the gap between material being deposited and picked up, the more chance it could be discovered. Harry Shergold suggested trying to combine the benefits of a dead drop with brush contacts. One way to do this would be at a cocktail party: as a Soviet official, Penkovsky would be expected to be invited to a few of these, and be allowed to attend without raising suspicion.

'He would know that the man who was going to pick up the material would be there,' Shergold explained to Kisevalter to translate. 'He would put it in place and the man would remove it.'

Variations of this could also be done in restaurants, essentially creating a dead drop that was immediately emptied.

Penkovsky was sceptical. 'Surveillance is very concentrated against your people in restaurants,' he said.

The problem would continue to exercise the team. It was all very well having a golden goose in Moscow – but they had to figure out a safe way to get at his eggs.

And there were a lot more eggs to grab. Most of the material Penkovsky had collected so far had been from the Dzerzhinsky Military Academy's library, but the academy had *another*, more prestigious library. Penkovsky and other high-ranking officers attended weekly lectures at the academy to keep up with their military knowledge, which was routinely tested. But as part of their studies they were also entitled to work in the GRU's library on the premises, which contained highly classified reference material under lock and key. Penkovsky had not accessed this library yet, but he could apply to do so for a few hours on Thursday afternoons. Penkovsky said that if he were given a Minox, he would try to photograph some of the documents he found. The team was keen; it was becoming clear that if they could find a way to keep in contact with him in Moscow, untold intelligence riches could be theirs for the taking.

Penkovsky also discussed the friction between Russia and its satellite states. He revealed that rockets had been delivered to all the satellite states, but without atomic warheads attached. An exception was the DDR, East Germany, where he said there were two brigades and two dumps of atomic warheads that were under the control of the Soviet Army.

This triggered one of his most intriguing parenthetical remarks, which nobody in the room could have known would foreshadow events to come. 'Speaking of Germans,' he said, 'you have seen how often Khrushchev threatened to make a separate peace with the DDR. He will not do this because it could invoke a war. He is not ready to fire missiles now and he will avoid a war at this time. Even though he is giving rockets and training personnel to the DDR, they are still far from being ready to use them.'

In 1961, the situation regarding Germany had still not been resolved since the Second World War. The four major victorious allies had agreed to share power in the country, with the eastern part becoming a Soviet zone and the west coming under the supervision of the US, Britain and France until a stable democracy was established. Berlin had also been split, with four sectors each controlled by a nation, again with the intention of this being an interim measure. However, Berlin was positioned in the east of the country, meaning that its Western sectors could only be accessed through Soviet-controlled territory. In 1948, objecting to currency reforms in the Western zones, Stalin had blocked all road and rail traffic into the Western sectors of Berlin. For a time, it had looked as if the situation might develop into a third world war: in late September, senior MI6 officer Dick Brooman-White had confided to journalist and sometime-MI6 instructor Malcolm Muggeridge that 'war now could more or less be taken for granted'.

The situation had eventually cooled, thanks to an airlift by the Western allies, but with a clear discrepancy in the standard of living between what was now two Germanys – the Soviets unilaterally declared the East a nation in 1949 – hundreds of thousands of people fled across the border from East to West Berlin every year. Since Stalin's death, Khrushchev had repeatedly called for the Western allies to resolve the issue by signing a peace treaty with the Soviet Union recognising East and West Germany as two separate nations. If they didn't, he said, he would sign a peace treaty with East Germany alone, which would once again threaten the access routes into western Berlin. However, according to Penkovsky, Khrushchev's demands could be ignored, because he would never risk waging a war over the issue.

As he had done in the first meeting, Penkovsky tried to press for payment for offering such intelligence, and disclosed that he was in financial trouble. 'I like to live freely and now and then take a lady out,' he said. 'I know how to approach them and I never drink to excess . . .' But he had debts, and wanted the team to help him out. 'I've already thought of buying odds and ends here that I can sell at a profit there,' he said. 'I know some wealthy Jews in Moscow who can even bundle diamonds.'

He argued that paying him would also smooth the wheels of access in Moscow. 'I must bring each and every friend of mine some small item,' he said, 'since they know that I am going abroad. It does not have to be an expensive item in every case but it would be extremely bad to neglect anyone.' Among the items he wanted were fountain pens, lipstick and neckties, as well as more expensive gifts for friends in the military. He was particularly keen to find cosmetics, stressing that he had to bring every secretary in his office at least one item, 'even though it may be the cheapest lipstick in England.'

Bulik suggested that such considerations be discussed at the next meeting. 'I just thought of something,' Penkovsky said, perhaps fearing he had overplayed his hand. 'If I could have a one-carat diamond, exactly one carat, not more or less, I am sure that I could cash it in for 1,200 rubles. Consider this, and possibly we can so work it out that you will not be concerned about passing any monies to me through contacts in Moscow for some time.'

Kisevalter assured him that it would be considered, and Penkovsky seemed satisfied. As two o'clock in the morning neared, the meeting broke up.

★

Penkovsky had once again provided a huge amount of raw intelligence, but the focus had shifted to a more blatant nego-tiation over payment. His claim that he needed to buy items in

London because they were necessary to smooth his work gathering intelligence once back in Moscow probably had some truth to it: in the Soviet Union, the cultivation of influence through favours and gifts was central to society. As one CIA officer involved in the operation later put it: 'Where one stood in the Kremlin hierarchy appeared to be part and parcel with what one was able to acquire from abroad.'

However, Penkovsky had also clearly realised that his intelligence was of great interest, and so was trying to pressure the CIA and MI6 into paying as high a price for it as he could get. But he didn't have all the leverage. His handlers knew that there was now no turning back for him, and that he was unlikely to find any other takers anyway. They didn't want to scare him off and have the intelligence dry up by low-balling him, but he couldn't risk them turning their back on him if he asked for too much.

These delicate negotiations depended to a great extent on George Kisevalter's charm and empathy, but the fact that they were happening was also reassuring. Penkovsky's remarks chimed with Bulik's earlier research into his time in Turkey, which had turned up reports of his approaching foreign diplomats trying to sell jewellery to them, and his desire for financial reward was more controllable than the more volatile question of his desire to exact revenge on his colleagues.

More troubling was his admission that he liked to 'now and then take a lady out'. It soon became obvious that this was an understatement, and that Penkovsky was repeatedly unfaithful to his wife and had a penchant for nightclub hostesses and prostitutes. Such behaviour posed a major security risk, as Penkovsky acknowledged, but it wasn't an easy problem to solve. It needed to be controlled: simply telling him to stop the practice wouldn't guarantee that he did.

★

Penkovsky and the rest of the delegation soon left London to visit factories in Leeds and Birmingham. The team followed, meeting him in hotel rooms. There were a few jumpy moments. In an episode reminiscent of a Laurel and Hardy film, when Kisevalter went into the street on one occasion to guide Penkovsky discreetly to the hotel where the team were staying the two men got in a muddle in the revolving door, with Kisevalter walking back through it to see what had happened to a dawdling Penkovsky just as the Russian was coming through – by the time they had extricated themselves, they had drawn the attention of most of the people sitting in the lobby. Penkovsky also made the mistake of going to the pub with Greville Wynne and drinking two pints of beer extremely quickly: his kidneys seized up and a doctor had to be summoned. Penkovsky was terrified of being hospitalised, as it would have been a black mark against him in Moscow, but luckily he soon recovered and it wasn't necessary.

On 28 April, the delegation returned to London, where the meetings continued at the Mount Royal. Penkovsky discussed the weight of launching fuel, the construction of containers for nuclear warheads, military vehicles, the development of fissionable atomic material, the preparation and use of codes and ciphers, radio intelligence within GRU *rezidenturas*, the Strela 4 mainframe computer and the bugging of foreign embassies. He was also shown around seven thousand photographs of Soviet diplomats that had been provided by the CIA, MI5 and MI6. From these, he identified around a thousand GRU officers and two to three hundred KGB officers, providing names, roles and operational histories for many.

This was unprecedented intelligence, but it was exhausting work extracting it, especially as Penkovsky was becoming increasingly pompous. 'I did not come to you to do little things,' he said at one point while reciting an almost comically egotistical speech he had prepared. The team let him deliver it:

a good case officer knows when to listen to his agent. Penkovsky said he wanted to be remembered as the greatest spy in history, and announced that he would like to meet the Queen. After all, Yuri Gagarin had met her when he had visited London, and unlike Gagarin he was working in Britain's interests.

According to Bulik, Shergold 'sweated crocodile drops' at this request. They had to appear to take it seriously, because the intelligence Penkovsky was providing was too valuable to risk alienating him. But introducing the Queen to a Soviet agent was out of the question: another solution would have to be found. Penkovsky claimed it was vital that he personally reassure those at the highest level in the West that he was genuine. 'I do not say that you do not believe me,' he said, 'you who are here and who are already my dear friends, my comrades in battle. This I reject. But perhaps somebody who does not know me, who cannot look into my eyes like you, will say, "Perhaps he copies all this about rockets out of *Pravda*," or something like that.'

Penkovsky spent 1 May, International Workers' Day, in high style: shopping at Harrods with Greville Wynne's wife, Sheila. He bought clothes for his wife and daughter and after-shave lotion for himself, and gave it all to Wynne, who would later bring it to Moscow. Penkovsky then returned to the Mount Royal for a debriefing session with the team. He put in another appeal for his intelligence to be evaluated in the event of his defection. He had heard that the CIA had paid a million dollars for a dossier from a South American country – he had now decided it was only fair that he should be paid $8000 into an account if he were to defect in eight months' time.

The team didn't want to commit to such an arrangement – not because they couldn't afford it, but because Penkovsky was far more valuable as an agent-in-place. The moment he defected he would cease to have access to current Soviet intelligence and strategic thinking. So they again avoided promising specific sums, and instead assured Penkovsky that he and his family would be extremely well looked after when they reached the West. Penkovsky emphasised how much he had already given them: 'I did not say to you, "Here is one rocket, two. This is a code. This is something else." I gave everything!' He wanted to agree figures because he was worried they could be replaced by other case officers later on, who could then change the terms if they hadn't been formally arranged. The team assured him that this would never happen: they would be his team from now until the end, come what may.

*

The team were processing the mountain of material at the command centre in Pall Mall, and bonded over lunches, often eating at a Lyons Corner House next door to the Mount Royal. Penkovsky, meanwhile, was enjoying his first trip outside the Soviet Union since his disastrous time in Turkey, and it was going to his head. After Wynne took him to the cinema to see *Roman Holiday*, he announced to the team that one day he would like to meet Audrey Hepburn.

He was also enjoying London's more illicit pleasures. At another meeting, he told the team about an evening he had spent with Wynne at a 'luxurious cabaret' and jokingly asked if they could extend his visit for another ten days. He had met a 23-year-old girl at the club. 'She has a pretty name,' he said. 'Zeph.' Wynne had introduced Penkovsky as 'Alex from Belgrade', which had caused him some difficulty when she had asked him to teach her a few words of his language. Penkovsky had said something in broken Russian, which Zeph had solemnly repeated.

Penkovsky had given fifteen pounds to Wynne, who had then arranged for him to spend two hours with Zeph at her flat. This had potential security implications, and it may be that Zeph received a discreet knock on her door shortly afterwards asking her not to talk about Alex from Belgrade to anyone – later in the operation, MI6 would make sure Penkovsky had access to women with security clearance, and Bulik personally arranged at least one meeting with a prostitute. It was no time for scruples about such matters.

Penkovsky was enjoying his time roaming London's *demimonde*, but he had not forgotten his request to meet someone of importance. He couldn't meet the Queen, so Dick White decided he would attend a debriefing session with him instead.

'Well, Colonel,' said the lean, patrician spy chief shortly after entering Room 360 late on the evening of 3 May, 'the message I have to deliver to you is from Lord Mountbatten, the chief of the Defence Department of England.'

Mountbatten was in fact chairman of the Chiefs of Staff Committee, but it had been felt that this would make more of an impact. White apologised that Mountbatten could not be there himself, but said he had been asked to relay his admiration for the great stand Penkovsky had made in choosing to serve the governments of Britain and the United States. 'I have also had reported to me the information which you have passed on to us,' he said. 'I can only tell you that it would be of the highest value and importance to the Free World.'

Penkovsky replied equally fulsomely, but ended by saying that he wished to swear his loyalty to Queen Elizabeth II and to President Kennedy. 'Although unfortunately due to circumstances this is not possible now,' he said, 'I hope that in the future I will be blessed by this fortune personally by the Queen.'

White neatly sidestepped the issue, saying that should the time come that Penkovsky would need to leave the Soviet Union, MI6 and the CIA would 'firmly and clearly' fulfil all its obligations to him. Wine was served, and Penkovsky's health and continued success was toasted. After this, Shergold escorted White out.

Penkovsky immediately turned to Kisevalter. 'Did I say everything properly?' he asked.

Kisevalter assured him he had done very well: 'You didn't overdo it.' He added that he was sure that Lord Mountbatten would tell the Queen about his work.

Despite this, it was obvious that the show had not gone down as well as had been hoped: Bulik later said Penkovsky 'was clearly not impressed'. White also sensed this, but felt it was unavoidable. 'I realised it was not what he wanted to hear,' he recalled. 'He wanted to be praised personally by the Queen for his monumental contribution and to have a medal pinned on his breast. There was no possibility of this.'

*

The same day Dick White met Penkovsky, George Blake had been sentenced to forty-two years' imprisonment at London's Central Criminal Court. With Blake behind bars and contact with a major new source in Soviet intelligence established, White may have sat at his desk in London and felt that MI6 had finally put its darkest days behind it. Despite Penkovsky's idiosyncrasies and demands, he was supplying a mountain of material about his colleagues, technical specifications and military secrets, the likes of which had never before been seen by the West.

For the team, elation was mixed with anxiety, because Penkovsky was soon due to return to Moscow. Also on 4 May, the team rehearsed a detailed communications plan, which had been codenamed YO-YO 51. It had several elements. One was the use of a radio set: this would be sent by diplomatic bag to the British Embassy in Moscow, and would be picked up by Greville Wynne to hand to Penkovsky at a later date. At designated times, the CIA would then broadcast messages via shortwave radio from one of their bases in Frankfurt. The messages consisted of numbers being read aloud: Penkovsky was told at which times these would be sent, and to disregard the random numbers transmitted either side of them. Once he had written down a message, he would decode it using a one-time pad. Kisevalter showed him how to make codes from the pads and the procedures for receiving and transmitting the messages, and tested him on both techniques with an expert named in the files as 'Paul' until he was totally fluent.

For simpler messages, there was the telephone, and several signals were agreed, including a regular check-in message on Mondays. Penkovsky was to set this in train as soon as he returned: at nine o'clock on the evening of Monday 8 May, he was to find a call box on the street and dial 948973. This was the number of John Varley, the assistant naval attaché at the British Embassy in Moscow. If all was well Penkovsky was to let the phone ring three times, then hang up, wait one minute, and repeat the process. If anything had gone wrong he was to do the same, but to let the phone ring five times in both bursts instead.

The team planned to provide Penkovsky with a miniature Minox camera, also via Wynne, with twenty rolls of film. At an earlier meeting, he had said he was worried whether he would be able to take good enough photographs with the Minox, as he had last used one in Turkey five years earlier. To make sure there were no problems, a photographic expert from MI6, referred to as 'Kingsbury' in the files, instructed him on how to use the camera to its best capabilities. After looking at several blown-up images by Penkovsky, Kingsbury pronounced himself impressed: 'I think he has gotten the idea fairly well. These are very good shots.'

The team also had to make arrangements regarding Penkovsky's meetings with Greville Wynne in Moscow – but

Penkovsky raised a potential problem. He sensed that Wynne was starting to resent him, feeling that Penkovsky was flush with money from MI6 and the CIA while he ran around as his errand boy, never receiving his fair share of the proceeds. Penkovsky urged them to tread carefully with Wynne, to pay him, and to make sure he was kept happy – he didn't want to jeopardise the operation with any weak links.

Wynne was not a professional intelligence officer, and nor could he be used too often without the KGB becoming suspicious. Several other methods of contact were discussed, some of them suggested by Penkovsky. The first was to use another dead drop he had identified and simply deposit material there. Then there was Shergold's idea to contact him at cocktail parties attended by Western diplomats. Penkovsky was told that any approach of this nature would be done by someone who would find a way to insert the name of Charles Peeke, the American military attaché he had known in Turkey, into the conversation. As a further means of identification, the contact would wear a distinctive tie clasp with red stones, which Kisevalter showed him.

If neither of these methods proved possible, Penkovsky could also pass material to them by throwing it over the wall of America House at agreed times: the old plan from the desperate COMPASS days. And if Penkovsky were suddenly sent abroad and didn't have an opportunity to warn them of it while still in Moscow, he should send a telegram to the address LABORICI LONDON, signing it ALEX. 'That's a nice name, Alex,' Penkovsky mused. It was in fact poor tradecraft to use it, as this was the name Wynne called him, a fact that could easily have been discovered by the Soviets – but in the event Penkovsky would never send any telegrams.

One final method of personal contact was suggested. Ruari Chisholm, MI6's Head of Station in Moscow, had worked with George Blake in Berlin, which meant Blake would almost certainly have given the KGB his name. As a result, Chisholm's MI6 file was marked 'Sovbloc Red', meaning there was a danger in using him in operations. Harry Shergold had an idea: why not use Ruari's wife Janet instead? Dick White thought it viable. She wasn't an intelligence officer, but had worked for MI6 – she had been Ruari's secretary and had given up the job on marrying him in 1954 – and although Blake had known her after that and her file was also marked 'Sovbloc Red' as a result, White's instinct was that the KGB would be unlikely to tail a woman, especially if she had young children with her: the Chisholms had three, and Janet often took them for walks in the city. It was decided that Penkovsky could meet her in a park in Moscow, the details to be worked out later.

It was nearly time to go. Penkovsky was keyed up, and at an egocentric peak. 'This is a historic room,' he announced. 'Someday there will be a memorial plaque here.' He was missing London already – at one point he began pining for Zeph. 'You know, she really fell for me,' he said. 'She was quite sincere, exceptionally so. Two hours was really very short. She was really a bit surprised that I left so soon.' Penkovsky had been impressed by her flat: 'I don't have such a nice one!' he said. It was perhaps a fitting note for the end of his trip, a reminder of the differences at stake: a Soviet colonel living with his wife, mother and teenage daughter was envying the living conditions of a London prostitute.

The team checked all the arrangements for Moscow one last time. Shergold drew up a set of detailed operational instructions, which ended with the following note: 'Arrangements for receiving material from Subject by the use of a lady, children and prams in a park will be passed to him via WYNNE, or failing this through DLB.'

On Saturday, 6 May, Penkovsky arrived in Moscow. He spent the weekend basking in the glow of his family, who were delighted with all the gifts he had brought from London.

Two days later he returned to work in Gorky Street, and on his way back from the office that evening entered a telephone booth close to his flat, placed a two-kopeck coin in the slot and dialled 948973. He let it ring three times, then hung up. He counted out one minute and repeated the process.

All was well, for now.

Russian Roulette

May 1961, Moscow.

Oleg Penkovsky walked into the Ministry of Defence complex on Frunze Street and showed his pass to the KGB guard on duty. After being nodded through, he strode down the lobby and took the stairs to the first floor, where he entered the library of the Artillery Command. He asked to be taken to the Special Collection, and showed another pass granting him access to the room containing shelves of top-secret material. Once inside, he quickly leaned the chair against the doorknob and took out his Minox. It was time to get to work.

Before he had left London, Leonard McCoy and an MI6 analyst had prepared a list of priorities – a 'requirements list' in the jargon – for Penkovsky to follow, and he now rifled through the files looking to fulfil it. He had told Marshal Varentsov that he wanted to write an article on nuclear strategy for a military journal, and Varentsov had immediately arranged for him to be given the relevant passes to access the material.

For the next couple of months, Penkovsky visited the library regularly, photographing hundreds of secret documents. He went well beyond the requirements list, looking for anything else that might be of interest. In his first meeting with the team in London, he had mentioned a defence journal, *Voyennaya Mysl* ('Military Thought'). McCoy knew from a previous operation that there were two versions of this journal, one for wider distribution and a classified edition, and so had suggested to the team that they ask Penkovsky to try to get hold of the secret version once back in Moscow. In response, Penkovsky had laughed and asked if they might not want the *third*, top-secret, version of it instead, which had been introduced in 1960 and was marked 'Only for Officers, Admirals and Generals of the Soviet Army'. Now Penkovsky took photographs of dozens of these issues of *Voyennaya Mysl*, which would become one of the CIA's most prized intelligence treasures. He also found a list of documents that had been stolen from American, French, British and Italian intelligence, and in four frames photographed all the Kremlin's classified telephone directories, which would eventually allow the West to create the most complete picture of the Soviet power structure to date.

★

On 27 May 1961, Greville Wynne arrived in Moscow, ostensibly for a French trade fair in the city. Penkovsky met him at the airport and helped him with one of his suitcases, which was stuffed with gifts Penkovsky had bought in London but had not dared bring through customs himself. Once they were in Penkovsky's car, the Russian passed Wynne three rolls of microfilm containing documents from the Special Collection library.

Wynne checked in to the Metropol, reputed to be the best hotel in Moscow but which he felt was on a par with 'some no-star hostel in the wilds of Cornwall', and then made his way to the British Embassy, where he asked for Ruari Chisholm. The two men conducted an exchange in silence,

Wynne handing over the microfilms and Chisholm passing him instructions to give Penkovsky that evening. As soon as Wynne had left the embassy, Chisholm's assistant Felicity Stuart sent a ciphered message to London to say that the exchange had gone as planned.

*

In Washington, Joe Bulik, George Kisevalter, Harry Shergold, Leonard McCoy and Mike Stokes were busy assessing the mass of intelligence from the meetings with Penkovsky in England. Instead of working out of CIA headquarters, they operated out of a warehouse in Alexandria, where the meeting tapes were transcribed and analysed.

To obtain a deeper understanding of Penkovsky's material, McCoy had been doing a lot of background research. He had visited the National Security Agency, the Strategic Air Command, Army and Air Force intelligence, North American Aerospace Defense Command (NORAD), the nuclear weapons design laboratory in Los Alamos and the Dugway military facility. As a result MI6 reassigned their own analyst, and their reporting and requirements division sent information directly to McCoy, as did the equivalent CIA division.

McCoy's careful probing within the intelligence community confirmed that Penkovsky's material was dynamite – but as a result it had to be handled extremely delicately. The team wanted the intelligence to reach all the appropriate officials in Britain and the United States, but without endangering Penkovsky in any way. As a result of George Blake and other cases, they were well aware of the risk of a security leak, and that if the Soviets got wind of the fact that so much high-grade intelligence was being passed to the West they could investigate and pinpoint the source.

To counter this, MI6 gave Penkovsky's material two code-names, RUPEE and ARNIKA, to try to disguise the fact that so much intelligence was coming from one source. In John le Carré's *The Russia House*, which was inspired by the Penkovsky operation, an MI6 case officer complains that the distribution list for the material from 'Bluebird', the novel's agent-in-place in the Soviet Union, is too large: 'There are two hundred and forty people on that list and every one of them has a wife, a mistress and fifteen best friends.' In Britain, 1,700 people eventually had access to Penkovsky's material, including members of MI5, the Foreign Office, the Joint Intelligence Committee and scientific research establishments. In May, Dick White also gave the go-ahead for a small group of very senior officers in MI5 to be briefed about other aspects of the operation: MI5's Director-General, Roger Hollis; his deputy Graham Mitchell; Martin Furnival Jones; and three other senior officers were informed that RUPEE and ARNIKA were in fact the same source, and were told Penkovsky's identity: in July, a further MI5 officer was similarly informed.

The CIA gave Penkovsky the codename HERO, and also gave his material two codenames. Material emanating from Penkovsky himself, such as his own opinions and analysis or information he had heard from others, was codenamed CHICKADEE, and was only distributed on a 'MUST KNOW' basis to the President, the Secretary of Defense, the Secretary of State and around twenty senior CIA officers. The raw material he provided, such as top-secret field manuals and military journals, was given the codename IRONBARK, and had a slightly wider distribution. Documents stamped with these two codenames were among the American government's most classified secrets.

The separate codenames were to help protect Penkovsky, but they also weakened the impact of his intelligence: some may have regarded it very differently had they known that the CIA and MI6 had managed to extract so much high-grade classified material from a single serving Soviet intelligence officer acting as an agent-in-place in Moscow. A later report by the US Senate called this the 'ultimate achievement' in the CIA's mission to collect intelligence clandestinely, but at the time very few of those who received it knew that this had been done. With the benefit of half a century's hindsight, it was probably also not the best idea to use a codename for the material that sounded like 'chickenfeed'.

Some of Penkovsky's most important intelligence, on Soviet missile strength, was greeted with great scepticism. At one of the meetings in London Kisevalter had asked him about Khrushchev's public claim that the Soviet Union had rockets with a range of 2000–4000 kilometres, and that production had begun on some with an even greater range. Penkovsky had replied that he knew from Varentsov that many of Khrushchev's proclamations on ICBMs and rockets were a bluff to fool the West: 'He lies like a grey stallion,' he said. This offered such a radically different interpretation of the situation that it was initially discounted. The US Air Force in particular had a vested interest in maintaining the perception that the Soviet missile threat was serious: the larger the threat, the greater its budget. Penkovsky's claims were not even mentioned in the subsequent National Intelligence Estimate, because the source had not been known and, perhaps more importantly, the information 'did not exactly fit the views of anyone at the meeting'.

In time, Penkovsky's intelligence was more widely accepted. A National Intelligence Estimate from September 1961 stated that new information had caused 'a sharp downward revision' in the estimate of Soviet ICBM strength, and a CIA report from 1975 concluded that while Penkovsky's intelligence alone had not been enough to close the missile gap argument, 'it tentatively supported the almost heretical argument for a limited Soviet ICBM program'.

A combination of sources finally led to a major shift in thinking: Penkovsky's information was corroborated by other intelligence, such as that provided by U-2 photographs. 'It is my view that in the field of intelligence you need both technical and human sources,' Joe Bulik later remarked. 'If you can get into the mind of the Khrushchevs of the world, then you've got a weapon that no technical amount of information can give you, and this is what Penkovsky was able to give us.'

★

While the team went through Penkovsky's material in the warehouse in Alexandria, close by John F. Kennedy was contemplating what to do in the wake of the Bay of Pigs humiliation. Kennedy was furious at the failed operation, declaring that he wanted to 'splinter the CIA in a thousand pieces and scatter it to the winds'. Both in public and via private diplomatic channels, Khrushchev and Kennedy professed themselves keen to work with each other to ease tensions between their countries, but both were also investing enormous resources into trying to discover the other's intentions, by fair means or foul. East and West alike claimed to be deeply shocked and outraged whenever they caught a spy on their territory, as though they never engaged in such activity themselves. But, as US Secretary of State Dean Rusk acknowledged a few years later, the reality of the Cold War was that behind the public statements and diplomacy, there was 'a tough struggle going on in the back alleys all over the world' in which there was 'no quarter asked and none given'.

On 3 June 1961, Kennedy and Khrushchev met for a summit in Vienna. The two men walked around the grounds of the American Embassy, followed by their interpreters, sizing each other up like boxers in the opening seconds of a round. The city was an appropriate venue for the confrontation: still conflicted and scarred by the Second World War, a place where East and West met uneasily every day.

On the surface, it wasn't a fair fight: Kennedy was young, handsome, new to office and still popular at home; the son of a diplomat, polished, articulate and leader of the world's greatest superpower. Khrushchev was a Ukrainian peasant, a former miner and metal-worker who had slowly ascended through Stalin's court. But the reality was rather different. Despite his glowing image of health, Kennedy experienced severe back pain as the result of Addison's disease and was taking a cocktail of methamphetamines and steroids – his so-called 'joy juice' – to stave off the agony.

Khrushchev was also a bare-knuckle fighter, prepared to hit below the belt. Although Kennedy's briefing documents had noted that Khrushchev was a volatile leader whose manner could veer from 'the cherubic to the choleric', the American was unprepared for the Russian's undisguised hostility towards him, and couldn't understand why Khrushchev was refusing to play by the usual diplomatic rules. The reason was simple: Khrushchev had estimated – precisely as Penkovsky had claimed – that the best way to deal with the Americans was to bluff about his own country's strength. When his son Sergei had asked him why he boasted of factories producing missiles like sausages when they in fact were doing nothing of the sort, Khrushchev had replied: 'The important thing is to make the Americans believe that. And that way we prevent an attack.'

The consequences of this strategy would play out in two crises to come, both of which took the world to the very brink of nuclear war. The first of these crises began in Vienna, and involved the tangled question of Germany. Khrushchev was pressing for his treaty with the West, but the Americans were anxious that this would result in restricting the freedom of movement in and out of western Berlin.

It was a stalemate, but it couldn't remain one forever. In a meeting with British Prime Minister Harold Macmillan on his yacht the *Honey Fitz* two months earlier, Kennedy had expressed surprise that Khrushchev hadn't made a move on Berlin, and wondered whether the hesitation had been due to a belief that the West would react firmly, triggering war. Penkovsky had also alluded to this with the team in London, claiming that despite Khrushchev's repeated threat to sign a separate treaty with East Germany he would not deliver on it because it might 'invoke a war'.

For a fortnight before the Vienna summit, Kennedy used back-channel communications with Georgi Bolshakov, a GRU officer working under cover as the head of the TASS news bureau in Washington, to inform Khrushchev that while he wanted to cool the tensions between East and West, he was not yet prepared to reach any agreement on the status of Berlin. Khrushchev was unimpressed. Kennedy had claimed in his inaugural presidential address that 'the torch has been passed to a new generation of Americans', but the Soviet leader was not convinced that this was for the better: he felt Kennedy was young, weak and inexperienced. Just before leaving for Vienna, Khrushchev told a secret session of the Presidium in Moscow he would insist on an East German treaty, because he didn't think the Americans would risk a nuclear war over the issue, partly because they could not rely on support from their allies. President de Gaulle and Prime Minister Macmillan would not side with the United States in unleashing war, he said, because 'the greatest detonation of nuclear weapons will be on the territory of West Germany, France and England'. Therefore, he concluded, the risk of pushing the issue was justified: 'If we look at it in terms of a percentage, there is more than a 95% probability that there will be no war.'

Khrushchev, then, went to Vienna with the aim of pressing for actions that by his own calculation involved a 5 per cent risk of war – a 5 per cent chance of the obliteration of many of the world's cities, and the deaths of many millions of people. It was an astonishing gamble, but it would not be the last Khrushchev would make. His sabre-rattling would lead to a battle of nerves with Kennedy, who would rate the odds of a nuclear war over Berlin rather differently: he privately estimated that there was a one in five chance.

★

In Vienna, Khrushchev was as good as his word to the Presidium, telling Kennedy brusquely that he planned to sign a treaty with the East Germans and settle the Berlin question by the end of the year, and that if the Americans refused to sign with them 'the Soviet Union will do so and nothing will stop it'. When Kennedy replied that this would mean war, Khrushchev responded ominously that if the US wanted to start a war over it, 'let it be so'.

Kennedy was shocked by the exchange. He had been aware that Khrushchev would press for a conclusion over Berlin, but was unprepared for the Soviet leader's forcefulness. A CIA memorandum a few days before the summit had reported a heated conversation on the issue that Khrushchev had had with Llewellyn Thompson, the US ambassador to Moscow, but concluded that the Soviet leader wasn't setting the stage for a showdown in Vienna, and that despite his scepticism that the West would resort to nuclear war over Berlin he was sufficiently uncertain about it that he would still prefer a 'negotiated solution' than risk forcing the issue.

Kennedy was indeed unwilling to resort to nuclear war, as he was keenly aware of the outcome of one, telling his brother Bobby that if it were to happen they could be grateful that they had led full lives, and were at least fully aware of the situation: 'The thought, though, of women and children perishing in a nuclear exchange. I can't adjust to that.' But when Kennedy mentioned to Khrushchev that a nuclear war between the US and the USSR could kill 70 million people in ten minutes, Khrushchev had looked at him as if to say, 'So what?' 'My impression was that he just didn't give a damn if it came to that,' Kennedy said.

This, of course, was precisely the impression Khrushchev wanted him to take away from the summit. He didn't want a nuclear war any more than Kennedy did – in July 1963, he would give a chilling speech in which he asked if survivors of such a conflict 'would perhaps envy the dead'. But that was still two years away: Khrushchev believed that by hinting that he might be prepared to go that far the Americans would cower. It was, just as Penkovsky had explained to the team in London, an enormous bluff.

*

While Kennedy stewed over the way he had lost control over the summit, the situation worsened. *Newsweek* claimed that Kennedy was convinced that war could break out as a result of the Berlin situation, and revealed secret Joint Chiefs of Staff proposals for that contingency. Kennedy was furious, partly because he hadn't even seen the proposals himself but also because he was concerned how the Soviets might react to them.

Khrushchev was not about to back down, but instead mixed conciliatory messages with open threats. On 2 July, at a performance by Margot Fonteyn at the Bolshoi in Moscow, he summoned the British ambassador, Sir Frank Roberts, to his box, and invited him to dine with him there. During an interval in the performance, Khrushchev told Roberts that the last time he had seen Harold Macmillan he had promised to take him on a hunting expedition, but that it would be impossible to honour the promise if the two countries had broken relations over Berlin 'and were perhaps shooting each other instead of elk'.

After this jovial opening, he added that the Soviet Union would ramp up its military strength in Germany if any other country did so, and that it could move forces to protect the territory of East Germany. However, he warned, this was not simply a matter of troop movements: modern wars would be fought with nuclear weapons, 'ten of which could destroy France or for that matter the United Kingdom'. Such a war would lead to the deaths of tens of millions of people, he said, but the Soviet Union was prepared to make that sacrifice if the Western allies attempted to force their way through to West Berlin following a Soviet treaty with East Germany. But he felt it would be 'ridiculous' for 200 million people to die over two million Berliners.

Three weeks later, Khrushchev adopted even starker rhetoric. He invited US envoy John McCloy to his *dacha* in the Black Sea resort of Pitsunda, where he warned him that if the US started a war Kennedy would be 'the last president of the United States of America'. On the same day, Kennedy gave a speech stating he would not allow the Soviet Union to drive the United States out of Berlin, 'an isle of freedom in a Communist sea', either gradually by using unilateral agreements or by force. He also announced plans to allocate funds for new air raid warnings and fallout shelters; strengthen the country's intercontinental ballistic missile forces; add five divisions to the Army; and increase military reserves and the capacity for sea and airlift in case Khrushchev tried to repeat Stalin's 1948 blockade of the city.

The United States already had extensive measures in place for the event of nuclear war. Its first Ballistic Missile Early Warning System, at the US Air Force base at Thule in Greenland, had become operational in January 1961, and would be joined by a counterpart at Clear Air Force base in

Alaska in September. If a report of incoming ballistic missiles from either base was deemed credible, members of Congress would be evacuated to a 112,544-square-foot bunker that had been built below the Greenbrier Hotel in White Sulphur Springs, Virginia, 250 miles from Washington. Codenamed CASPER, the bunker had two-foot-thick steel-reinforced concrete walls and a cafeteria, dormitory and clinic. If an attack was thought to be extremely imminent, the President and a small group of senior figures would head for one of the two shelters below the White House, but otherwise they would embark for Camp David, with the Pentagon evacuating to a facility nearby. In February, the Strategic Air Command had launched LOOKING GLASS, the maintenance of a fleet of specially equipped Boeing EC-135 jets that could act as airborne nuclear command and launch facilities if the country's ground centres were critically damaged. For the next three decades, one 'Doomsday Plane' was in the air at all times.

Unlike the US, Britain didn't yet have a dedicated method for detecting incoming ballistic missiles. In 1960, the Joint Intelligence Committee had noted with alarm that their previous estimate that they would have up to a week's warning of an attack was wrong, and that in fact they couldn't rely on receiving any warning at all until the British addition to the Ballistic Missile Early Warning System was ready. That was still being built at RAF Fylingdales in Yorkshire, having been held up by a series of strikes, and would not become operational until late 1963. As an interim measure, the telescope at Jodrell Bank in Cheshire was adapted: the idea, as with Fylingdales, was to detect any incoming missiles at least four minutes before they landed, giving the RAF enough time to get its bombers in the air to launch a retaliatory strike. The 'Four Minute Warning' would also trigger emergency broadcasts by the BBC on television and radio, as well as sirens across the country, all of which would advise people to stay in their homes and move to their fallout rooms. After a nuclear strike on Britain, BBC radio planned to combine its Home, Light and Third Programmes into 'the National Programme', which would air updates on the situation from studios in Corsham, Wood Norton in Worcestershire and thirteen other bunkers. In late 1961, £72,000 was put aside to spend on a stockpile of records for the studios, as sustained live broadcasting would probably be 'impracticable'. A later plan also proposed airing reruns of panel games such as *My Word!*, but as listeners would only be able to listen on battery-powered transistors that would fail within a few weeks it's hard to imagine many survivors chuckling at Frank Muir's witticisms.

The grim reality was that even with a warning very few people in Britain would have survived a nuclear strike by the Soviet Union. Even if they managed to scramble to shelter in time, once their stockpiled food and water had run out there would have been nowhere to find more without risking contamination. British contingency plans had originally envisioned large-scale efforts to protect the public during an attack, but the costs had been so prohibitive that by 1961 the primary goal was to protect those who would be needed to rebuild and rule the country following a nuclear strike. An early plan for the Prime Minister and a select few to retreat to a honeycomb of rooms under Whitehall had been scrapped after two secret reports in 1955 painted a horrific picture of the consequences of an H-bomb attack on Britain. A detailed analysis of Whitehall's 'citadels', as the bunkers were called, had revealed that they might not withstand a direct strike, and that a single explosion might even block their exits, entombing the country's leadership below ground. The experts had also estimated that an attack on Britain with ten hydrogen bombs would turn much of the country into a radioactive wasteland, and kill or seriously injure 16 million people – around one third of the population.

As a result of these grim prognoses, a new plan had been devised: if the political situation deteriorated to the extent that an attack seemed imminent, the Cabinet, members of the royal family and senior members of the military and scientific communities would be evacuated to a thirty-five-acre blast-proof bunker that had been built in the old limestone quarries in Corsham, Wiltshire, with a few hundred others retreating to underground operational bases around the country. In the summer of 1961, government departments were asked to draw up lists of whom they would wish to have in their group in the Corsham bunker. A civil servant within the Treasury responded that, along with typists, a doctor and a solicitor, his department would also require a 'Welfare Officer', for which he provided a job description: 'The kind of person we want is a kindly, fairly fat motherly sort of soul with a broad pair of shoulders on which people can weep. She need have no welfare experience so far as I can see, but be prepared to work hard in what would undoubtedly be very trying circumstances.'

*

As the situation in Berlin moved closer to the undoubtedly trying circumstances of a nuclear war, senior officers at the CIA's headquarters in Washington turned their eyes to Oleg Penkovsky, wondering if their agent-in-place might be able to provide intelligence on the unfolding crisis. But CIA director Allen Dulles first wanted to know if Penkovsky could really be trusted – was there any chance he had either been turned or was part of a deception operation?

One man whose opinion held sway with Dulles and many others in the agency was its chief of counter-intelligence, James Angleton. Lean, tall and hollow-cheeked, Angleton's vulturous demeanour and studied mystique had made him both revered and feared among the intelligence community in the United States and Britain. Within the CIA, he was nicknamed The Gray Ghost, The Fisherman and The Scarecrow.

Angleton was the dean of the shadowy world of counter-intelligence, which he termed a 'wilderness of mirrors', a place where bluff and counter-bluff were plotted like chess moves across continents. His first taste of it had been in blacked-out London, where he had served with the CIA's precursor, the OSS, in its counter-intelligence unit X-2, sharing offices with MI6 and becoming friends with Kim Philby. The later revelation of Philby's treason scarred him: shocked that he had failed to see the conspiracy in front of his eyes, and that he had been deceived by such an apparently warm and charming friend, Angleton devoted much of the rest of his life to trying to find other moles, with disastrous consequences.

In the summer of 1961, the molehunts were still to come. Angleton read some of the transcripts of the first meetings with Penkovsky in London, and was convinced that he could not be under Soviet control: a controlled agent simply would not have talked the way Penkovsky had done, for example his vicious remarks about Khrushchev and his damning reports about the rampant corruption, diminishing food supplies and dissatisfaction across the country.

In Angleton's view, the operation was 'undoubtedly the most important case that we had for years', and he felt it would be dangerous to distribute the intelligence widely in case it got back to the Russians that they had such a major source. However, he also felt it was 'terribly important that the President, who was now faced with crucial problems regarding Berlin, should have the benefit of the full story'. He recommended that Kennedy not just be briefed about Penkovsky's intelligence, but given the raw transcript of the London meetings, because their full impact and obvious authenticity could only be appreciated by reading them directly. The transcript, Angleton said, 'revealed so much about the agent's access and the validity of his information that this should be made available to the man who had to make crucial decisions regarding the Berlin crisis'.

Sunday in the Park with Oleg

The CIA's power-brokers had given the operation the green light to continue, but Penkovsky was now back in the Soviet Union and therefore out of direct American control: for the foreseeable future his fate rested in the hands of a few Brits in Moscow, and in particular a 31-year-old mother of three.

The idea to use Janet Chisholm as Penkovsky's contact has been characterised as a 'fit of intelligence lunacy' by one writer on Cold War espionage. Apart from the fact that George Blake had known her in Berlin, she was not a professional intelligence officer and so had never worked in the field, let alone one as intimidating as Moscow. It was home to KGB headquarters, tens of thousands of whose officers roamed the city, many of them under cover conducting surveillance on the small pool of foreign diplomats. Walls in apartments, offices and public locations across the city contained microphones, and entire floors of buildings were given over to command posts listening in to and recording conversations. It was not for nothing that COMPASS had become paranoid, and that the CIA still didn't have a station there: in 1961, Moscow was perhaps the most dangerous city for espionage in the world.

How to meet Penkovsky in such an environment? The plan depended on simple, brazen double bluff. Shergold had reasoned – and Dick White had agreed with him – that the sheer improbability of using Janet Chisholm was the best reason to do so, as the Russians would never consider the possibility. White would later say he had felt that the alternatives of using dead drops and safe houses in Moscow would have been even riskier – especially as, thanks to Blake and other traitors, the Russians knew MI6's 'complete order of battle'.

Janet Chisholm was no longer in MI6, but as a result of her brief time at the agency she had a keen sense of discretion and understood what it meant to work for her country's interests. Born in India, the daughter of a colonel in the Royal Engineers, she was naturally reserved and patient: both good characteristics for intelligence work. She had learned Russian at school and French at Grenoble University, immediately after which she joined MI6 as a secretary, and was posted to the Allied Control Commission in Germany.

Her boss there turned out to be a charming and 'immensely likeable' Roman Catholic Scot. Ruari Chisholm's father had been a Highlander, then a *gaucho* in Argentina, but had returned to Europe to fight in the First World War, during which he had lost a leg and been imprisoned by the Germans. Ruari became a cold warrior, joining MI6 after studying French and Russian at Cambridge. Berlin had been his first posting, and after marrying Janet he had worked back in London for a while, and then in Singapore.

In May 1960 he had arrived in Moscow as Head of Station, working under diplomatic cover as a visa officer at the embassy. He was soon joined by Felicity Stuart, fresh from a three-year assignment at the MI6 station in Paris. After learning Russian from MI6-approved *émigrés* in London, Stuart had been offered the posting in Moscow, which she had jumped at. 'I was dying to go there,' she says. 'I had an aunt who'd had some marvellous experiences during the Revolution and I wanted to follow in her footsteps.'

Stuart, under cover as a junior attaché in the embassy, was Chisholm's secretary and cipher clerk. Despite the lack of creature comforts compared to Paris, she remembers her time in the city fondly: there was usually a party on somewhere to stave off the 'Moscow twitch', the feeling of isolation that came from being far from home and under constant surveillance, unable to discuss one's feelings or work with friends or even spouses for fear of being bugged.

Stuart was certain her flat was bugged, and fairly sure her car was, too. 'I had a little black Austin A30 I used to bomb around in,' she says, 'but the battery failed shortly after I arrived in the city and a new one was fitted by Russians.' This may have afforded an opportunity for a microphone to be fitted somewhere in the car but, miraculously, the new battery also worked, even in sub-zero temperatures. 'It made me incredibly popular. The big American cars like the Chevrolets never used to be able to start, but my Austin did so I was always giving people lifts home from parties.'

She soon learned to spot surveillance on the street, usually a muddy green Pobeda with no number plate in front, and perfected a move to lose it: 'A quick turn round Arbatska Square meant you could get behind the Pobeda and even spot its rear number plate as it waited by traffic lights to follow you. But it was a tricky manoeuvre and not to be recommended with innocent passengers.'

At the British Embassy – a former sugar baron's mansion directly opposite the Kremlin – Stuart and Ruari Chisholm shared an office, and both took it as given that this too was bugged. 'Ruari was a marvellous story-teller, but sometimes he would get halfway through an anecdote and suddenly realise that he was about to say something incriminating about someone he knew, and that it might be used for blackmail. So he would finish the story by scribbling the crucial point down on paper and we'd have a good laugh about it, before rushing off to burn the paper.' There was a pan especially for this purpose in the nearest bathroom – the ashes were then flushed away.

If they wanted to discuss sensitive matters at greater length they would leave the office, as it was believed that the KGB's microphones picked up much less if one kept moving. Loudspeakers were strategically placed around the embassy's corridors, and at the touch of a button would play random snatches of speech or music to confuse the eavesdroppers. Another technique was to talk while strolling across the tennis courts at the back of the embassy. And like the Americans, the British had built a 'bug-proof' room. John Miller, a Reuters correspondent in the city at the time and a friend of the Chisholms, once visited it and felt it resembled a combination of 'a "portakabin" toilet, bank vault and boardroom'.

Ruari Chisholm took his work seriously, but he also had a mischievous sense of humour. Miller remembers how after they had once been unable to book a table at the Praga restaurant, Ruari had hammered on the plate-glass door. When a doorman angrily approached, Ruari grandly proclaimed he was the King of Laos, who was on a state visit to the Kremlin at the time. He and Miller had been shown to a table at once.

Miller and Stuart were both frequent visitors to the Chisholms' home on the eighth floor of 12/24 Sadovo-Samotechnaya Street, a beige block of flats built by German POWs after the war. It was nicknamed 'Sad Sam' by its residents, all of whom were foreign diplomats and journalists – no Russians lived there, and the courtyard had a ten-foot-high cement wall closing it off from surrounding houses and apartments. But the KGB, or 'the Nasties' as Ruari called them, were again ever-present. During a spot check the Chisholms found a bug in a hollow spot in one of their walls, but when they tried to remove it found themselves in a surreal tug of war with the KGB men at the other end, eventually coming away with the microphone and a piece of snipped wire. Cleaners were provided by a Soviet agency that was clearly a KGB front: Janet discovered their first maid going through their drawers and sacked her, but when the next did the same realised it was futile. An exception was the family's nanny, Martina Browne, a young Irish Catholic whom they had brought with them from London.

The Chisholms had quickly adapted to life in the city. Janet enrolled in ballet classes at the American ambassador's residence, Spaso House, while the children attended the city's Anglo-American school. Ruari would often dip into the bar at the British Embassy, where staff and visiting Brits would usually drink to avoid getting into trouble elsewhere – apart from the alcohol and the company, it was a good way to keep his ear to the ground.

Along with John Miller, the Chisholms were also close friends with the *Daily Telegraph*'s correspondent, Jeremy Wolfenden, who lived in the Ukraina Hotel. Janie, the couple's eldest daughter, who was five when the family arrived in Moscow, remembers Wolfenden as a charming and funny visitor to their flat in Sad Sam. 'He used to tell us children that he was Jeremy Fisher from Beatrix Potter,' she says.

Wolfenden was precociously clever: reputed to have been the cleverest boy at Eton (and, in the school's estimation, therefore the country), he had taken a congratulatory first in PPE at Oxford, with one of his examiners complaining that even when being brilliant he acted as though it were beneath him: 'He wrote as though it were all such a waste of his time.' As well as being charming and clever, Wolfenden was gay, an irony as he was the son of Sir John Wolfenden, who had chaired the 1957 committee recommending the decriminalisation of homosexual acts in Britain (although the law would not be changed until 1967).

Jeremy Wolfenden may also have worked for MI6, at least informally. Journalists were even more prized assets than businessmen, as they were trained to ferret out information and had permission to do so. After Eton, Wolfenden had learned Russian as part of his National Service, and at Oxford had been recommended to MI6 by a fellow undergraduate. Following the interview, Wolfenden confided in a friend that he believed that only the secret services could make the most of his talents, adding: 'And they don't seem to mind me being homosexual.'

After a spell at *The Times* Wolfenden had been poached by the *Daily Telegraph*, a paper rumoured to have close links with the intelligence services. One former correspondent on the paper has claimed he was told to report to MI6 officers in Moscow when he was posted there, and it may be that Wolfenden received similar instructions before he arrived in the city in April 1961. If so, he would have been able to inform with relative ease on other expatriates, as he himself noted in a 1965 article about Moscow life: 'Everyone knows the private affairs of everyone else.'

But Wolfenden was not a natural spy, mainly because he spent most of his days in an alcoholic haze. Moscow's expatriate village was cosy, but could also lead to strange interconnections: as well as being friends with MI6's man in Moscow and his family, Wolfenden was close to one of the most notorious traitors of the time, Guy Burgess. Since his defection in the early 1950s, Burgess lived in a flat in the city under the alias Jim Andreyevitch Eliot, pottering around it in blue silk pyjamas from Fortnum & Mason. Burgess and Wolfenden had a lot in common: both were Old Etonians, had worked for *The Times*, were flagrantly gay and were heavy drinkers – after his death in 1963, Wolfenden inherited many of Burgess's books and was one of the pallbearers at his funeral.

★

This was the cast of the British community in Moscow, but for now the leading player was Janet Chisholm, who had been given the codename ANNE (her middle name). On Sunday 2 July 1961, as Margot Fonteyn and her company prepared to perform at the Bolshoi, Janet gathered up her three children and walked with them towards Tsvetnoy Boulevard. The location for the brush pass with Penkovsky was the park just off the boulevard, which had been chosen to avoid drawing suspicion on either of them if they happened to be seen there. It was just a few minutes' walk from Sad Sam, so an unsurprising spot for Janet to take the children for an outing, and a plausible place for Penkovsky to wander during his lunch break from his office at the State Committee on Gorky Street, while also being far enough away that it was unlikely any of his colleagues would do the same.

Summers in Moscow are short and sultry, and on that Sunday the threat of rain was in the air. Janet was wearing a brown suede jacket, as she had been instructed by Ruari, and pushed her youngest child, Alastair, in a pram. Once they had reached the park she found a bench by the main path, opposite a circus and a cinema and near some kiosks selling fast food and ice cream, and kept one eye on the pram and another on her two daughters as they ran around playing.

Penkovsky arrived shortly after. He had brought his 'red book' with him as a safety precaution – if a militiaman challenged him he intended to brandish his GRU credentials to bluff his way out of the situation. Approaching the middle of the park he soon recognised ANNE from her jacket and the photograph Greville Wynne had shown him. He didn't much like the spot she had picked: there were too many people milling around for his liking. He wandered about for a while until, as he had hoped, it started to rain. The crowd began to thin out, and Penkovsky approached the bench. He casually admired the baby in the pram, then smilingly offered the older children a box of multi-coloured vitamin C tablets, commonly eaten as sweets by Russian children because of the climate. Janet thanked him, took the box, swiftly placed it under a blanket in the pram, then brought out an identical box and offered those to the children instead. Penkovsky was impressed by how naturally she had acted, and with his typical flamboyance called her a 'heroine' when later relating the encounter to MI6. He chatted with the children a little while longer, then moved on. Just a friendly stranger saying hello.

All told, the pass had taken less than two minutes – but it was one of the most significant moments of espionage during the Cold War. Hidden inside Penkovsky's box of sweets were seven rolls of undeveloped film and two typewritten sheets of paper, dated 26 June and marked 'Especially Important and Urgent'.

A few days later, Maurice Oldfield, MI6's senior officer in Washington, informed the CIA of the take from this meeting, noting that it included 'an important statement on Berlin'. Penkovsky told how he had visited his mentor Varentsov's *dacha* in Babushkino for a party to celebrate his having been promoted to Chief Marshal. Penkovsky reported that during a private conversation at the party Varentsov had told him that Khrushchev had now decided to sign a treaty with East Germany in late October, immediately after the next Party Congress.

Khrushchev apparently recognised that this was a risky tactic, but felt that the US, Britain and France would back down over the issue rather than risk conflict. By acting tough, he hoped to force Western leaders to recognise East Germany, at least in part, and to accept his terms for access routes. The treaty would not entail cutting off access to Berlin completely, but would introduce new restrictions over movement in and out of the city. In case the West objected to this and decided to try to consolidate communications with Berlin, Varentsov had revealed, on signing the treaty Khrushchev would declare a combat alert, and East German troops would block the Helmstedt highway and other 'dangerous roads' with tanks. Air patrols would also be strengthened, and Soviet troops in East Germany and Czechoslovakia would be put at battle readiness. The Soviet Union was prepared to use tanks 'and other weapons' if necessary. 'However,' Varentsov had said, 'we would want any clash to be brief and limited in scope.' The intention was not to start a world war, but at worst a local one restricted to a small area inside Germany.

Penkovsky had his own view of this, which he appended to his report: 'The treaty will be signed. The firmness of Khrushchev must be met with firmness.' He reiterated that Khrushchev was not prepared for a major war, and suggested that the West immediately let it be known that they were redeploying NATO troops and that they simulate the bringing of their own forces to combat readiness. Once again, Penkovsky was providing intelligence indicating that Khrushchev was using belligerence as a psychological tactic to try to bend the West to his will, and once again he was advising that if his bluff was called firmly, rapidly and clearly, he would back down.

On receiving this material from MI6, Dick Helms, head of the CIA's clandestine operations, sent a memorandum to the Department of State summarising its message, and on 13 July senior members of the CIA met to discuss its implications. Penkovsky's tendency to present his intelligence as a warning had intensified, and they had to consider how much this was because the international situation was changing and how much might be a result of Penkovsky's pride: simply relating the facts with no real consequences or escalating effect attached to them might not have suited his own sense of worth as the greatest spy of all time. MI6 had backed Penkovsky's report to the hilt, stating that his bona fides had been established 'beyond any reasonable doubt'. But although Dick Helms had been convinced that Penkovsky was genuine several months before MI6 had become involved in the operation, he now felt that the agency had to be careful about 'going bail' for such major and controversial intelligence. The head of the Soviet Russia division, Jack Maury, remained confident that Soviet deception was out of the question, but Helms felt that Penkovsky's latest material might have been influenced by personal bias, and that there was a risk of him 'overreading' information he had picked up through hearsay.

More troublingly, James Angleton, who only a fortnight earlier had called the operation the most important the agency had had in years and advised informing Kennedy of it at once, now turned cold on HERO. Angleton still felt it impossible that the Russians would want to feed such information to them, but he didn't trust it nevertheless. He told his colleagues, including CIA director Allen Dulles, that he suspected Penkovsky was 'an anarchist or crank' who for reasons of his own was trying to get the West into a war with the Soviet Union.

*

Angleton's concerns were overruled, and his earlier suggestion for the President to be told about the operation was carried out instead. Dulles met Kennedy in the Oval Office; he didn't reveal Penkovsky's name – nobody outside the small team directly involved in the operation knew that, as was standard practice – but informed him that the CIA, in conjunction with MI6, had a spy within the Soviet General Staff, and briefed him on his information from Varentsov. Kennedy, still smarting from the Vienna summit, anxious about the crisis and in excruciating pain from his back, read the report, rapt. As well as the specific intelligence regarding intentions for Germany and the advice that Khrushchev's firmness 'be met with firmness', at several points Penkovsky had said that Khrushchev was deliberately overstating the Soviets' military capacity. As Kennedy had suspected, Khrushchev was trying to manipulate him psychologically. Penkovsky's report gave a strong signal to hold his resolve.

However, despite Kennedy's enthusiasm for Penkovsky's report, there was still hesitation among senior figures to trust the CIA's sudden flood of intelligence from the USSR. As a result, on 18 July the Soviet Russia division circulated an 'operational history' of their source to its distribution list to explain why his intelligence was so significant. He was described as 'a senior-grade Soviet Army staff officer presently in intelligence, whose career up to a certain point was successful and indeed brilliant'. The details of his career, the evaluation stated, had been independently corroborated, and his motivation was probably through having been sidelined due to 'disagreements on matters of principle with his superiors', which was a kind interpretation of his squabbles in Turkey. 'His tour of duty in a Western country was abruptly terminated,' the document noted, and having become attracted to Western comforts while there, he had started preparing to contact the US government. The document was accompanied by a CIA evaluation of his material, which noted that he had provided unique and unprecedented information on the structure and aims of Soviet intelligence, including the identification of 'more than 300 Soviet Intelligence officers and of more than a dozen Soviet Intelligence agents active in the West'.

This document may have helped convince senior US policymakers that IRONBARK was genuine – but it was also a very risky move. It revealed that IRONBARK was a human source, and gave several clues as to his identity. Goleniewski had known that the KGB had an agent in British intelligence, but had not known his name – however, the documents he had seen had provided enough information for Harold Shergold to narrow the list of suspects until he was certain it was George Blake. If anyone who received the CIA's operational history of IRONBARK was working for the Soviets and passed the document to them, the KGB would have several valuable leads. A Soviet Army staff officer who was in intelligence suggested a member of the GRU. He was currently serving, and of a senior rank, which would disqualify many candidates. How many of the remainder had served in Western countries, and how many of those had had their tours 'abruptly terminated'? If the number of suspects was small enough, the KGB could then place surveillance on all of them.

*

On 18 July 1961, the same day the CIA sent out documents clarifying the importance of their agent, Penkovsky arrived back in London. A few weeks earlier he had been appointed deputy head of the foreign section of the State Committee, and his first task in his new role was to arrange a scientific delegation to take to the Soviet trade fair in Earls Court, which had started in early July. Khrushchev had decided another forty or fifty specialists should be sent to London, including chemists and metallurgists, and as Penkovsky had been there before and apparently performed his tasks well he was given the three-week assignment.

This, of course, was a perfect opportunity for MI6 and the CIA. Penkovsky checked into the Kensington Close hotel, where a room had been booked for him by the Soviet Embassy, and called Greville Wynne – now referred to by the codename TARRY in MI6–CIA documents – to tell him he had arrived. Wynne immediately informed Mike Stokes and gave him a rendezvous point away from the hotel. Stokes booked into the Kensington Close, then proceeded to the rendezvous point and picked up Penkovsky to drive him to the flat of fellow MI6 officer John Collins, which would be used as a safe house.

As well as his work with the trade fair, Penkovsky had been given another, unofficial assignment, which was potentially much more important: the wife and daughter of GRU chief Ivan Serov had decided to use the occasion to visit London, and Serov had asked Penkovsky to take care of them as a personal favour. He took up the task with relish. On one evening, he treated them to dinner in a restaurant, and in the taxi back to their hotel Svetlana, Serov's 22-year-old daughter, flirted and 'squeezed up to him'. Despite the deep waters he was now swimming in, Penkovsky was living life to the full – perhaps even enjoying the feeling of operating in such danger.

He was unaware that, behind the scenes, frantic discussions about him were taking place. Ironically, just as the President of the United States was starting to appreciate the value of his intelligence and the CIA were insisting on its significance, the doubts about him within the agency had resurfaced, leading to the suggestion that he should be 'fluttered' – given a polygraph test, possibly supplemented with the use of sodium pentothal or other truth drugs. On the one hand, it seemed inconceivable that the Soviets would sacrifice so much top-secret strategic intelligence for a deception operation. On the other, they had done just that with the Berlin tunnel to protect George Blake.

One cause for the suspicions about Penkovsky was the quality of his photographs: the MI6 expert training appeared to have worked almost too well. George Kisevalter later estimated that Penkovsky had produced around five thousand perfect frames. This had led to the question: could the KGB be taking the photographs for him? The team had tested Penkovsky out, surprising him at one of the meetings in May by giving him a Minox and asking him to take photographs of magazines, maps and pound notes on the spot. They had left him alone for fifteen minutes while they had taken afternoon tea, and then returned. 'I'm done,' Penkovsky had said, throwing the camera back. The next day they developed the prints. They were masterful, Kisevalter remembered: 'Out of this world.'

Penkovsky had been right to be worried in April: some were indeed wondering if he was copying his rocket information out of *Pravda*, or perhaps worse. Up close, it was easy to understand that he was genuine, but thousands of miles away in CIA headquarters all such estimations could be, and were, second-guessed.

MI6 took exception to the Americans' proposal to flutter Penkovsky, and unofficially asked CIA analyst Leonard McCoy for his opinion. From previous experience McCoy felt that polygraph tests could be unreliable; he was also certain from his own analysis of the material that Penkovsky was bona fide. The polygraph idea was dropped, partly because MI6 were emboldened by McCoy's analysis, and partly through fears that such an exercise might humiliate Penkovsky and that he could withdraw his cooperation as a result.

Agreement on the polygraph had been reached, but it had left a cloud over the operation: around this time, suspicions between the Americans and the British erupted. McCoy remembers being summoned to see the CIA's London Chief of Station, Frank Wisner. 'I went into his office and he handed me a HQ cable, asking for my comment. It was from Joe [Bulik], charging that MI6 was trying to steal the operation. It seemed a very negative approach to take, and I told Wisner that I saw no basis for it, and that MI6 was in fact responsible for everything we had received from Penkovsky in Moscow. The main unexpected evidence was that the MI6 man in Moscow had worn the jointly agreed signal to an event which Penkovsky had attended, and Penkovsky had observed the signal.' This was a reference to the tie clasp Kisevalter had shown Penkovsky in May, but it is not clear what meeting this refers to.

As soon as Bulik and Kisevalter arrived in London, Wisner called a meeting with Shergold at MI6's Pall Mall base. He asked Bulik to present his case, and after he had done so asked for Shergold to respond to what he had heard. 'When Shergie finished,' McCoy recalled, 'Wisner declared the meeting over, directed that the matter not be discussed further, got up and left.'

Oblivious to all this, Penkovsky began his debriefing sessions, unloading everything he had picked up since he had last met the team, including insights he had gleaned from Varentsov and others, how the meeting had gone with Janet in the park and more. At a meeting on 28 July, he told them that there was 'a secret opposition' to Khrushchev in the Kremlin. This group was still in a minority, he claimed, but its existence could lead to a serious split in the Soviet leadership as a result of doubts over the way Khrushchev was handling the Berlin crisis.

Penkovsky was soon due to return to Moscow. He repeated the request he had made in May that Wynne be paid a fair sum for his contributions to the operation, and suggested that the team also be given bonuses for their work. Decoration and prestige were often on Penkovsky's mind. As part of his continuing efforts to have his own contribution recognised, he had asked to be made a colonel in both the British and American armies, with uniforms to match. Bulik knew the American military attaché in London, who was about Penkovsky's size, and borrowed his uniform: using a Polaroid, he took photographs of the Russian posing proudly in both outfits.

Before Penkovsky left again, the team held a small going-away party. In the midst of effusive toasts and speeches of thanks to one another, it was stressed that however important the intelligence he obtained was, his own safety took priority and he was not to run any unnecessary risks. 'For me it is not only your respect,' Penkovsky replied in English, 'for me it is your order.' In the event that he were to come under suspicion, he suggested an alternative method of escape than those they had discussed at earlier meetings, which had included escaping via Berlin. 'If you say, "Penkovsky, go to the Far East and working from there we'll collect you by submarine and take you to Japan when necessary; go with your family to such and such a harbour for a fishing trip and then row out a few miles in a rowing boat." That is also an alternative!'

★

The Berlin fuse was still burning. On 4 August, Khrushchev sent notes to the governments of the United States, Britain, France and West Germany, saying he was ready to negotiate a settlement, but with a classic sting in the tail: in his note to the West Germans, he warned them that they would not survive 'even a few hours of a third world war if it is unleashed'.

Kennedy, meanwhile, was shown a document Penkovsky had photographed: the Russian transcript of his summit with Khrushchev in Vienna, which had been distributed within the Soviet intelligence and military community. Kennedy was 'most enthusiastic' about this, and asked to be informed on precisely how it differed from the American transcript. Perhaps that could offer clues as to Khrushchev's real intentions.

On the evening of Saturday 12 August 1961, taxi drivers in western Berlin started radioing in to their dispatcher at headquarters that they were being stopped from taking customers into the eastern sector of the city. At around two o'clock in the morning of 13 August, the dispatcher told his drivers to refuse any further requests to drive into the eastern sector, for fear they would have difficulties getting back across. An hour later, East German troops started work on an operation codenamed ROSE: fortifications were placed around western

Berlin, including concertina wire, and the border between the east and the west of the city was soon sealed.

As the month went on, fortified barricades and watchtowers were also erected, and construction began on what would become known as the Berlin Wall. The Iron Curtain had been made physical . . .

'Atomic Hitler'

The Aeroflot TU-104 skimmed across the tarmac at Le Bourget airport on the outskirts of Paris, and came to a standstill. It was 9.50 p.m. on Wednesday 20 September 1961. Oleg Penkovsky, a member of a visiting delegation for the Soviet trade fair, stepped on to the stairs of the aircraft and looked out across the City of Light.

Once he had gone through customs, Penkovsky was greeted by the familiar face of Greville Wynne, who drove him to his hotel, the Cayré in Saint-Germain-des-Prés. Along the way, Penkovsky handed Wynne eleven cassettes of undeveloped Minox film, which Wynne later passed to Roger King, a former racing driver who was MI6's support officer in the city. King was used as a liaison in this way so that Wynne remained in the dark about the identities of Penkovsky's case officers.

Joe Bulik, George Kisevalter and Mike Stokes were waiting for Penkovsky at an MI6 safe house at 6 Hameau Béranger in the 16th *arrondissement*. They were irritated and tense. Shergold had stayed behind in London while they had been living cheek-by-jowl in the cramped apartment for what had seemed an eternity: Penkovsky's visit had been delayed by three weeks while the French authorities dithered over granting him a visa. On arriving in the city, Leonard McCoy was surprised to find that the three men were now barely speaking to one another, 'except with hostility and antagonism'. The chief point of contention, McCoy remembered, was whose turn it was to return the Perrier bottles for the deposits. Kisevalter, who snored, had been banished to the living-room sofa. McCoy had attempted to act as peacemaker, but to no avail. On one visit to the apartment – he was accommodated elsewhere – he suggested they all visit the American military Post Exchange store in Fontainebleau. The excursion briefly lightened the mood, but the hostility lingered: 'By the time Penkovsky arrived, they were not speaking to one another, and I became the messenger between them.' Roger King, who as well as acting as the link with Wynne was managing the safe house, had become so irritated by his guests' behaviour that he had taken to calling them the 'Amcraps' and the 'Britshits'.

Penkovsky, by contrast, was in a buoyant mood: his wife was pregnant again, and expecting in seven months. He had also brought with him a long shopping list from GRU head Ivan Serov and his family. After looking at the list, Bulik joked, 'I can see now why you need twenty-five days in Paris.'

Penkovsky also had important material to share with the team. Shergold was due on a flight from London that evening, so while they waited for him to arrive, Penkovsky distributed gifts, including caviar and hollowed Georgian cow horns, and asked if the last batch of Minox cassettes he had passed to Wynne in Moscow had turned out alright. Shergold then arrived from Orly, and after they had warmly greeted each other Penkovsky started to debrief. Since his last meeting with the team he had had several discussions with Varentsov and other high-ranking figures. They had confirmed that in early October major military exercises would begin, and would last up to a month. These were partly training in case there was a war over Berlin, checking everyone's readiness and ability to coordinate, but they were also a way to have forces in a state of combat readiness. Khrushchev was planning to sign a peace treaty handing the control of Berlin to East Germany – if the West made any moves after the treaty was signed, Soviet forces would then already be mobilised and able 'to strike a heavy blow'. Khrushchev, Penkovsky said, saw the sealing of the border between East and West Berlin as 'the first pill' for the West – they had swallowed it, so now a second pill would come in the form of a treaty.

Penkovsky now revealed that he had learned in advance of plans to close the Berlin border, including the precise date and time it would happen. 'I knew about this closing four days before the fact,' he said, 'and I wanted to pass this information on to you but had no means for doing this, since the phone call arrangement was only good for Monday and this took place on a different day. I did not want to risk putting the information into the dead drop and calling by chance. We will have to work out a system that will permit me to pass critical information to you quickly in future.'

One imagines that both the team and the analysts who studied Penkovsky's words later can only have agreed. It would have been an enormous intelligence coup to have known about the closing of the border in advance (some felt it was an enormous failure that nobody did), although it would probably have needed more than hearsay for Kennedy to have acted on it, especially as it came from just one source, and with only four days' notice. But it's a tantalising what-if. Had Penkovsky managed to pass this information to his case officers in time, and had it been taken seriously enough in Washington, Kennedy might just have found a way to cow Khrushchev – perhaps by preempting it in a speech and threatening firmer retaliation than tanks in rubber treads – and the Wall might never have gone up. But it wasn't to be. Penkovsky did *not* get information about the closing of the border to the team in advance, and the Wall was built without any real resistance from the West, dividing Europe for the next twenty-eight years.

Penkovsky said he had been told about the closing of the Berlin border by one of Varentsov's aides. Four days earlier, Penkovsky and his family had attended Varentsov's sixtieth birthday party at his *dacha*. As with the party in June, it had been an idyllic affair, with sunshine, cold cuts and plenty of booze. Penkovsky had presented Varentsov with several gifts before the party, including a rocket-shaped lighter, a cigarette box and a very expensive and rare vintage cognac from 1901. It was supposed to be sixty years old, brewed on the date of Varentsov's birth, but was in fact several years younger, and the label had been specially prepared with the help of four case officers in the CIA. The cognac had been rapturously received by the guests at the party, among whom had been Rodion Malinovsky, the minister of defence. 'The minister,' said Penkovsky, 'wanted to drink only that cognac.'

At one point, Penkovsky's mother had asked Malinovsky if there would be a war over Berlin. Malinovsky had replied that it was hard to say and that he didn't want to talk about it, as it was something he had to consider all the time. However, he added, the closing of the border between East and West Berlin had been handled well, and 'we are keeping everything in readiness'.

Leonard McCoy immediately began preparing a report: Penkovsky's information about Khrushchev's plans for October was highly significant, if true. MI6 were very keen to make sure it was, McCoy remembers: 'MI6 sent the chiefs of its Soviet and European divisions to Paris to interview me and the MI6 team to assure that we were reporting correctly.' On 5 October, the US Board of National Estimates prepared a Special National Intelligence Estimate, in part to evaluate the claims Penkovsky had made in the 20 September meeting – a 'highly unusual' step according to a CIA history of Cold War operations in Berlin. The report's writers concluded that they didn't believe that 'firm decisions of this kind' had been made by the top Soviet leadership, and that they felt instead that the information had been 'construed' by the source, i.e. Penkovsky, from knowledge of military preparations alone. Behind the bureaucrat-speak, the message to the CIA was clear: 'Your source is over-reaching.'

★

Back in Paris, the team questioned Penkovsky more closely on 22 September. It was difficult to keep him pinned to concrete matters because he was worked up about Khrushchev, at one point even suggesting that the West consider assassinating him. Penkovsky was an intelligence-collecting machine with a remarkable memory for details, but his hatred of the Soviet leadership sometimes threatened to derail debriefings. 'Khrushchev today is the new Hitler, an atomic Hitler,' he said, 'and with the help of his stooges who support him he wants to start a world conflict so that prior to his death as he has said, "I will bury Capitalism."' But when pressed by Shergold on whether Khrushchev would try to trigger a world war if the West forced access to Berlin despite the Wall, Penkovsky said he didn't think he would in that case, and would instead try to defeat the West in a localised conflict. 'But,' he added, 'if he feels that he has sufficient strength to knock out the USA and England, who are the leaders of NATO, it is possible that he may strike first.'

Penkovsky said that such strength was a long way off: the figure of 30,000 atomic weapons, which had been published in the Soviet press, was hugely exaggerated, and the R-14 range of intermediate-range ballistic missiles was still not in mass production. Nevertheless, he said, it might be a large enough arsenal for 'this maniac' to chance his hand and to launch an attack – 'that is what all Russian people are afraid of'.

Shergold and Kisevalter carefully went through each piece of intelligence Penkovsky had revealed, asking him to name his sources for each item, and the circumstances in which he had heard it: the more it could be substantiated, the more useful it would be in London and Washington.

★

On 27 September, the team had a surprise for Penkovsky. Much to his delight, Janet Chisholm entered the room, and they arranged a detailed schedule of times and locations to meet in Moscow during the next three months, with alternates if either couldn't make an appointment.

Three days later, there was another surprise visitor, Quentin Johnson from CIA headquarters, who was introduced to Penkovsky as 'John'. Johnson was the Soviet Russia division's Chief of Operations, and had flown in for two reasons. The first was to show Penkovsky a miniature short-range transmitter he was to use when he returned to Moscow. In a charming piece of spycraft, Johnson greeted Penkovsky, then revealed he had been recording him and removed the transmitter from his clothes and played it back. After this, Johnson briefed him on how to use the device – the idea was that he could carry it around Moscow with him and, when within range of the American Embassy, send a signal in a rapid burst. Penkovsky was impressed.

The other reason Johnson was in Paris was to smooth over the tensions that had built up between the four case officers. These had only been exacerbated by the arrival of Penkovsky, who loved Paris, a city that in its unapologetic delight in pleasure and comfort was the polar opposite of life in drab, grey Moscow. This had made him even harder to manage – the team felt he was operating 'at the highest egotistical pitch ever noted'. As Kisevalter spoke French, Bulik had asked him for his help in hiring a prostitute for Penkovsky to keep him happy; when Kisevalter refused, Bulik arranged it himself. Kisevalter would later say that he felt that Bulik was trying to curry favour with Penkovsky, and to impress the British with his operational skills.

The tensions had finally boiled over. After one of the debriefing sessions, Kisevalter and Mike Stokes had gone out on the town and found a bistro. Kisevalter got drunk, started buying other customers drinks, and at one point began discussing Penkovsky, including information he had revealed in the latest session. On their return to the safe house, Stokes informed Shergold, and the two gave McCoy the bad news. McCoy, ever the messenger, informed Bulik.

'He was thoroughly shocked,' McCoy remembers, 'but said he could not bring himself to report it to HQ, but that he would leave that to me.' McCoy sent the message. Two days later Johnson arrived, and Kisevalter was quietly removed from the front line of the operation. To make sure Kisevalter was not offended, the chief of CIA's Paris Station presented him with a Certificate of Merit and Distinction and a cheque for $1000 at a small ceremony at the American Embassy. Bulik was privately awarded the same medal.

From then on, Kisevalter took a backroom role in the operation, and was replaced by another officer, whose name has never been declassified. It was a sad end to the great Teddy Bear's sterling work on the operation.

*

The huge amount of material Penkovsky was handing over was now becoming difficult to process, so McCoy proposed to Shergold that a dedicated task force be set up to handle it all. Shergie readily agreed. 'He proposed that I come to London, interview translators, and produce the intelligence reports for both CIA and MI6,' says McCoy. 'I sent that proposal to HQ and immediately received a reply stating that the task force would be set up in Washington, under my jurisdiction, with translators selected by me. That then happened, and Mike

[Stokes] came and worked as my deputy for a year and a half, as we managed a task force in the Central Building of the original CIA address, 2430 E Street.'

The CIA was now firmly in the driving seat of the operation. Under McCoy's direction, the task force pored over Penkovsky's material, trying to figure out what light it could shed on the situation in Berlin. The crisis could flare up again at any moment, especially now there was such an obvious sign of the problem in the form of the Wall. In September, Kennedy had been given a proposal to launch a limited first strike on Soviet military targets if necessary, but had rejected it. NATO officials would later propose a similar option, codenamed BERCON BRAVO, which involved a 'nuclear demonstration' to make it clear that the West was prepared to act. The plan had two variations: one was to detonate a nuclear weapon over selected areas in such a way as to minimise deaths but make sure that the explosion could be seen from the ground, while the second was to drop a nuclear weapon on a military target away from populated areas – potential targets included aircraft, airfields, surface-to-air missile sites and troop concentrations.

Due to the tense international climate, MI6 and the CIA decided that until the situation died down they needed a sure way to be in touch with Penkovsky – just as he had earlier heard about the closing of the Berlin border but had been unable to tell them in time, he might learn that the Soviets were planning a nuclear strike and be able to warn them of it sooner than the early warning stations. At a meeting on 2 October, the team discussed plans with him for how he could contact them in the case of such an emergency. Penkovsky said he was prepared to use a telephone signal provided he didn't have to speak on the line: he was worried about leaving incriminating evidence for any KGB listeners, who might be able to identify his voice and use it against him if he were later accused of being a traitor.

They agreed the procedures – later given the codename DISTANT – with Penkovsky orally, but as it was vital that there should be no confusion about their use, before leaving Paris the team handed him a document that described them in detail. He should signal them only in three sets of circumstances. The first was the most important: if he received credible intelligence 'from responsible Soviet officials' that the USSR had decided to launch an attack on the West. In this case, he should immediately leave in his dead drop details of the plan, the date and time of the intended strike, and how he had come to know about it. The second situation was only marginally less critical: if he learned that the Soviet Union would launch an attack if the West carried out – or didn't carry out – particular actions or policies. Again, he was to place all the information he had, and how he had found out about it, in the drop. The third situation was almost trifling in comparison, and seems to have been tacked on as an afterthought: if he learned that he was due to be posted out of Moscow, but that it was to happen before his next scheduled meeting with Janet Chisholm, he was also to place the information in the drop. The instructions emphasised that the drop should only ever be used for one of these emergencies, as material could only be safely taken from it once.

In any of these three circumstances, after loading the drop with his material Penkovsky was to make a black mark on a lamp post near a trolleybus stop on Kutuzovsky Prospekt, and then call the flat of Captain Alexis Davison, which overlooked the lamp post on Kutuzovsky Prospekt. Davison was a US assistant military attaché and the embassy's physician – he had no prior intelligence experience but was co-opted by the CIA to check the lamp post every day, which he usually did when he drove past it on his way to work. Now his wife, Claire, was instructed to be on standby regarding Penkovsky's early warning signal, which could come at any time of the day or night. If he heard her answer 'Hello, Mrs Davison speaking', he was to replace the receiver without saying anything, count out a minute, then redial the same number and hang up again. If there was no reply or their Soviet maid answered instead, he was to call a second number, which was that of the flat of William C. Jones III, a CIA officer under cover as a second secretary at the embassy – his wife was also on standby, and someone would always be there to answer one of the numbers. As soon as the CIA received this signal, they would go to check the drop. In February 1962, Jones was replaced by Hugh Montgomery, Deputy Chief of the CIA station, who lived in the same flat, and Penkovsky was correspondingly informed that instead of 'Jones', the answer would be 'Montgomery'.

There was one final emergency procedure. If Penkovsky learned that the Soviet government was about to go to war but didn't have time to load the dead drop, he should try to leave a mark on the lamp post and then call either number. If a man answered, he was to 'blow three times into mouth piece and hang up'. (It wasn't specified what he was to do if a maid or one of the wives answered, but presumably he was to try the other number.) This signal was only to be used in the event of an imminent Soviet act of war.

*

In Britain, civil servants were continuing to revise contingency plans for a nuclear conflict. On 5 October 1961, Harold Macmillan was asked by one of his civil servants to divide his ministers into categories in the event of an imminent war: those who would stay in London, those who would leave for the bunker in Wiltshire and those who would leave for regional headquarters scattered elsewhere around the country. Macmillan also appointed two senior ministers, Rab Butler and Selwyn Lloyd, as his nuclear deputies: in the event he was

killed in an attack they would be authorised to order a retaliatory strike. The first deputy would be authorised to issue the
order from London, while the second would be in Corsham if
the capital were, as one memorandum described it, 'silenced'.
Both agreed to take on the roles, and a letter was drawn up for
them that explained the points and agreements that would
need to be discussed with the American President and NATO's
commander in Europe before launching a strike – an eerie
'don't forget to turn the lights out' checklist for nuclear war.

The Americans' equivalent plans were starker still: in 2012,
a declassified White House meeting report from 1968 revealed
that US policy at this time had been that if the President were
killed or couldn't be found following any kind of attack from
the Soviet Union or China, a 'full nuclear response' would
automatically be ordered.

★

On 17 October 1961, the telephone rang twice in Felicity
Stuart's flat in Moscow, then went dead.

Penkovsky had been instructed to call her, she says, only in
the event that he was about to travel to the West. The call
came three days after Penkovsky had arrived back in Moscow.
However, there was a problem with it. Penkovsky's pre-
arranged signal to Stuart's number consisted of *three* rings, not
two. 'I wasn't a hundred percent certain that it was the signal,'
she says. 'But I knew this was an important signal if he was
going to go to the West, and that the office in London wanted
to know when that would be, so the following morning I sent
a telegram to say I'd received it.'

★

Autumn was turning to winter. In Berlin, the crisis took a new
turn, with tensions over access to the eastern part of the city:
on 22 October, East German guards at the Friedrichstrasse

crossing – 'Checkpoint Charlie' – stopped a blue Volkswagen belonging to Allan Lightner Jr., the US State Department's most senior official in Berlin, as he and his wife tried to cross to attend the opera, and demanded to see identification papers. The four-power agreement stipulated that no German could stop Allied personnel in this way so Lightner refused, insisting that a Russian official inspect his papers instead. When this didn't happen, he informed Kennedy's personal adviser in Berlin, General Lucius Clay, who sent armed military police to escort him to the opera and back.

This triggered a war of nerves, and after two similar incidents Clay deployed tanks near Checkpoint Charlie to assert the Allied powers' right of movement. The Soviets responded by sending six armoured tanks to within less than a hundred yards of the Americans, and everyone braced themselves for a possible confrontation – both sides' tank commanders had orders to fire if they were fired upon. The standoff went on for eighteen hours until finally, at around half past ten on the morning of 28 October, the Soviet tanks started retreating – half an hour later, the Americans followed suit, and the world breathed a sigh of relief.

In Moscow, there were also small signs of a thaw. On 31 October, Stalin's body was moved to a new resting place near the Kremlin Wall, leaving just Lenin at the more prestigious Mausoleum in Red Square – suggesting an official relegation of Stalin's importance. His name was painted over at the Mausoleum's entrance, but the paint wasn't strong enough to withstand the Russian cold, and it soon peered through again.

In Washington, Dick Helms and James Angleton had become uncomfortable with the idea of operating Penkovsky by remote control via MI6 using Janet Chisholm, but they didn't fancy sending another 'singleton' to Moscow: memories of COMPASS were still sore. The solution, they decided, was for the CIA finally to set up a station in Moscow, and in late

November Paul Garbler arrived in the city as its first chief, taking the cover of a naval attaché in the embassy. A lean, handsome former dive-bomber pilot, Garbler had previously been stationed with the CIA in Berlin and Seoul: in the latter city, he had occasionally played tennis with George Blake. Like Kisevalter, his family had Russian roots: his father was Russian and his mother Polish.

Garbler was unaware that he was walking into a hornet's nest of office politics. Joe Bulik had not wanted him to be appointed Chief of Station – he had favoured Hugh Montgomery, who was instead appointed Deputy Chief. Montgomery had served with the OSS in the war and, after taking a doctorate in Russian studies from Harvard, had joined the CIA: he had been one of the officers working on the Berlin tunnel operation.

In most US embassies, the CIA station is a separate entity, closed off from the rest of the staff. In Moscow there was no separate station, just a handful of intelligence officers working alongside embassy officials. When Garbler arrived, the first thing the ambassador, Llewellyn Thompson, did was summon him into the Tank to ask him who in the embassy was CIA. Garbler brought some order to affairs, but it was a long process. All meetings between CIA officers were held in the Tank, and organising them was akin to arranging a rendezvous with an agent on the street, complete with an elaborate signal system – it could sometimes take two days for Garbler to set up a meeting with one of his own officers inside the embassy.

Garbler was also hamstrung by the fact that headquarters didn't inform him about all aspects of the operation. This was because shortly after he arrived in Moscow Angleton's paranoia erupted into full bloom: doubts about Penkovsky's reliability were now joined by doubts about the trustworthiness of the CIA's own officers.

Unaware of these developments, Garbler settled in for the winter ahead: in December, the temperature fell to minus twenty Celsius. For the Westerners already in the city, the season was always tense. 'Bugging is funny in summer when you can get out,' says Felicity Stuart, 'less so in the white-out and dark evenings.'

The Man in the Black Overcoat

In late 1961, MI6 and the CIA had another problem on their minds: they had established procedures for a telephone signal with Oleg Penkovsky, codenamed DISTANT – but what would they do if he activated it? As it was principally to provide warning of an imminent nuclear strike on the West, the new CIA station in Moscow had been instructed to report any such signal directly to headquarters in Washington, without waiting to pick up the details from the dead drop first. From there, the message would be transmitted to the President and his advisers for evaluation. However, Maurice Oldfield, head of MI6's station in Washington, was worried that this might lead to the signal being misinterpreted, which could inadvertently trigger a nuclear war. He proposed to SR head Jack Maury that in the event of a DISTANT call being received, the Joint Intelligence Committee in London be informed first – the head of the CIA's London Station sat in on JIC meetings. If they evaluated that the signal was a genuine threat, military and political leaders in Britain and the United States would then be informed.

This debate led to a top-level meeting in London in late October 1961, with Dick White, Allen Dulles and Dulles's appointed successor John McCone all present. It was decided that if the DISTANT signal were received, the British Prime

Minister, the American President and the Joint Intelligence
Committee would all be informed simultaneously.

★

Bizarrely, British fears were tested less than two months later.
On 25 December 1961, the telephone rang in the Moscow flat
of Alexis Davison. His wife Claire, who despite it being
Christmas was on duty monitoring the line, picked up. There
was no answer, and the caller hung up. Three minutes later,
the same thing happened again.

As with the earlier calls to Felicity Stuart, this didn't corre-
spond precisely to agreed procedures, which in this case stipulated that the gap between calls should be one minute rather
than three. But there seemed no other way to interpret it than
as the DISTANT signal from Penkovsky. The procedure had
been put in place as an alert system for when the international
situation appeared to be unstable and a nuclear strike might be
a possibility: it would have been impractical to have someone
in reach of either number for prolonged periods. But *now* was
such a time – indeed, the procedure had only been set up a few
weeks earlier – and one of the numbers had received two
voiceless calls. The probability of one voiceless call happening
by chance when the early warning procedure to receive it was
in place seemed extremely slim: when someone calls a wrong
number, for example, they usually say something before hanging up. Two calls left little doubt: the most logical explanation
was that it was the emergency DISTANT signal, and that
Penkovsky had simply mistimed the gap between rings.

Alexis Davison immediately called Spaso House, the
American ambassador's residence, and, after some trouble as
there was a party going on, got through to Paul Garbler. There
were two variants to the DISTANT signal, one with three
breaths into the phone and one without. This was the latter
variation, which indicated that the dead drop had been loaded

with material. After a suitable pause so that the other guests would not make any connection with the call he had just received, Garbler feigned drunkenness and left the party with the embassy's security officer, John Abidian, the man who had first received Penkovsky's documents from Eldon Ray Cox over a year earlier. Abidian and Garbler drove to the lamp post at Kutuzovsky Prospekt to check it, but it was dark and they couldn't tell if it was marked. Garbler decided they should check the dead drop at Pushkinskaya Street, and sent Abidian to do so. But it was empty.

Harry Shergold was informed of the calls to the Davison house two days later. He recommended not servicing the dead drop, saying that the calls must simply have been a false alarm. But the drop had already been checked by then, so it seems there was a communications breakdown about this. They were becomingly increasingly common.

*

The Penkovsky operation was in full swing, but the CIA was also being kept busy by startling developments elsewhere. On 15 December 1961, Major Anatoli Golitsyn, a senior officer in the KGB's First Chief Directorate, rang the doorbell at the home of the CIA's Chief of Station in Helsinki and offered to defect to the United States. Golitsyn had been getting ready for the day for two years and he came well prepared, claiming to have memorised dozens of KGB files related to NATO countries.

Suddenly, Penkovsky was not alone: there was another walk-in. He shared Penkovsky's self-importance, too, announcing immediately that he was 'the most important defector in history'. He wanted a private jet to escort him and his family out of Finland at once, and demanded that as soon as he landed in the US he be taken to see the President so he could share his intelligence with him directly. He didn't get his way, but once in the US he was eventually introduced to Robert Kennedy.

Golitsyn had fifteen years of experience as a serving KGB officer, which made many of his claims credible. He stated that Soviet intelligence had succeeded in recruiting dozens of agents in the West, including a ring in France codenamed SAPPHIRE and an agent within the CIA codenamed SASHA. His intelligence was remarkable in its value and precision, and many in the CIA were staggered by it, as it indicated that Soviet intelligence had penetrated the West to a far greater degree than feared. In March 1962, James Angleton introduced two senior British counter-intelligence officers to Golitysn, who informed them that the KGB had a group of agents in Britain, known as the 'Ring of Five'.

This shocking claim coincided with fresh intelligence that convinced Dick White to reopen the file on Kim Philby. Despite all the suspicions about him over the years, Philby had never been arrested by the British, perhaps because to some the idea that such a senior officer could have been a traitor for decades was unthinkable – he had headed MI6's Section IX, meaning he had been responsible for the agency's entire counter-intelligence efforts against the Soviet Union. Some had even tipped him for a future 'C'. However, when the evidence against him was re-examined it became clear that he *was* a Soviet agent, and in January 1963 MI6 finally decided to act on it, sending an officer to confront him in Beirut, where he was working as a journalist for the *Observer*, with the aim of extracting a confession that would help assess the damage he had done. Philby reacted by defecting to Moscow, confirming his treason unequivocally – MI6 went into a tailspin, and were soon hunting for moles in every corner. Suddenly, anything seemed possible.

★

All that was still to come. Back in Moscow, Penkovsky was now carrying out brush contacts with Janet Chisholm on an almost regular basis: at a delicatessen above the Praga restaurant, in the park, in the Kommission store, in a second-hand clothes shop and in the hallway of a block of flats in a small lane near Arbatska Square. Janet would sometimes duck inside the hallway under the pretext that she was adjusting her clothing or tending to her son out of the wind and cold. The Arbat neighbourhood was home to GRU headquarters, so the operation was being conducted right under the noses of Soviet intelligence, but it was also home to the American ambassador at Spaso House, where Janet attended ballet classes on Fridays and Mondays. These were her cover for her meetings with Penkovsky in the area, as they gave a plausible reason for her to be there. If either had strayed too far from their expected areas of movement, suspicions might have been raised.

But while these meetings had all seemed to run smoothly, senior officers at CIA headquarters in Washington were anxious: was Penkovsky overdoing it? Joe Bulik was particularly concerned at the frequency of contact with Janet. 'I tried to urge Shergold to cut down on the meetings,' he later said, 'but I couldn't persuade him to do that. It's in a sense like being married and your wife has equal opportunity to sell this house, but you can't sell it without her signature and I couldn't get the meetings to slow down without [Shergold's] signature.'

As a result of the CIA's qualms, in late January the Soviet Russia division's Quentin Johnson flew to London to meet Shergold to discuss the operation, and to find out for himself just how the British were conducting their end of it. Janet Chisholm attended one of these meetings, and told Johnson that although her husband was 'heavily surveilled' by the Russians, she herself was 'seldom followed'. Listening to her assessment of the situation, Johnson felt confident she could detect surveillance and was impressed and reassured by her grace under pressure, feeling she was 'fairly relaxed about her part in the operation'. 'She might have appeared so,' her daughter Janie says today, 'but she was probably terrified.'

Shergold told Johnson that the Chisholms would be withdrawn from Moscow around June, as Janet was once again pregnant. They agreed that it would be appropriate to make a 'handsome present', probably in the form of cash, to the Chisholms after they had left Moscow as a gesture of appreciation for the dangerous and valuable work they had done, and that the two agencies would share the cost.

Shergold planned to replace the Chisholms with another couple, Gervase and Pamela Cowell: he was an MI6 officer, and she, like Janet, was a former MI6 secretary. 'She has three children,' Johnson noted in his memorandum of the meeting. 'Two are too old for cover use, but the third will be "pram age" at her arrival in the area.' MI6 was also considering supplementing these clandestine meetings with 'a cover', meaning another member of the Station, who would presumably be given a job at the British Embassy. Shergold had someone in mind with very good Russian, whom he thought he could send to Moscow a few months after the Cowells. Johnson had 'speculated whether George Blake might know of him', and suggested that in the meantime all personal contacts with Penkovsky be slowed down. The mention of Blake confirms that MI6 and the CIA were aware that the KGB might know the identities of their people in Moscow as a result of his treachery. But they had nevertheless decided to use Ruari and Janet Chisholm, both of whom Blake had known in Berlin.

And Bulik had been right to worry. On 5 January, after Penkovsky met with Janet in the hallway of the apartment building in the Arbat, he spotted a car entering the lane, violating traffic regulations. He watched as the car, a brown saloon, swung around, and saw that one of the two men in it was looking intently out of the window. After a couple of minutes, the car moved off the lane and turned into Arbatskaya Street.

Could it be surveillance from the KGB? At his next meeting with Janet, on 12 January, Penkovsky saw nothing untoward, either before, during or after their contact, and didn't mention the car to her. But after his meeting with her the following week he walked down Arbatska Square and just as he turned on to Bolshaya Molchanovka he saw the same brown saloon. This time there was only one man in it, wearing a black overcoat. Penkovsky moved along quickly, and didn't turn up for his next three appointments with Janet. On 20 February, Maurice Oldfield informed Jack Maury at the CIA: 'I have just heard from Shergie that there was no sign of HERO at the reserve RV scheduled for today.'

Penkovsky finally made contact with Janet again on 28 March. The occasion was a cocktail party at the home of Dr David Senior, the British Embassy's scientific attaché, and his wife Sheila. Improvising, Penkovsky suggested that Janet lie down in a bedroom, as she must be tired from her pregnancy. A few minutes later he joined her there under the pretext of being shown around the apartment by Sheila Senior and, as he was leaving the room, quickly passed her a pack of cigarettes behind his back. It contained eleven rolls of exposed Minox film and a letter.

The letter explained Penkovsky's vanishing act, and even gave the licence plate number of the brown saloon. He had concluded that surveillance was being conducted on ANNE, 'perhaps periodically', and suggested calling off all meetings on the street for three or four months, proposing instead that he hand over material once or twice a month at diplomatic functions. If he had anything urgent, he would place it in the dead drop.

It seemed the most sensible course of action, and the operation was put on ice.

*

On 26 February 1962, at a meeting in the White House, US Attorney-General Robert Kennedy told General Edward Lansdale to wind up all plans for covert actions against Fidel Castro, which had been codenamed Operation MONGOOSE: none of the efforts were getting anywhere, and so he should instead submit a plan 'for an initial intelligence collection program only' in Cuba.

Kennedy's order was ignored. The Joint Chiefs of Staff had previously noted that the United States could only intervene militarily in Cuba if they were provoked – in March, they proposed ways in which they could create the appearance that this had happened. While none of the proposals, codenamed NORTHWOODS, were put into action, they make for shocking reading even today, as they show that senior figures in the US military considered, among other things, blowing up an American ship in Guantanamo Bay and blaming it on Castro, and killing and wounding Cuban refugees living in the United States and pretending it was part of 'a Communist Cuban terror campaign in the Miami area, in other Florida cities and even in Washington'.

*

Penkovsky was on ice, but he was no longer the West's only human source of intelligence about Russia. Anatoli Golitsyn was unloading his knowledge of Soviet deception and penetration in Washington, and there was more to come. In May 1962, during an interval in an arms control conference at the Palace of Nations in Geneva, a first secretary from the Soviet foreign ministry, Yuri Nosenko, sidled up to an American delegate and, glancing around to make sure he was out of earshot of anyone else, told him that he urgently needed to make contact with American intelligence.

The CIA's station in Bern was notified at once, and two days later Nosenko met CIA officer Pete Bagley at a safe house in the heart of the city's Old Town. Bagley was a CIA case officer working under diplomatic cover. Within minutes of shaking hands with Bagley, Nosenko revealed that his job as first secretary was cover for his real role: he was a KGB officer, previously deputy head of the Second Chief Directorate section responsible for operations against the American Embassy in Moscow, now assigned to its Tourist Section. His current role was to oversee the security arrangements of the Soviet delegation in Geneva. But Nosenko had a problem: he had spent so much money in bars in Geneva that he had eaten into the official advance he had been given for the trip. On returning to Moscow, he would have to pay it back or he would be in serious trouble. He offered to give the Americans classified information in exchange for their paying his debt immediately.

Pete Bagley was a young man going places. Born in Annapolis, he was from a noted naval family: his father was an admiral, as were both his brothers and two of his great-uncles. He had enlisted in the Marines in 1943 aged seventeen, and after the war had studied political sciences, taking a PhD at the University of Geneva. In 1950, aged twenty-five, he had joined the CIA. In a few months he was due to take the position of head of counter-intelligence in the Soviet Russia division, aged just thirty; some in the agency already regarded him as a potential future director.

And now Bagley had what seemed to be a boost for his already stellar career: Nosenko felt like a major catch. He immediately cabled CIA headquarters informing them of what had happened, and George Kisevalter – no longer in the front line of the Penkovsky operation following his indiscretions in

Paris – flew to Geneva at once. Bagley met him at the airport and took him to the safe house, where Kisevalter swiftly installed hidden microphones.

For the next week the two men questioned Nosenko, who was given the codename BARMAN, which was coincidentally appropriate considering his drinking debts. During these meetings, the Russian claimed that the KGB had detected the CIA's former agent-in-place Pyotr Popov by chance as a result of routine surveillance on an American diplomat in Moscow, who had been seen delivering a message via a dead drop.

This was major news to both Kisevalter, who had been Popov's chief case officer, and Bagley, who had also worked on that operation. Nosenko's story seemed to confirm what Penkovsky had said at his second meeting in London, when he had recalled a lecturer saying that the KGB had spotted American intelligence operations being conducted in the Krasno-Presnensky Rayon area of Moscow, and that this had led to the expulsion of a US attaché after a meeting on a bus.

Nosenko's debriefings have yet to be declassified, and Bagley and Kisevalter's accounts of what he said differ on some points, but there are puzzling aspects to it whoever's memories one accepts. For example, according to Kisevalter at one of these meetings Nosenko claimed he had personally overseen surveillance in Moscow of the American Embassy's security officer, John Abidian, for several months and that this had led to the discovery of a dead drop in the lobby of a block of apartments in the city in December 1960.

Abidian was the man who had scolded student Eldon Ray Cox in August 1960 when he had turned up at the embassy with two sealed envelopes he had been given by a strange Russian on Moskvoretsky Bridge. The discovered dead drop had to refer to Pushkinskaya Street, the only apartment block in Moscow that contained a CIA dead drop. That was Oleg Penkovsky's drop: he had recommended using it, and had even drawn a diagram and explained how to do so, in one of the letters he had given Cox.

But there was a problem with the dates. That letter had been read by Abidian and others in the Tank shortly afterwards, but the CIA and MI6 hadn't managed to regain contact with Penkovsky until April 1961, and so had had no need to visit the drop until then. Before that first meeting in the Mount Royal Hotel in London, neither the CIA nor MI6 had even been completely certain that Penkovsky was genuine. As far as the CIA were aware, the dead drop had only ever been visited by them once. That had indeed been by John Abidian, but his visit had taken place a whole year later than Nosenko claimed, in December 1961, just after the mysterious silent phone calls to Alexis Davison's number. Might Nosenko simply have been mistaken about the dates, and meant 1961? No, Nosenko said, he had not been involved in surveillance work in December 1961, but had been preparing for his current assignment in Geneva. The drop had been discovered in December 1960, he insisted.

As well as these mysteries, Nosenko also mentioned that he had once recorded the conversations of an Indonesian diplomat in Moscow by the name of Zepp. In time, Bagley would come to believe that this was a crucial piece of information – but for different reasons than Nosenko would have wanted him to.

*

A few days later, Bagley walked through the marble-floored lobby of the CIA's new headquarters, past the imposing inscription from the Book of John: 'And Ye Shall Know The Truth, And The Truth Shall Make You Free.' Allen Dulles – the son of a Presbyterian minister – had picked out the verse.

Although located in 225 acres of woods in McLean, just eight miles from downtown Washington, the whitish-grey concrete complex would soon become better known as 'Langley', the previous name for the neighbourhood.

Bagley and Kisevalter had both been recalled to Langley after debriefing Nosenko, taking different flights with records of the conversations just in case anything happened to one of them. Bagley was also due to move to Langley in a few months to take over as chief of the Soviet Russia division's counter-intelligence section. He took the lift to the fifth floor, where he and Kisevalter debriefed SR chief Jack Maury on Nosenko. Maury felt the case had potential, but told Bagley about Anatoli Golitsyn's defection six months earlier and suggested he see James Angleton, who had all the data on that operation, so he had a wider picture. After speaking to Angleton, Bagley retreated to a sparse conference room and sat down to read the transcripts of the briefings with Golitsyn.

As he did, a shiver crept up his spine. Most of the information Nosenko had revealed in Geneva had already been given by Golitsyn. While it was plausible that there would be some overlap, Golitsyn and Nosenko claimed to be working in completely different departments of the KGB, and it didn't make sense that they would both know so many of the same details about such a range of agents and operations.

It looked like one of them was lying, and of the two, Nosenko seemed to Bagley to be the more suspect. Could it be that Nosenko was simply exaggerating his knowledge to impress them – or could it be something worse? In his first debriefing with the CIA in January 1962, Golitsyn had predicted that the KGB would try to discredit him by sending false defectors to muddy the waters. Looking at the information Nosenko had given him with fresh eyes, it seemed to Bagley that his versions of the intelligence Golitsyn had handed over either downplayed their importance or negated their validity completely. What if, he wondered, Yuri Nosenko was a KGB plant?

Colonel Oleg Penkovsky in dress uniform. (CIA)

First contact: the typed letter Oleg Penkovsky handed to American student Eldon Ray Cox on 12 August 1960. (CIA)

Мой, дорогой Господин!

Прошу довести до соответствующих компетентных лиц Соединенных Штатов Америки следующее.

[...]

Всегда Ваш ....

19.7.60.

The team: Mike Stokes, Harry Shergold, Joe Bulik and George Kisevalter in the Mount Royal, London. (CIA)

Penkovsky, left, toasts CIA officer Joe Bulik in the Mount Royal Hotel in London. (CIA)

Harry Shergold listens intently as Penkovsky expands on a point during a debriefing. (CIA)

Penkovsky poses in the uniform of a US colonel, left, and a British colonel, right: prestige and acceptance were extremely important to him. (CIA)

Military passes used by Oleg Penkovsky, 1961: top, his pass for the General Staff and Ministry of Defence buildings in Moscow; bottom, his pass for the Intelligence Directorate of the Ministry of Defence. (CIA)

Soviet premier Nikita Khrushchev examines the wreckage of Gary Powers's U-2. (CIA)

East German workers reinforce the new wall dividing the city near the Brandenburg Gate. Bunkers, spotlights and firing and observation posts were also added. (NARA/IPS)

Behind the Wall . . . East German troops and police behind the new frontier. (NARA)

SS-4 on parade in Red Square, Moscow. In combination with the manuals provided by Penkovsky, CIA analysts determined that these missiles were on Cuba. (National Security Archive)

Crisis trigger: a Soviet truck convoy deploying missiles near San Cristóbal, Cuba, on 14 October 1962. This photograph, taken by Major Richard 'Steve' Heyser in a U-2, was the first picture that proved Russian missiles were being placed on Cuba. (The image is dated the day it was printed.) (US Air Force)

A map of Cuba showing US targets that Soviet intermediate- and medium-range ballistic missiles could reach. (CIA)

18 October 1962: Soviet foreign minister Andrei Gromyko, on the right of the sofa, meets with Kennedy in the White House and tells him the Soviet Union has no offensive weapons on Cuba. But Kennedy has already seen the U-2 photographs, so knows this is untrue. (John F. Kennedy Presidential Library and Museum)

CIA director Allen Dulles. (NARA)

Following the Bay of Pigs disaster, Kennedy replaced Dulles with John McCone, here being sworn in. McCone became convinced the Soviets had offensive weapons on Cuba – and was proven right. (John F. Kennedy Presidential Library and Museum)

EXCOMM meeting, 29 October 1962. Kennedy and his advisers, including John McCone, try to hammer out a solution to the crisis. (John F. Kennedy Presidential Library and Museum)

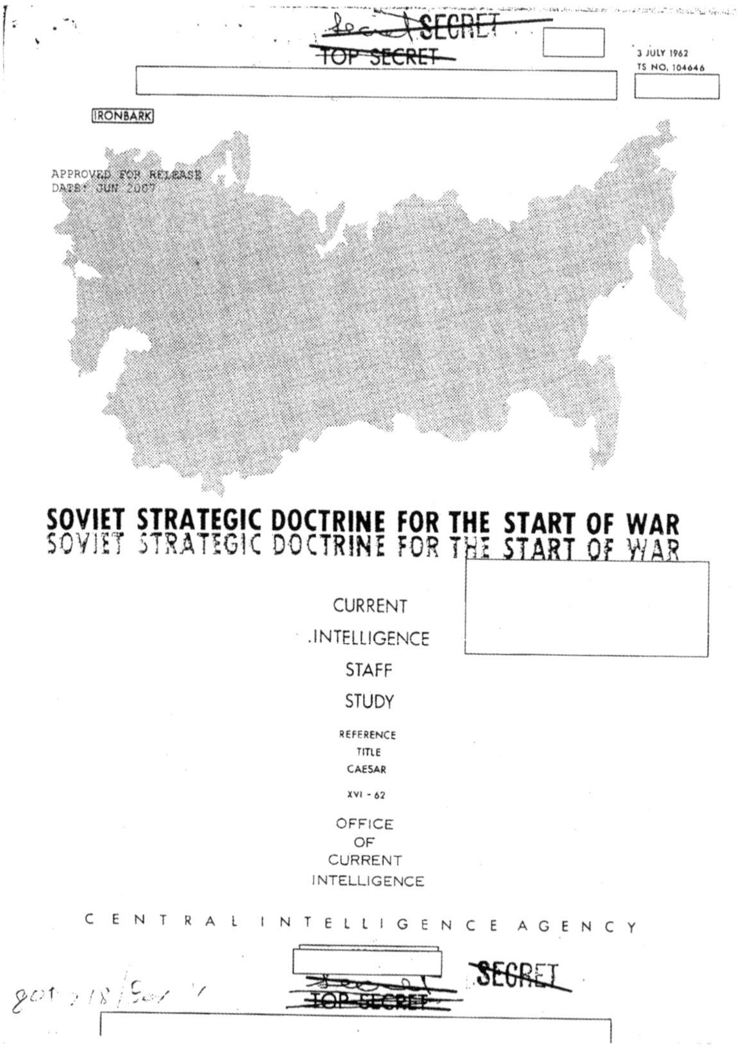

SECRET

TOP SECRET

3 JULY 1962

TS NO. 104646

IRONBARK

APPROVED FOR RELEASE
DATE: JUN 2007

SOVIET STRATEGIC DOCTRINE FOR THE START OF WAR

SOVIET STRATEGIC DOCTRINE FOR THE START OF WAR

CURRENT
INTELLIGENCE
STAFF
STUDY

REFERENCE
TITLE
CAESAR

XVI - 62

OFFICE
OF
CURRENT
INTELLIGENCE

C E N T R A L I N T E L L I G E N C E A G E N C Y

SECRET

TOP SECRET

CIA document outlining US intelligence's perceptions of the Soviet strategy for nuclear war – including the possibility of preemptive strikes – from July 1962. Note the stamp 'IRONBARK' in the top-left corner, indicating that it used intelligence from Oleg Penkovsky. (CIA)

Bagley and Kisevalter continued to work together to get information out of Nosenko, and Kisevalter was also involved in debriefing Golitsyn. But as more information emerged from both defectors, the atmosphere of suspicion grew. Oleg Penkovsky was no longer alone as a source, but Golitsyn and Nosenko were troubling. Like Penkovsky, they provided a wealth of intelligence on how the KGB and other organisations operated, the identities of officers, technical details and insights into Soviet capabilities and intentions – Golitsyn also claimed that the KGB was involved in deception on a grand scale. But while Golitsyn's initial intelligence had been highly valuable, as time went by it seemed as if he believed that the KGB had agents, and were operating conspiracies, everywhere. He claimed that the Sino-Soviet split wasn't real, but was instead a grand ruse designed to lure the West into a sense of false security, and that the leader of Britain's Labour Party, Hugh Gaitskell, had been assassinated by the KGB in order to make way for its own agent, Harold Wilson. As Maurice Oldfield, who would later become head of MI6 and who was also a wine connoisseur, once remarked: 'The first pressings from a defector almost always have the most body. The third pressings are suspect.'

In time, Nosenko and Golitsyn would become locked in a surreal war of words to convince the CIA of their bona fides, with Golitsyn claiming Nosenko was a KGB plant. Two factions emerged within the agency, one side convinced that Nosenko was a valuable defector and the other that he was fake. As a result, nothing would ever be seen the same way again – the Penkovsky operation included.

*

On 20 May, Khrushchev told his foreign minister, Andrei Gromyko, that he was considering placing nuclear ballistic missiles on the island of Cuba, just ninety miles from the coast of the United States.

In retirement, Khrushchev said that he had had two goals in mind: to defend the island from further American attempts to invade it, and to try to equalise the balance of power with the West by establishing a 'tangible and effective deterrent' to wider American involvement in the Caribbean.

He may have felt he needed such a deterrent because he had been warned that the United States was considering a surprise nuclear attack on the Soviet Union. In March, the GRU had produced two reports that supported an earlier assessment by the KGB that the Pentagon was planning a nuclear first strike, even though this was not in fact the case. The GRU even claimed that the US had planned a nuclear attack in September 1961, but had abandoned it shortly beforehand because they had discovered that the Soviet nuclear arsenal was far more powerful than they had believed.

Ironically, at almost the same time as Khrushchev was mulling this over, the Americans were presuming something very similar, and equally false, about Soviet intentions. In July 1962, in a report that examined a range of intelligence, including some provided by Penkovsky, CIA analysts concluded that the Soviet military had received approval from the political leadership to consider 'a doctrine of pre-emptive attack'.

This was never Khrushchev's intention – but he did want a credible deterrent. His attempt to force the West into agreeing to his terms over Berlin had failed, but they had called his bluff. Now he was going to be one step ahead of them, and threaten them in a much more dramatic manner. After a Soviet delegation returned from an exploratory mission to Cuba, Khrushchev unveiled his grand plan at a meeting of the Presidium on 8 June 1962. Codenamed ANADYR, after a river in Siberia, the project was to transform the island into a major Soviet military base. The plan was to send forty nuclear missiles to Cuba, including R-12 medium-range ballistic missiles and R-14 intermediate-range ballistic missiles. A submarine base would also be built on the island, and over fifty thousand Soviet troops stationed there.

ANADYR was an extremely well-kept secret, with messages about it hand-delivered to those in the know, making sure it was totally compartmentalised. But it wouldn't stay secret long.

*

Penkovsky had kept a low profile since March – but now he reappeared. On 31 May, he attended a reception for 600 people at the British Embassy in Moscow to celebrate the Queen's official birthday. In the alcove of a cloakroom in the embassy's eastern wing, he quickly conducted an exchange with Janet Chisholm: she passed him unexposed film for his Minox and a letter with further instructions from the team, while he in turn handed her a package containing seven rolls of exposed film and three letters.

In his letters, Penkovsky revealed that his wife had given birth to a second daughter, but that was the extent of the good news. He had heard that towards the end of 1961 the KGB had been unable to locate his father's grave and now suspected he was still alive, possibly overseas. As a result, his permission to accompany an upcoming trade delegation to Seattle had been refused. He felt that he might be discharged or arrested at any moment, and asked for advice: should he move to another city where it might be easier to escape to the West, or stay put? He also asked the team to 'send film and a small pistol that can be conveniently carried', adding: 'We will continue to work until the last opportunity.'

On 2 July, Greville Wynne arrived in Moscow again: his trading company, in which his old MI6 contact Dickie Franks was conveniently a sleeping partner, owned England's longest articulated lorry, and Wynne had set up meetings with the State Committee to discuss bringing it to Moscow to show off British products. Penkovsky picked Wynne up from the airport and accompanied him to his room at the Ukraina. After his customary procedure with the taps in the bathroom, Penkovsky told his friend that Ivan Serov, the head of the GRU, had just cancelled an application he had made to travel with his job to Cyprus, apparently because they feared he might be targeted by a Western provocation there.

Wynne gave Penkovsky some records by Alexander Vertinsky, a popular émigré singer whose music was very hard to find in Moscow: Penkovsky had asked the team to get them for him when he was in Paris, so he could give them to Varentsov, Serov and others. In return, Penkovsky handed Wynne a letter, two rolls of exposed film and six passport photos of himself. He was visibly under pressure, fearing he was under KGB surveillance, and thinking of escape – he told Wynne that the team had considered various means of getting him out of the country, including by submarine. According to the files, this had in fact been his own idea at the last meeting in Paris, but perhaps they had agreed while toasting wine with him that it was possible and their comments were not recorded. Or perhaps Penkovsky was clutching at straws. Echoing his last letter to the team, he asked Wynne if he could get him a gun: it seemed he was thinking of another way out if the KGB came for him in the night.

Unsurprisingly, Penkovsky's bleak mood appears to have affected Wynne. The Chisholms' nanny, Martina Browne, would later say she had once had dinner with Wynne and come away with the impression that he was 'too nervy to take the pressure'. Perhaps he was starting to sense just how high the operation's stakes were and was experiencing, as John le Carré's character Barley Blair does when faced with a similar position in the novel *The Russia House*, 'the Moscow fear': the sudden realisation of the terrors that lay behind the façade of life in the city, and the reality of what might happen to him at the hands of the KGB if he were arrested.

★

On 4 July, Penkovsky visited Spaso House for an Independence Day lunchtime reception. He was accompanied by Vassily Petrochenko, another senior member of the State Committee, who was a last-minute addition to the invitation list. One of the cisterns in a toilet inside had been prepared by a CIA officer so that Penkovsky could deposit material there: Rodney Carlson, a bespectacled assistant attaché at the embassy, had been given the task of retrieving it.

Penkovsky, looking relaxed, mingled on the lawn and chatted easily with other guests. Paul Garbler, in pressed uniform in his cover role as a naval attaché, shook his hand: the Russian had no idea he was the head of the CIA station. In the latter stages of the party, Penkovsky managed to engineer a very brief one-on-one conversation with Carlson, whom he recognised on account of his red tie clasp, which matched the one Kisevalter had shown him in London, as well as a photograph Wynne had shown him a couple of days earlier. In a quiet moment, Penkovsky told Carlson he had nothing to hand over, and both men left empty-handed.

The CIA analysed every moment of the party. Why had Petrochenko turned up? Was it simply protocol that he had insisted on coming, or was there something more sinister behind it?

The following evening, the noose seemed to tighten again. Wynne met Ruari Chisholm at the bar in America House and followed him to the bathroom, where he handed him Penkovsky's material. He then took a taxi to the Hotel Pekin, where he and Penkovsky had arranged to meet for dinner. He got there early and so wandered around the neighbourhood, circling back every few minutes to check if Penkovsky had arrived yet.

Then he saw them: two men standing in a doorway. He walked towards the restaurant, and the men walked after him. He saw Penkovsky coming the other way, wearing a raincoat and heading for the entrance of the restaurant. But Penkovsky didn't greet him and instead walked in, looking for a table. In an echo of the Laurel and Hardy routine he had performed with Kisevalter, as Penkovsky came out of the restaurant Wynne was going in, and pretended to look around himself. As he followed Penkovsky back out, he saw the two men from earlier standing across the road. Wynne stopped a taxi and asked to be taken back to the Ukraina, but the driver refused, as it was just a short walk away. In his peripheral vision Wynne saw Penkovsky turning into a small alleyway, and left the taxi and ducked in after him.

Penkovsky was waiting for him by the wall as he turned the corner. 'You are being followed,' he hissed. He told Wynne he would have to leave the country immediately, and promised to arrange a flight the next morning – he would pick him up from his hotel and take him to the airport to make sure he got on it.

The World Holds its Breath

The operation seemed to be unravelling. The surveillance at the Pekin couldn't be ignored, and inevitably led to questions about the reliability of Penkovsky's most recent material – was it of the same calibre as his earlier intelligence, or could they now be dealing with the same situation they had faced with Pyotr Popov, who had come under KGB control in 1959? On 20 July, John McCone, who had recently replaced Allen Dulles as head of the CIA, met with President Kennedy in the White House and informed him that they thought the CHICKADEE source was in trouble. 'We conclude he is under suspicion, possible surveillance, and even might have been compromised to the point where he could be acting as a counter-agent,' McCone noted. As a result, he told Kennedy, none of the source's most recent reports were being distributed, pending a more thorough analysis of them.

This review took place over the next six days, and examined Penkovsky's entire security history. It concluded that he had not been compromised, but recommended that the following six measures, which had been agreed with MI6, be taken:

1. Communications with HERO must be maintained in any event.

2. No pressure will be brought on HERO to produce intelligence, particularly in the event he should be retired.

3. If HERO goes abroad, we recognize that he may wish to defect and we will not induce him to return to the USSR.

4. If HERO should remain in the Committee [i.e. the State Scientific Technical Committee], we will make every effort to restrict personal communications with him to a social-professional context.

5. We will examine the possibilities of clandestine exfiltrations from the USSR for the eventuality of his retirement.

6. WYNNE's role will in future be one of support for HERO's position in the Committee and his clandestine communication role will cease.

On 30 July, Howard Osborn, now chief of the Soviet Russia division, requested an authorisation for £15,000 to be used in support of their 'covert agent'. This was the CIA's share of the cost for 'one special phase of operations' regarding Penkovsky – the other £15,000 was to be provided by MI6. This was Wynne's pay-off for his work in Moscow, although he would later receive considerably more compensation. The assumption was that only Wynne had been blown, and removing him from the sphere of the operation would lance the boil and allow it to continue.

With a lesser source, the operation would have been wrapped up the moment it was clear the KGB had spotted contact between the liaison and the agent-in-place. But Penkovsky had become too important for that to happen, and was gaining importance by the day: by now the CIA had realised that something was going on in Cuba. Reliable reports suggested that the Soviets were dramatically increasing the number of their ships heading to and from the island's ports. John McCone was concerned, and stepped up the number of overhead flights by U-2 spy planes to try to get a sense of what was happening. On 10 August, McCone examined intelligence that included U-2 photographs and reports of cargo ship movements from the Baltic and Black Seas to Cuba: he was also well aware of the material Penkovsky had given about the Soviets' nuclear capabilities, strategies and plans.

Later that day, in a meeting of a National Security Council subcommittee overseeing covert actions in Cuba, McCone suggested that the Soviets might be bringing electronic and military equipment to the island, 'including medium range ballistic missiles'. The same day, he dictated a memorandum to President Kennedy in which he stated: 'The only construction I can put on the missiles going into Cuba is that the Russians are preparing to introduce offensive missiles.'

This theory was greeted with scepticism by Kennedy's advisers. McCone had been brought in to clear up the CIA after Dulles's resignation following the Bay of Pigs disaster, but he was a lifelong Republican, and a conservative tycoon to boot. He had a reputation for being a militant anti-Communist, and from the start was deeply mistrusted by liberals in the administration. In addition, there was no solid evidence for his assertions of Soviet intentions. Indeed, his subordinates advised him to leave out his suggestion about offensive missiles in his memo to Kennedy until there was proof of it.

McCone insisted it stay in, because he was convinced he was right – and he soon had some circumstantial evidence to support the idea. On 29 August, a U-2 plane photographed surface-to-air missiles and seven KOMAR guided-missile patrol boats on Cuba. However, even this didn't rouse Kennedy to action. After the Republican senator Kenneth Keating started publicly asking questions about 'rocket installations in Cuba', Kennedy issued a statement on 4 September saying that despite a clear build-up of weapons on the island, there was no evidence that any had an offensive purpose. 'Were it to be otherwise,' Kennedy said, 'the gravest issues would arise.'

★

A new crisis was rapidly emerging, but for a handful of people within MI6 and the CIA there was an additional worry: Oleg Penkovsky had now missed his last three scheduled appointments. Just when they most needed to know what was happening in the corridors of the Kremlin, their man in place had dropped out of touch.

In late August, Penkovsky finally reappeared, at a reception in the apartment of the US agricultural attaché Bill Horbaly. The reception was for an American tobacco delegation, and Rodney Carlson was again present. As with the meeting at Spaso House on Independence Day, it had been decided to use a toilet cistern as a dead drop.

Penkovsky turned up around half an hour into the party, and this time he was alone. He mingled and made his way towards Carlson, who was talking to one of the State Committee's interpreters and an American embassy officer. Carlson felt he was 'obviously somewhat nervous', but that nothing otherwise seemed amiss.

After some chit-chat, Carlson moved away and headed to the bathroom. Once inside, he locked the door and removed a small oilskin-wrapped package from his pocket. He taped it to the underside of the lavatory's water tank cover, then flushed the toilet and rejoined the reception. He found Penkovsky, and the Russian informed him he had a package for him and asked if he had anything in return. Carlson told him he did, and that it was in the bathroom.

As he had done at the Seniors' party, Penkovsky expressed interest in the apartment, and Carlson and two other Americans showed him around it. Penkovsky asked if he could use the bathroom and walked in – the others moved away and Carlson quickly followed and locked the door. Penkovsky immediately handed him a package from his pocket, and Carlson removed his from the tank and handed him it. They left separately and rejoined the party.

Penkovsky's package included a letter in which he discussed his anxiety that he would be discovered, and which asked several questions about what would happen if he were to defect to Britain or the United States. He had calculated that, within the terms they had already agreed, he would have around forty thousand dollars in his bank account, but he felt this would not be enough to start again from scratch with his family. He asked for his contributions to be assessed by the heads of MI6 and the CIA and an offer for a lump sum to be made. Worried about the implications of this, the CIA quickly prepared a forged Soviet internal passport in the name of Vladimir Butov for Penkovsky to use if he needed to escape suddenly.

*

The Chisholms had left Moscow in June, and Gervase – 'Gerry' – Cowell had now taken over as the head of MI6's Moscow Station. Cowell was a slight 36-year-old with a somewhat shy demeanour but a sprightly sense of humour. In 1948, he had studied Russian at St Catharine's College, Cambridge with Ruari Chisholm; they had even performed in the same production of Pushkin's *Boris Godunov*. While at Cambridge, Cowell had been spotted by MI6 and recruited by his tutor. He had been warned that espionage primarily consisted of dreary paper-pushing but, as he drily observed many years later, 'happily my career henceforth was quite hairy and turbulent'.

The plan was now for Penkovsky to meet with Pamela Cowell, codenamed PANSY, at parties in British diplomats'

flats. All these flats had tins of Harpic detergent in the bathroom, and MI6 had built a replica of one with a false bottom
in which they could insert instructions and microfilm. PANSY
would visit the bathroom and replace the Harpic tin with her
own. Some time later, HERO would retrieve its contents, and
PANSY would then switch back the tins.

On 6 September, Penkovsky attended a screening of *A
Taste of Honey* at the British Embassy. Gervase Cowell was
there, and Penkovsky made eye contact with him, but he
could see no sign of Pamela, who had in fact not yet arrived in
the Soviet Union, and so he shook hands, watched the film
and left. The scheme with the Harpic tins was never used.

Four days later, the CIA and MI6 drafted a letter to
Penkovsky asking him if he had any 'concrete information as
to military measures being undertaken by the USSR to convert
Cuba into an offensive military base'. More specifically, they
asked if he knew whether there were any plans to place surface-
to-air missiles on the island. And in an indication of how
urgent this had become, the letter responded to his previous
request for clarity on financial remuneration by stating 'our
leadership has authorized an award of $250,000, which is being
set aside for you until you come to the West'.

This letter was given to Pamela Cowell to pass to Penkovsky
at another reception hosted by David Senior. But Penkovsky
didn't appear at the reception, and on 16 September a cable
was sent to Washington that read simply: 'HERO NO
SHOW'.

*

On 18 September 1962, General Matvei Zakharov, Chief of
the Soviet General Staff, and Admiral Vitaly Fokin, deputy
head of the Soviet Navy, sent a top-secret message directly to
Nikita Khrushchev informing him of the Navy's plans to send
ships to Cuba. These included a brigade of torpedo submarines

and a division of missile submarines, which would travel submerged by day and only surface at night. A week later they sent another message to Moscow, stating that 114 ships had now been sent to Cuba, with 35 still scheduled to be sent. They also reported that they now planned to equip the four torpedo submarines with nuclear warheads, and that on 7 October a transport ship, the *Aleksandrovsk*, would also embark for the island, accompanied by a Project 627 nuclear submarine.

In Britain, civil servants began drafting the documents that would be given to those selected to retreat to the massive bunker in Wiltshire if a nuclear attack seemed imminent. The documents often read like a caricature of the British stiff upper lip, with suggestions for preparing for a journey that involved abandoning one's family with no likely return phrased as though discussing a school outing: 'Food cannot be provided on the journey, and you are advised to take something to eat, such as chocolate or biscuits, with you.' Those reading the document would have been informed that they would need 'only pocket money' while they were away, but could withdraw twenty-five pounds in advance of their salary.

In September 1962, the government took part in FALLEX 62, a major NATO war exercise, and tested how Britain would survive a 200-megaton attack on missile sites, airfields and centres of population. The exercise suggested that there would be major breakdowns in communications and law and order and, perhaps most disturbingly, that dealing with the latter would be seriously hampered as many of the police and Army would have their radiological lives 'used up in the first few hours and days after attack', thanks in part to a lack of protected accommodation. While the politicians headed for the bunkers, others would be above ground trying to save lives, and becoming contaminated in the process. For now it was all being conducted on paper and by telephone, but beneath the surface lay the nightmarish possibility of a world plunged into darkness.

The Soviets were also preparing for war, but with rather more purpose. The United States' National Security Agency – an organisation so secretive it is sometimes referred to as 'No Such Agency' – was keeping a very close eye on the Soviet forces' readiness. On 11 September 1962, the Kremlin suddenly put its strategic forces on the 'highest readiness stage since the beginning of the Cold War'. They were kept at that level for the next ten days. The reason for this remains unclear, but it may be that Khrushchev was worried that the Americans had discovered the missiles on Cuba.

*

The tension was ratcheting up, but the public still had no idea what was happening. On 5 October 1962, the first James Bond film, *Dr. No*, had its première in London, featuring Sean Connery as Ian Fleming's suave British agent unravelling the eponymous villain's plot to divert the course of American missiles from his base on an island sixty miles south of Cuba, thus upsetting the balance of power and potentially triggering a nuclear war. He outlines his plan to Bond, who remarks sardonically, 'World domination – the same old dream.'

In the real world, world domination was no dream but an ongoing struggle between the superpowers. And as in *Dr. No*, the focus point was the Caribbean. John McCone was still convinced that the Russians were intending to use Cuba as an offensive military base, and was making himself increasingly unpopular among Kennedy's circle of advisers and even among his own staff. On 8 October, GRU officer Georgi Bolshakov – the same back-channel who had been used for the Vienna summit – met with Robert Kennedy, and relayed a personal message from Khrushchev: the Soviet Union, he said, was only supplying Cuba with *defensive* weapons. However,

Bolshakov was taking part in what a former State Department analyst would later characterise as 'unwitting deception' – he hadn't been told that the weapons were in fact offensive.

Bolshakov's assurances soon crumpled to ashes. In the early morning of 14 October, Major Richard Heyser flew his U-2 over western Cuba, and took two large rolls of film with the plane's high-resolution camera. The next afternoon, analysts at the CIA's National Photographic Interpretation Center in Washington pored over Heyser's photographs and noticed images of missiles that looked longer than surface-to-air missiles. Nothing like them had been seen on Cuba before. The crucial question was if they might be medium-range ballistic missiles, or MRBMs – offensive, rather than defensive missiles.

The Center had loose-leaf volumes called 'black books' that compiled all the available information. They contained hundreds of photographs taken at the Soviets' May Day parades, as well as the field manuals that had been photographed by Penkovsky in Moscow. In looking through the black books, the team came across a photograph of the Soviets' R-12 MRBM, designated the SS-4 by NATO forces. Penkovsky had provided a manual for the SS-4, and checking it they realised that it was the same missile as in Heyser's photos.

John McCone had been right all along: the Soviets *did* have offensive missiles on Cuba, and they could strike the United States. The SS-4 had a range of around 1,100 nautical miles, meaning it could reach anywhere between Dallas and Washington. It carried a one-megaton nuclear warhead, which would create a blast equivalent to around 1 million tons of TNT. Hiroshima had been around 14,000 tons of TNT.

*

On the morning of Tuesday 16 October, McGeorge Bundy, the President's national security adviser, entered Kennedy's

bedroom in the White House, where he was in his pyjamas
reading the *New York Times*, and informed him of the news.

Kennedy immediately set up a group to deal with the situa-
tion, the Executive Committee of the National Security
Council, or EXCOMM, which held its first meeting in the
Cabinet Room of the White House later that day. After a brief
interruption by his five-year-old daughter Caroline, the meeting began just before noon. Art Lundahl, the director of the
National Photographic Interpretation Center; Sidney Graybeal,
the chief of the CIA's Guided Missile division; and General
Marshall Carter, the deputy director of the CIA, took the
President and his advisers through the evidence they had found
so far, using photographs displayed on easels.

'This is the result of the photography taken Sunday, sir,'
Carter began, referring to Heyser's U-2 flight. 'There's a
medium-range ballistic missile launch site and two more military encampments on the southern edge of Sierra del Rosario
in west central Cuba.'

Once Kennedy was satisfied that the CIA were certain that
the missiles were MRBMs, he asked if they were ready to be
fired and, if not, how long it would take before they would be
ready. Graybeal fielded the question, answering that they
didn't believe the missiles were ready to be fired, as there was
no evidence of nuclear warheads in the immediate vicinity,
which would need to be 'mated' to the missiles, and which in
itself would take a couple of hours.

Robert McNamara, the Secretary of Defense, asked
Graybeal if he could comment on 'the position of nuclear
warheads'. Graybeal replied that they had found 'nothing that
would spell nuclear warhead in terms of any isolated area or
unique security in this particular area'. This was a crucial point
– the time it took for the Soviets to develop 'the readiness to
fire capability' was essentially the amount of breathing space
they had. To estimate that time, Graybeal added, they needed

to know where the warheads were, and as they had not yet found any probable areas for the storage of warheads on the island, 'It seems extremely unlikely that they are now ready to fire, or may be ready to fire within a matter of hours, or even a day or two.'

With the established information having been presented, Graybeal and Lundahl left the room and the members of EXCOMM set about trying to come up with a solution to what was clearly a major problem. They had various proposals, from a surprise airstrike on the missile sites and surrounding airfields to a full-scale invasion of Cuba. After listening to the arguments, Kennedy felt that the missiles had to be removed from the island, but was not yet prepared to order an airstrike or an invasion. This was perhaps in part because he had received assurances from the Soviets that the missile sites were defensive, and so was still unsure about precisely what was happening on the island. McNamara had also pointed out that, with no evidence of nuclear warheads anywhere on Cuba, it could be a day or even two before the Soviets would be able to fire the missiles.

As the crisis developed, several of Kennedy's advisers expressed the view that the Soviets were unlikely to retaliate to an invasion of Cuba with military action, buoyed by the CIA's estimate that there were only 10,000 Soviet troops on the island. In fact, the situation was even more perilous: at a conference on the crisis in Moscow in 1989, it was revealed that there had in fact been 43,000 Soviet troops on the island at the time, along with 270,000 Cuban troops. The Russians and Cubans at the conference also made it clear that they would have reacted to an invasion with military action – this would, in all likelihood, have escalated to a full-scale conflict.

*

On the evening of 16 October, a further meeting took place in the White House in which Marshall Carter showed the President and several others the latest photographs from Cuba. 'This is a field-type missile,' Carter told them, 'and from collateral evidence, not direct, that we have with the Soviet Union, it's designed to be fielded, placed and fired in six hours.' Carter explained that the U-2s had taken the photographs at what seemed to be a very early stage of deployment. 'It would also appear that there does not seem to be the degree of urgency in getting them immediately into position. This could be because they have not been surveyed. Or it could be because it is the shorter-range missile and the radars and the oxygen has not yet arrived.'

Kennedy's ears pricked up. 'There isn't any question in your mind, however, that it is an intermediate-range missile?' he asked, although he had confused the terms: the missile under discussion was in fact medium-range. Carter assured the President that there was no doubt about it, but now that the issue had been raised others around the table also started asking questions: was it possible that the CIA was discussing a threat to the United States that was not based on proof? Carter assured the assembled company that there was no doubt about the evidence, and that in addition there was no possibility that the Soviets had tried to use camouflage or some other means to deceive them over the evidence.

McGeorge Bundy was unconvinced. It would be 'really catastrophic', he said, if they were to make a judgement on 'a bad guess'. He pressed Carter to explain precisely how the CIA knew which missiles these were, and what their range was. Carter explained that the CIA's analysts and a committee of guided missile and astronautics experts had 'fully verified' the information. Bundy wanted more detail on what had decided the verification: 'How do we know what a given Soviet missile will do?' Carter replied that the information on range had been vetted for over two years, and that the CIA had accepted the specifications regarding this family of Soviet missiles. Bundy leaped on his choice of words. 'I know that we have accepted them,' he said, talking over Carter as he tried to explain once again, 'and I know that we've had these things in charts for years, but I don't know how we know.'

'Well,' Carter replied, 'we know from a number of sources, including our IRONBARK sources, as well as from range firings, which we have been vetting for several years, as to the capabilities. But I would have to get the analysts in here to give you the play-by-play account.'

The conversation moved on to other matters. In the tense atmosphere of the time, it was vital that the CIA could support its analysis under close questioning. But the agency had a problem. Even with the looming risk of global nuclear war, Carter could not simply say to the country's national security adviser: 'We know because we have a spy: a Soviet military intelligence officer in Moscow has taken photographs of their missile manuals and given them to us.' Even while Penkovsky's intelligence was being relayed inside the White House during the greatest crisis of the Cold War, his own identity had to be protected – even to the extent of claiming that he represented more than one source – because if this crisis abated, he might be crucial in stopping the next one.

★

On the morning of 18 October, the CIA concluded from examining the latest U-2 photos that as well as the MRBM sites on Cuba there also appeared to be two intermediate-range ballistic missile (IRBM) sites 'with fixed launchers zeroed in on the Eastern United States'. That afternoon, Kennedy met with Soviet foreign minister Andrei Gromyko in his office in the White House for two hours, during which Gromyko repeated Georgi Bolshakov's assertion that the USSR's assistance to Cuba 'pursued solely the purpose of contributing to the defense capabilities of Cuba and to the development of its peaceful economy'. Kennedy smiled tersely.

That same day, Leonard McCoy was hard at work at the CIA task force centre at 2430 E Street, when he was called in by the director of the agency's science and technology division to look at a document. It was a report that John McCone was about to hand the President, and it was stamped IRONBARK. It drew heavily on the material Penkovsky had provided on the Soviet MRBM characteristics. McCoy was asked to review its accuracy, check that all the essential details were included, and ensure that the document didn't compromise Penkovsky in any way. He did so.

McCone handed Kennedy the report that evening. It made grim reading. 'The magnitude of the total Soviet missile force being deployed,' it stated, 'indicates that the USSR intends to develop Cuba into a prime strategic base, rather than as a token show of strength.' It spelled this out in specific terms: 'A mixed force of 1020- and 2200-nm missiles would give the USSR a significant strategic strike capability against almost all targets in the U.S.' – a map showing these targets was also included. The document concluded that the Soviets were making a 'major military investment in Cuba with some of their most effective guided missile systems', and that the planning for the operation to place the missiles on the island 'must have started at least one year ago and put into motion last spring'. Kennedy now knew that Gromyko had just lied to his face.

At a meeting with the Joint Chiefs of Staff, the President admitted that the Soviets had outfoxed him. 'I think we ought to think of why the Russians did this,' he said, and then gave his own answer.

Well, actually, it was a rather dangerous but rather useful play of theirs. If we do nothing, they have a missile base there with all the pressure that brings to bear on the United States and damage to our prestige. If we attack Cuba, the missiles, or Cuba, in any way then it gives them a clear line to take Berlin, as they were able to do in Hungary under the Anglo war in Egypt. We will have been regarded as – they think we've got this fixation about Cuba anyway – we would be regarded as the trigger-happy Americans who lost Berlin. We would have no support among our allies. We would affect the West Germans' attitude towards us. And [people would believe] that we let Berlin go because we didn't have the guts to endure a situation in Cuba. After all, Cuba is five or six thousand miles from them. They don't give a damn about Cuba. And they do care about Berlin and about their own security. So they would say that we endangered their interests and security and reunification and all the rest, because of the preemptive action that we took in Cuba. So I think they've got . . . I must say I think it's a very satisfactory position from their point of view.

Kennedy didn't much like the options open to him. A quick air strike might eliminate the danger that the missiles could be used from Cuba, but it increased the chance of reprisal from the Soviets – most likely their trying to take Berlin by force. 'Which leaves me only one alternative,' Kennedy said, 'which is to fire nuclear weapons – which is a hell of an alternative – and begin a nuclear exchange, with all this happening.'

Another option was a blockade, but that might provoke the Soviets to create a blockade of their own in Berlin, and be seen to be justified in doing so. However, Kennedy recognised that something had to be done. 'Because if we do nothing, we're going to have the problem of Berlin anyway.' It was estimated that the IRBMs on Cuba would be operational within two months, so any inaction would simply delay the inevitable until then.

The next day, 19 October, Kennedy visited Chicago for a campaign trip – the public still didn't know about the crisis and he was going about his business as usual. However, he returned to Washington the next day, a Saturday, with the press being told that he had a cold, and that afternoon called his wife Jacqueline, who was in Glen Ora in Virginia with their children and expecting him to join them for the rest of the weekend. Kennedy suggested that they instead return to Washington, and Jackie noticed 'something funny in his voice' as he made the request.

That evening, with his family safely back in the White House, the President told his wife about the situation regarding Cuba. Jacqueline asked him to promise that he would not send her or their children to Camp David or anywhere else if there was no room in the bunker in the White House. 'If anything happens,' she later remembered telling him, 'we're all going to stay right here with you.' If a nuclear strike were too imminent to find shelter, she wanted to be on the lawn of the White House with him: 'I just want to be with you, and I want to die with you, and the children do too – than live without you.' Kennedy swore he would not send them away.

*

With the CIA identifying yet more missile sites, it was time for others to be informed, too. On 21 October, Kennedy wrote to Harold Macmillan about Cuba, informing him of the identification of '21 medium-range ballistic missile sites and eight intermediate-range ballistic missile sites capable between them of covering the whole of the United States'. In the early hours of the morning of 22 October, Kennedy called Macmillan personally to discuss the crisis and stated his belief – which echoed Penkovsky's – that 'firmness offered the best chance of avoiding the outbreak of a third world war', and recalled the consequences of not standing tough early against Hitler. However, he still hadn't decided what precise course of action to take, other than the idea of a naval blockade of the island.

A lot has been made of the close coordination between the Americans and British during the missile crisis. Kennedy was an anglophile and had a particularly close friendship with the British ambassador to Washington, David Ormsby-Gore, who was related by marriage to both him and Macmillan and had even been promised a place in Camp David if it came to war. But despite this, and the fact that CIA analysts had figured out that MRBMs were on Cuba partly as the result of intelligence from an MI6–CIA operation, Kennedy didn't consult Macmillan before deciding on his initial response to the crisis. In his letter to Macmillan, Kennedy regretted the lack of consultation, saying he had judged 'speed of decision to be essential', but the reality was that he had known about the missiles since the morning of 16 October, and had not consulted with any other government: as a result of Cuba's location, the administration regarded this as a threat primarily to the United States. Charles de Gaulle in Paris and Konrad Adenauer in Bonn were informed of the situation at the same time as Macmillan – less than a day before the rest of the world found out.

Kennedy had also been right about the reaction in Europe to events thousands of miles away. On 24 October, the *Daily Express* published a cartoon by Osbert Lancaster pointing out many Europeans' perception of the threat: a severe Englishwoman in a cocktail dress examines a globe and says to her drinking partner, 'Of course, one does see why President Kennedy's just a little nervous – after all, Washington's not all that much further from Cuba than London is from Russia.' The threat that was spiralling into a global crisis was one that had been in place for other Western nations for years. In addition, as Khrushchev would point out, in April the United States had placed Jupiter IRBMs on Turkey, and those threatened the Soviet Union.

★

On 22 October, the evidence of the missiles was shown to congressional leaders, and shortly afterwards the United States placed its military forces at DEFCON-3, signifying: 'Forces on standby to await further orders.' At 7 p.m. Eastern Standard Time, Kennedy finally made the crisis public in a television address in which he accused the Soviet Union of transforming Cuba into a major strategic base that threatened the United States with 'large, long-range, and clearly offensive weapons of sudden mass destruction'.

The only purpose to this, Kennedy said, could be to provide the Soviets with 'a nuclear strike capability' against the Western hemisphere. He excoriated Gromyko for his bare-faced lie to him in his own office a few days earlier, and announced that the US Navy would stop all Soviet ships travelling to Cuba and inspect them for weapons.

At the close of the seventeen-minute speech – perhaps the most tense ever delivered by an American president – Kennedy's speechwriter Ted Sorensen struck a note that was simultaneously accusatory and conciliatory and which, in its soaring rhetoric, also sought to signal to the Soviet leader and the world that he was not a greenhorn president, but a mature and visionary statesman: 'I call upon Chairman Khrushchev to halt and eliminate this clandestine, reckless, and provocative threat to world peace and to stable relations between our two nations. I call upon him further to abandon this course of world domination, and to join in an historic effort to end the perilous arms race and to transform the history of man.'

An alternate version of this speech was also prepared in the event Kennedy decided to take more serious action. Revealed in 2002, it offers an insight into an alternate history that very nearly happened, and if it had been delivered it might now be more famous than the speech that was delivered, or perhaps not known at all, as it could have been one of the last public speeches given before the onset of an all-out nuclear war, which could have led to the destruction of civilisation: 'My fellow Americans, with a heavy heart, and in necessary fulfillment of my oath of office, I have ordered – and the United States Air Force has now carried out – military operations, with conventional weapons only, to remove a major nuclear weapons build-up from the soil of Cuba . . .' It is not known if there were versions of the speech that informed the American public and the world that Kennedy had ordered either a full-scale invasion of Cuba, or a nuclear strike.

*

The world listened to Kennedy's speech in offices, homes and bars. In Langley, CIA HQ, it was now clear that the international situation was once again perilous. There was, however, still no sign of Oleg Penkovsky. Joe Bulik cabled the CIA station in Moscow: 'SUGGEST HERO EARLY WARNING PROCEDURE BE IN ALERT SITUATION WITH PERSONNEL IN PLACE.'

Nuclear Gun-barrel

Directly after Kennedy's speech, the National Security Agency's signal intelligence indicated that the Kremlin had put its military forces on an 'extraordinarily high state of alert'. Unlike in September, it was mainly defensive forces that were affected – offensive forces were not placed at the highest level 'as if to insure that Kennedy understood that the USSR would not launch first'. Nevertheless, the Russians' tactical air forces and air defence units were now at the highest state of alert ever observed by the Americans.

The most significant step Kennedy had announced was the naval blockade, or quarantine, which went into effect two days later. Khrushchev immediately condemned it as illegal and told Kennedy in a letter on 24 October that the Soviet Union would not stand by and watch 'piratical acts by American ships on the high seas'.

At 10 a.m. Washington time on 24 October 1962, as the quarantine went into effect, General Thomas Power placed the US Strategic Air Command at DEFCON-2, the defence condition one step short of imminent nuclear war: it was the first time in history that the United States had been at such a position.

*

Khrushchev had come on strong early in the crisis, but as it progressed he became worried that such a hard line might lead to the situation escalating, and slipping out of control. At a meeting of the Presidium on 25 October, he suggested proposing a solution to the crisis: if the US promised never to invade Cuba, they would in turn agree to remove their missiles from the island. Such a deal would represent a massive climb-down for the Soviet Union but, typically, Khrushchev presented it as a great victory, claiming that the Americans had been shown to be cowards and joking that Kennedy 'slept with a wooden knife', a reference to a crude Russian proverb that said that when someone goes bear hunting for the first time, they take such an instrument with them so they can clean their soiled trousers.

Khrushchev composed a letter to Kennedy outlining his proposal, but judging from declassified Soviet files it seems the nub of it may have been transmitted in advance, either on Khrushchev's instructions or someone in his inner circle, to Alexander Feklisov.

Feklisov was the head of the KGB *rezidentura* in Washington, working under cover as a counsellor at the Soviet Embassy using the alias Alexander Fomin. On 26 October, he called the American journalist John Scali, whom he had met several times before, and invited him to lunch. Scali had already eaten but, noting the Russian's urgent tone, agreed. They met at the Occidental restaurant, just two blocks away from the White House. Scali later recalled what happened next: 'When I arrived he was already sitting at the table as usual, facing the door. He seemed tired, haggard and alarmed in contrast to the usual calm, low-key appearance that he presented.' After the waiter had taken the two men's orders, Feklisov 'came right to the point and said, "War seems about to break out; something must be done to save the situation."'

The previous afternoon, at an emergency session of the UN Security Council in New York the American ambassador

Adlai Stevenson had humiliated his Soviet counterpart Valerian Zorin, challenging him to deny that the USSR had placed missiles on Cuba and then showing the photographic evidence of it. According to Scali, 'Fomin' now suggested that the Soviet Union would be prepared to dismantle the bases on Cuba, and that they would not provide Castro with any further offensive weapons, if the US pledged never to invade the island. Scali's report of his lunch with Feklisov soon reached the State Department, and from there made its way through Washington's decision-makers.

At the time, it was thought that Feklisov's message might have been a peace feeler directly from the Kremlin, but even today the story remains unclear. Feklisov's proposal was the same as the one Khrushchev had presented to the Presidium the day before, and yet in his report back to the KGB he made no mention that he had proposed anything, and instead claimed that it was Scali who had suggested the way out of the stalemate through fear of the 'horrible conflict' that might lie ahead. It may be that Feklisov had been affected by the stream of ciphered messages he was sending to Moscow about the Americans' preparations for war and decided to take diplomacy into his own hands, perhaps prompted by someone close to Khrushchev. Or it may be that he or someone else decided that the KGB was not to be informed that he had made the peace overture.

Whether Feklisov was acting on his own initiative or on instructions from the Kremlin, his meeting with John Scali and his reports on it illustrate that even with the stakes as high as nuclear war, wires were being crossed on the Soviet side.

★

Meanwhile, the Americans were trying to track down Castro's forces in Cuba, but with little success. A CIA report from 26 October suggested that Che Guevara had established a military command post in the province of Pinar del Río. In fact, he was in la Cueva de los Portales, a command and control centre hidden in a network of limestone caves in the mountains, fitted with the latest in Soviet communications equipment.

The crisis reached perhaps its most dangerous point on the evening of 26 October, although this didn't become public until 2002. In enforcing the US quarantine, American aircraft carriers south of Bermuda were trying to track and stop a Soviet submarine, known as B-59 to the Russians and C-19 to the Americans. The USS *Randolph* located the submarine and the Americans dropped practice depth charges to tell the Russians they should surface and identify themselves. There was no response. Other American warships soon surrounded the scene, and the USS *Beale* dropped five hand grenades as a further challenge. But there was still no response.

This was because, unknown to the Americans, B-59 was carrying nuclear-tipped torpedoes. In addition, the submarine's captain, Commander Valentin Savitsky, exhausted and stressed, had assumed that the bombardments they were experiencing meant that a third world war had broken out above the surface. According to testimony from Vadim Orlov, a communications intelligence officer on board B-59, Savitsky ordered the submarine's nuclear torpedoes to be assembled for battle readiness. 'Maybe the war has already started up there while we are doing somersaults down here,' Savitsky apparently screamed. 'We're going to blast them now! We will die, but we will sink them all – we will not disgrace our Navy!' Luckily, Savitsky was eventually talked down from giving the order to fire the torpedo by Second Captain Vasili Arkhipov, who was also captain of the submarine fleet, and deputy political officer Ivan Maslennikov, and B-59 came to the surface shortly after.

*

The next day another crisis occurred, and this one was public: just hours after Khrushchev had delivered a speech on Radio Moscow offering to remove the missiles from Cuba if the United States withdrew its Jupiter missiles from Turkey, the Soviets shot down a U-2 on a reconnaissance flight over Cuba, killing the pilot, Major Rudolf Anderson. Kennedy and Khrushchev found themselves once more, in Ted Sorensen's memorable phrase, 'staring at each other down a nuclear gun-barrel'.

On the evening of 27 October, Robert Kennedy met with Anatoli Dobrynin, the Russian ambassador to the US, and told him that the shooting down of the U-2 had ratcheted up the pressure on his brother. In a ciphered telegram to Moscow that night, Dobrynin reported that Robert Kennedy had told him that the Americans felt their reconnaissance flights were necessary to monitor the building of the missile bases in Cuba, but that if their planes were to return fire, the situation might cause a 'chain reaction' that would be very hard to stop. Kennedy had added that much the same logic applied to the missile bases: '"The US government is determined to get rid of those bases – up to, in the extreme case, of bombing them, since, I repeat, they pose a great threat to the security of the USA. But in response to the bombing of these bases, in the course of which Soviet specialists might suffer, the Soviet government will undoubtedly respond with the same against us, somewhere in Europe. A real war will begin, in which millions of Americans and Russians will die."' He stressed that he and his brother wanted to avoid this if at all possible, and that he was sure that the Soviet Union felt the same. But he warned that some of the American military leadership were 'itching for a fight', and that the situation was in danger of spiralling out of control. He had a potential solution: to accept Khrushchev's demand to remove the American Jupiter missiles in Turkey.

The snag was that this would only happen afterwards, and would remain secret.

On 28 October, Khrushchev announced on Radio Moscow that missiles would be removed from Cuba. Although it was not made public until some time after, the US agreed to withdraw their Jupiter missiles from Turkey. This was not unilaterally well received – General Curtis LeMay, the Air Force Chief of Staff, banged the table and told Kennedy it was the greatest defeat in American history. 'We should invade today!' he yelled. Kennedy overruled him. The Cuban missile crisis was over.

★

Although his intelligence had been heavily used during the missile crisis, Penkovsky himself had gone missing. On 2 November, MI6 and the CIA team were jointly composing a letter to him asking for an analysis of the crisis the world had just lived through when the phone calls came. One was placed to the CIA's Deputy Chief of Station, Hugh Montgomery, and the other to MI6's Head of Station, Gervase Cowell. Three short breaths being blown into the mouthpiece, before the caller hung up and the line went dead.

Both men were sceptical of the signal, but reacted differently. Although the crisis finally appeared to be over, Soviet MRBMs were still on Cuba and US forces remained at DEFCON-3, while British V-bombers were at Alert Condition 3. Gervase Cowell felt sure the call was a false alarm and, deciding it was not worth jangling highly jittery nerves, didn't send it up the line as the procedure dictated but simply sat on the information. Sir Gerry Warner, a former deputy chief of MI6, recalled the incident in a 2012 interview with the BBC: 'He did nothing – which was exactly the right thing to do. He didn't tell his ambassador, he didn't tell London, he didn't tell anybody, because he was morally certain that Penkovsky was captured so this was meaningless. But had he told anybody else, he might have started the most enormous panic. And I think it is the most wonderful example of coolness under fire – of real, real bravery and judgement.'

The CIA, however, *did* send the signal up the line: Hugh Montgomery drove to the American Embassy and sent a flash message to Langley saying that the early warning signal for war had been received. 'While we have serious reservations about its authenticity,' Montgomery cabled, 'nonetheless we are obliged to inform you in case you have any other relevant information.'

Alexis Davison was sent to see if there was a mark on the lamp post on Kutuzovsky Prospekt. He set out in his Ford at 9.20 on the morning of 3 November, wearing a sports jacket and with a hood pulled over his head. There was no black mark on the post.

The CIA then decided to check the dead drop to see if Penkovsky had provided any further details, just in case. Montgomery summoned a junior CIA officer, Dick Jacob, to the Tank, and gave him instructions to clear the drop. Jacob then conducted what was known in the jargon as 'dry cleaning', taking a circuitous route through the city and walking through a bookshop with two exits to lose any possible tails until he reached the drop in Pushkinskaya Street. But as soon as he retrieved the matchbox from behind the radiator, he was seized by waiting KGB officers.

Pushed into a waiting Volga, he was taken to a nearby *militsiya* station, where he asked to be put in touch with the embassy. According to Jacob's later debrief by the CIA, an official then asked him, 'somewhat indifferently', which embassy he meant, and Jacob specified that he was an American diplomat.

The Russians soon placed Jacob on a plane out of the country. The message was clear: Penkovsky had been 'rolled up' – exposed and captured. McCone reported that HERO in all probability had been compromised, adding: 'this source will be of no further value'.

Robert Kennedy came out of the meeting and slumped on to a bench in the garden of the White House next to his sister-in-law. 'It's just awful,' Jacqueline Kennedy later remembered him saying, 'they don't have any heart at CIA. They just think of everyone there as a number. He's Spy X-15.' Bobby Kennedy was angry that the CIA had apparently kept pumping Penkovsky for intelligence even though he was in obvious danger. 'Why didn't someone warn him?' he'd asked McCone. 'Why didn't someone tell him to get out?'

Everyone's worst fears were confirmed a few days later, when it was announced that Greville Wynne had been arrested at a trade fair in Budapest.

*

Unlike Harry Shergold, Oleg Gribanov didn't conduct interrogations in elegant conference rooms overlooking parks. He operated from within the confines of the Lubyanka, the tallest building in Moscow.

Gribanov, head of the KGB's counter-intelligence directorate, had arrested and interrogated Popov in 1959. Now he had Penkovsky, and his British accomplice Wynne, although neither arrest was made public for a while: the idea was that they might 'start a game' with their handlers to find out more, as they had done years before with Pyotr Popov. Assisting him in the investigation were two deputies, Alexander Zagvozdin and Nikolai Chistyakov. According to Zagvozdin, Wynne was utterly terrified after his arrest, and in his first interrogation session asked for time to consider how he could cooperate – for his second session, he told them all he knew about his contacts with Penkovsky. It seems he also offered to cooperate by working for the KGB as a triple agent for two years, pleading 'but give me my freedom after this'.

According to Zagvozdin, when confronted with the paraphernalia taken from his desk Penkovsky gave a limited and
misleading confession, claiming he had been recruited in Paris
and significantly downplaying how much material he had
handed over. But in his second interrogation session, he had
talked about his contacts with Greville Wynne and revealed
that he had handed material to someone Zagvozdin remembered as 'Anne Chiskow'.

The day after his arrest, Penkovsky had also offered to turn
triple agent, suggesting that as the Americans and British
trusted him he could 'be useful again to the Soviet Union'. A
rare KGB file declassified in 2007 confirmed this.

The KGB decided not to use Penkovsky as a triple agent –
he had betrayed too many secrets for that – so Zagvozdin
instead told him that if he confessed everything they might
consider it later. Zagvozdin had in fact been largely in the dark
about his activities: 'I didn't know much, but I used the bits
that I knew, and they helped.' Initially, he didn't even know
whether Penkovsky was working for British or American
intelligence, or both. The 'most important thing' he learned
from questioning Penkovsky was that he had a dead drop on
Pushkinskaya Street, so it seems plausible the KGB would
want to use that information. It seems likely that at some point
Penkovsky also revealed details of his emergency signal procedure, and that coupled with the location of the dead drop this
resulted in the KGB calling Hugh Montgomery and Gervase
Cowell. The KGB doesn't seem to have understood the
purpose of the signal, and that it could have led to nuclear
annihilation. For this reason, it seems probable that Penkovsky
hid that from them. Joe Bulik would later say that he felt the
calls had originated with Penkovsky and that, 'since he knew
he was doomed, he figured that he might as well take the
Soviet Union down with him', and had told the KGB that the
signal meant something else to try to force the United States to

launch a nuclear strike. Such a strike would, of course, have had a high chance of being detected by the Russians, who would have retaliated, and so would probably have led to the destruction of a large part of the West as well.

There is one compelling piece of evidence to suggest that Penkovsky gave the KGB the wrong idea about the DISTANT signal in order to provoke a nuclear war. An article in *Izvestia* in December 1962 stated that Penkovsky had two ways of contacting the Americans. One was to call Alexis Davison, followed by another call to Hugh Montgomery. The other method, 'in case of unexpected danger', was to put a black mark on the pole at Kutuzovsky Prospekt, then dial both numbers, but 'blow three times into the mouthpiece'. The KGB would not have risked triggering a nuclear war simply to expose a CIA officer, but the much vaguer 'unexpected danger' would not have worried them. The spy who some feel helped save the world looks likely also to have tried to destroy it.

*

Greville Wynne's arrest, unsurprisingly, received widespread attention in the British press. 'Reds arrest Briton' proclaimed the *Daily Express*; 'Director suspected of spying' said the *Guardian*. The *Daily Mirror* took another line, implying the arrest might be the result of a prank by Wynne, and that he had earlier been ordered to leave West Germany after offending some influential people there.

MI6 and the CIA knew better. The arrests of Wynne and Jacob indicated that Penkovsky was by now almost certainly in KGB custody, but there was no way of knowing if he were being interrogated, tortured or was even still alive. But Robert Kennedy was wrong – not everyone saw Penkovsky as a number. Joe Bulik repeatedly pressed the agency to try to find a way to save his life. In November, he sent a memorandum to James Angleton and Howard Osborn, suggesting that they send letters to the KGB *rezidenturas* in Paris, London, Rome and Copenhagen, and to GRU *rezidenturas* in four other cities, stating that if Penkovsky was not treated considerately the CIA would leak information about the operation and the enormous amount of intelligence he had provided to embarrass them. Osborn returned the memo to Bulik as though it had never been read.

Bulik then took the proposal to Angleton in person, and was told by the counter-intelligence chief that the CIA never directly conversed with the KGB. Bulik was furious, recalling in an interview in 1998 that Penkovsky had provided intelligence worth 'billions of dollars' and that his proposal had entailed very little danger: 'The only risk was to have some kid take the memo to the Soviet Embassy and give it to the guard, that was the only danger.'

However, unknown to Bulik, Angleton forwarded his idea to the British. Dick Helms also initially approved of the idea in principle, and suggested to MI6 that it could covertly pass a message to the KGB or GRU.

The British objected strongly to the idea – and then abruptly changed their minds. On 10 December 1962, Howard Osborn sent a memo to Helms outlining a fortnight of tense negotiations with the Brits. 'Quite recently,' he wrote, 'in communications from SIS Headquarters in London through Maurice Oldfield, we were informed that they had indeed reversed their position and proposed discussions with the Foreign Office which, in the opinion of Mr. Angleton and me, went much too far and proposed a detailed exposé of several categories of substantive information that [Penkovsky] had provided during his tenure as a joint agent of SIS/CIA.'

In addition, Osborn wrote, the British were now proposing to make an official approach to the KGB/GRU on behalf of MI6 and the CIA. Osborn and Angleton had strongly objected to this idea, stating that the CIA could not under any circumstances establish 'official contact with any intelligence organ of the Soviet Union'. Angleton and Osborn also pointed out that if they revealed too much of Penkovsky's intelligence to the Russians it could backfire, because far from being cowed into affording him softer treatment they could instead use it in his trial and score a massive propaganda coup against Britain and the United States.

MI6 were peeved: they had initially disagreed with the CIA proposal, but now that they had changed their mind it seemed the CIA had decided it was a bad idea after all. In response, MI6 told the CIA that it would take 'official unilateral action', which might include retaliating by expelling Soviet intelligence officials in Britain. The CIA objected to this on several grounds. A unilateral approach to the Soviets would not work, they claimed, as the Soviets would know from Penkovsky that it had been a joint MI6–CIA operation. The CIA didn't wish to PNG anyone, as this would merely provoke retaliatory expulsions of their own officials by the Soviets. Osborn and Angleton were prepared to countenance either a letter to the Russians 'couched in general terms' or the use of a 'cleared British attorney' who would ostensibly be working on behalf of Greville Wynne's wife Sheila, but drew the line at official contact.

But no contact of any sort was ever made.

★

On 11 December, the TASS news bureau announced Penkovsky's arrest, saying that he had passed scientific, technical, political and military secrets to British and American intelligence. The report added that Penkovsky had used a dead drop in number 5/6 Pushkinskaya Street and that Richard Jacob of the American Embassy had been apprehended on 2 November in the midst of retrieving espionage material from it. In Moscow, Reuters' bureau chief Peter Johnson wondered aloud to his colleague John Miller what precisely the link was between Penkovsky and the businessman Greville Wynne, who TASS had also reported had been arraigned for trial. Miller had met Wynne at a function in Moscow, and had found him pushy and self-important, but could he really be a spy? The British government had responded to the charges against him with a muted denial: an under-secretary in the Foreign Office had stated in the House of Commons that Wynne had no connection with intelligence 'so far as I know'.

In researching an earlier story, Miller had discovered that the KGB had a telephone number for citizens to call around the clock if they had any information. Johnson suggested he call the number and ask whether Wynne was now in the Lubyanka, and if so what condition he was in. Miller didn't think much of the idea. 'It's not as though he is being kept in Bradford General Hospital, and we need to know his condition,' he replied, proposing politely that Johnson make the call himself. Predictably enough, the KGB switchboard clerk who responded claimed never to have heard of Wynne and suggested he direct questions to the Ministry of Foreign Affairs. Johnson wrote a four-paragraph article on the denial, and was no doubt noted down in a black book as being a troublemaker.

*

John Miller was soon to find out what really lay behind the arrests of Wynne and Penkovsky – and that his friends the Chisholms had played a key role in the affair. In the meantime, details were scanty, with the TASS report providing the bare bones from which most stories were being written.

The CIA and MI6 were equally in the dark. There was little doubt in their minds that Wynne would be transferred to Moscow: the more troubling question was what the Soviets would do after that. A CIA analysis written in May 1963 presented best- and worst-case scenarios. The best was separate trials for Wynne and Penkovsky, with Wynne's in open court but Penkovsky's *in camera*, with only the verdict announced. There was felt to be no hope for this for Wynne, because his abduction in Hungary had been represented as extradition. The worst was a show trial, although from a propaganda perspective it was thought that this would present 'more problems to the Soviets than to us'.

The Trial

After six months of silence, TASS announced the news. It was the CIA's worst-case scenario – a show trial. Penkovsky and Wynne were both charged with espionage, and the trial was set for 7 May 1963.

Reuters had been assigned one press pass for the courtroom, so Peter Johnson and John Miller took turns in court and back at the office, the one calling the other with the latest to transmit back to London. The courtroom was packed, and intensely hot from banks of spotlights placed around it: a Soviet television crew filmed the whole trial.

Greville Wynne, Miller remembers, was a far cry from the brash businessman he had met on the cocktail party circuit, and looked 'haunted'. Oleg Penkovsky, on the other hand, appeared calm, and spoke clearly and lucidly. Under questioning from the burly prosecutor, Artem Gorny, he gave a largely accurate account of his actions, demonstrating how he had photographed documents with the Minox and giving names and dates for several points. This included his meetings in London and Paris, as well as with Janet Chisholm – usually referred to in the trial as either 'Ann' or 'Anna' Chisholm – and her children in the park.

This revelation created a storm of coverage in the British press. It was immortalised by the *Daily Express* in a Giles cartoon that depicted Janet Chisholm trying to carry out an exchange of secret documents with a swarthy Russian in a doorway of an apartment block in Moscow interrupted by her eager young son exclaiming at the top of his voice in the street 'Don't forget the fruit gums, Mum!', a reference to Rowntrees' slogan at the time.

The Chisholms were besieged by the press at their home in Sussex, and as a result gave interviews that ran on the front pages of the *Express* and the *Mirror*. Janet poured scorn on the idea that she had been 'Mata Hari in a woolly skirt and sensible shoes', and she and Ruari both strenuously denied having ever worked for British intelligence. Ruari took one precaution: he visited his eldest daughter's school and told the headmistress the truth. He asked her to make sure that no reporters would be able to walk in and speak to Janie, because if they showed her a photograph of Wynne or Penkovsky she might recognise them, unwittingly revealing the truth. The headmistress agreed but, as Janie relates today, there was little danger she would have remembered either man even if asked.

Felicity Stuart, who had left Moscow in early 1962, was also called by the *Express* and asked if she had been a member of a Moscow spy ring. 'I cannot make any comment,' she said. Privately, being named in the trial had been a shock. 'Suddenly friends knew what one did,' she says.

But Penkovsky didn't name everyone. He revealed his actions and those of British and American intelligence, sometimes in detail, but held some information back on the stand, claiming that his case officers had, rather improbably, been named 'Grillier', 'Mille', 'Alexander' and 'Oslaf'. This was never corrected by the prosecutor, and their real names were not revealed in the trial. Had the Soviets known them it seems strange they did not name them, as they had no compunctions about doing so for others. Penkovsky had never been told any of the team's real identities for precisely this eventuality, but the names he gave at the trial were not even similar to the cover names they had given him. Either he had managed to hold back enough information to avoid the KGB identifying them from their files, or the KGB's dossiers on MI6 and CIA officers were not extensive enough to use the information he did give, and they invented four names for him to use. Either way, the fact that they didn't even know the names of his case officers punctures the idea of the all-knowing KGB having the entire order of battle of MI6.

★

Greville Wynne's assigned defence lawyer, Nikolai Borovik, argued that his client had simply been a 'chauffeur', an unwitting go-between rather than an active agent. To a degree, this was accurate. Wynne later claimed the Russians had forced him to rehearse his answers beforehand, but it seems odd if so that they didn't make him admit to being more important than he was – especially considering his potential use for a future prisoner swap.

Instead, Wynne's role appeared to have been minimal, and he claimed to have been duped and pressured by British intelligence into a role he had not fully understood or wanted. 'A thousand miles from here there are my own people,' he said, 'responsible people who have landed me in this dock.' This comment also made headlines, and was widely believed in Britain; in 1964, the *Observer* theorised that Wynne had had the same kind of 'vague and bullied relationship' with MI6 as Alec Leamas had had with his superiors in le Carré's *The Spy Who Came in from the Cold*.

It's surprising that Wynne suddenly turned on MI6, but the tone of voice seems to be all his and it would be a natural reaction on discovering that, after all, with none of the diplomatic immunity afforded the Chisholms or the Cowells, or simply sitting safely in London like Dickie Franks, he was instead facing long imprisonment in the Lubyanka with no apparent hope of rescue from the British government. It may be that he stubbornly held out on the question of whether he had been a spy but that the KGB tried to play on his feelings of having been betrayed. It worked well enough as propaganda, although it would have presumably suited them more if the roles had been reversed, with Wynne the great imperial master-spy and Penkovsky his small-time source who had been duped into revealing a few snippets.

But it seems that to at least some degree Wynne was acting the role of injured businessman in order to avoid compromising MI6. He claimed that he had been approached by Oleg Penkovsky in Moscow in April 1961 and that when he had returned to London he had spoken to a security officer called Hartley in one of the companies he represented, dining with him and a man called Ackroyd from the Foreign Office. Ackroyd, Wynne said, later took over the case with one Roger King, also from the Foreign Office. Ackroyd and Hartley were invented names, and had Wynne genuinely felt betrayed he could have named Dickie Franks. Roger King was the MI6 officer who had acted as his contact in Paris, and Wynne mentioned reporting to King on Penkovsky's arrival there – but the real King had no role in London. As far as possible, Wynne presented a muddle of generic names that would be impossible for the KGB to trace, and provided no information about any of the men beyond useless details. When asked if Ackroyd had any children, Wynne said he thought he had one child. 'Married?' asked Gorny. 'That would come with it in our country,' Wynne responded.

Despite his subterfuge with names, like Penkovsky Wynne also revealed several real operational details, including having visited the flat of a British diplomat to deliver material: when pressed, he said he thought this was Ruari Chisholm. This was in contrast to his protection of Dickie Franks, suggesting he may have had no choice in the matter: the KGB had probably told him they knew Chisholm was MI6's man in the embassy, and it would then have been pointless to pin it on someone else or invent a name that could be easily checked.

Wynne also revealed that at a meeting in his room at the Ukraina, Penkovsky had ushered him into the bathroom and, after running the taps to drown out their voices, told him that the British had proposed several possible ways for him to escape from the Soviet Union, 'one of them by submarine'. It seems likely that he had had little choice but to reveal this. Wynne later claimed that, following his arrest, the KGB had accused him of organising agents within the Soviet Union. Wynne had stuck to his cover story that he was a businessman, but one of the interrogators had brought in a tape recorder and played back his conversation with Penkovsky in the Ukraina Hotel on 2 July 1962. Despite having turned on the television, radio and taps, their voices could clearly be made out, and Wynne listened as Penkovsky talked about the submarine escape plan.

*

The trial lasted four days, and trawled through all the dirt on the operation the Russians had, from the range of spy equipment they had found in Penkovsky's apartment, which was shown in court, to a string of witnesses who testified to the baseness of their former friend's character. Although he had initially appeared confident and smart, after a couple of days Penkovsky appeared pale-faced and anxious, with large bags under his eyes. The trial was world news: the revelations were dramatic, and it was the first time such a full account of espionage activity had become public. The *Boston Globe* said the operation 'had all the makings of a fictional spy thriller', and they weren't the only ones to notice. After the trial, dozens of TV shows and thrillers featured spy agencies sending businessmen behind the Iron Curtain to make contact with an important agent.

But for all the sensational details about microfilm hidden in boxes of sweets and lamp posts marked with crosses, the trial revealed next to nothing about the content of Penkovsky's material. His betrayal of his country was presented in an abstract way, and the extent and grade of the secrets he had passed over were seriously downplayed. The prosecution instead focused on his moral failings – he was a degenerate, greedy, a womaniser, a drinker – and argued that this had led him into the arms of the West. In his closing speech, Gorny claimed that American intelligence 'spread its tentacles everywhere in the world and carries out murder and provocation'.

Joe Bulik was enraged by the Soviets' hypocrisy – and his own agency's unwillingness to intervene. On 10 May, he wrote a second memorandum, urging once again that efforts be made to negotiate over Penkovsky's life. He pointed out that even if the effort were to fail, it would send a message to the rank and file of the KGB and GRU that the CIA tried to protect its own. This in itself might prove useful because 'the need for other Oleg Penkovskiys' was greater than ever. He stressed again the enormity of Penkovsky's contribution, citing the fact that at one point in the operation headquarters had authorised 'an unusually large sum of money' to be given to him in the event that he defected, and that they owed him a huge debt. 'For us not to consider ways and means of saving his life is to me a reflection of low moral level,' he wrote, and asked to be formally told if his proposal were rejected or accepted. He received no reply, something he never forgave.

On 11 May 1963, the sentences were handed down – the verdicts, of course, had never been in any doubt. Wynne was found guilty of acting as the chief link between Penkovsky and British and American intelligence and was given eight years, with the first three years to be served in prison and the remaining five in a labour camp. Penkovsky was found guilty of high treason for having passed state and military secrets to British and American intelligence, including 'Anna Chisholm, an intelligence agent and the wife of the second secretary of the British embassy', and was sentenced to 'death by shooting'. There was 'a long roar of applause' in the courtroom at the announcement. His family was not mentioned in the verdict. A supplementary ruling named the Chisholms, the Cowells, Felicity Stuart, Ivor Rowsell and John Varley at the British Embassy, and Davison, Montgomery, Carlson, Jacob and Jones at the American Embassy as having engaged in espionage. Most had already left the country, but the Cowells had stayed. On 13 May, they were expelled from the Soviet Union.

Shortly after being sentenced, Wynne was allowed a half-hour meeting with his wife, Sheila, in which he tried to put a brave face on it. He joked to her that he was 'not expecting a Butlin's holiday camp', but that it would be like being back in the Army. A possible way out for him was already being aired, however, with the *Observer* reporting on 12 May that there was already 'talk in Moscow' that the Soviet authorities might wish to exchange him for Konon Molody, the Russian agent who had operated in Britain under cover as a Canadian businessman called Gordon Lonsdale before being arrested by MI5 in 1961. The *Guardian* also speculated that the trial had been a Soviet 'masquerade' in order to imprison Wynne so he could be used for a swap with Lonsdale.

★

As dawn broke on 16 May 1963, sentries came to Oleg Penkovsky's cell in the Lubyanka. He knew why they were there. His hair had become increasingly grey in the last few months, and had now turned white. As he was walked across the courtyard, he sensed he was being watched. He glanced up for a moment and saw dozens of windows high in the walls surrounding the small asphalt courtyard – every single one of them had a face peering out, watching the procession.

Penkovsky was taken to Butyrskaya prison, and shot by a firing squad. He was executed at 4.17 p.m., and incinerated at 9.45 p.m. the same day. The next day, *Pravda* reported that the Presidium had rejected a 'request for mercy' from Oleg Penkovsky, and that his death sentence had been carried out.

PART II

The Fallout

In the Cold

The fallout from the Penkovsky operation descended swiftly in the Soviet Union. On 12 March 1963, the Presidium demoted Varentsov to the rank of major-general for 'loss of vigilance and unworthy conduct', and Serov suffered the same fate. Some three hundred Soviet agents were also reported to have been recalled to Moscow, rumoured to be all those who had ever come into contact with Penkovsky, and whose covers he could therefore have blown.

Nikita Khrushchev, it seems, either misinterpreted or misrepresented the damage done by Penkovsky. In a one-on-one meeting with President Lyndon Johnson in February 1964, John McCone stated that satellite photography suggested that the Soviets were stepping up their construction of 'hard sites' – extremely protected launching sites, often housed underground – for their ICBMs. In a memorandum of the conversation, McCone noted:

> I explained that after Penkovsky was apprehended, Khrushchev had stated, and we had learned, that he had told the Presidium that Penkovsky had revealed the location of their missile sites, therefore he had to spend an enormous amount of money – 50 billion rubles – to relocate the missiles because we now knew where they were. This was

untrue because Penkovsky had not told us the location of a single missile site. However Khrushchev knew that through satellite photography we were learning the exact location of missile sites. He was not relocating them – what he was doing, he was hardening them, and this was costing them an enormous amount of money.

Khrushchev was deposed in October 1964, with Kosygin and Brezhnev taking over the reins of power: his reckless gamble with nuclear war played a significant role in his downfall.

★

There was fallout of a different sort in the United States. Ironically, John McCone's standing with Kennedy fell as a result of the crisis. The President disliked the fact that once it was over the CIA's director made it clear he had been right about the Soviets' intentions on Cuba all along, sometimes in public. Kennedy was also disturbed that it had been possible for the intelligence community at large, and the CIA in particular – with the exception of McCone – to miss the problem for so long. This left McCone in the awkward position of having to argue that his men had done a good job even though he had disagreed with their judgements and overruled them. What should have been a great success for the CIA began to seem like the opposite.

It is still not clear today why McCone was so convinced that the Soviets were planning to place offensive missiles on Cuba, when nobody else thought it plausible and there was no proof of it. McCone clearly had an enormous body of intelligence about the military build-up in Cuba at his fingertips, and it may simply have been that the combination of all this material led him to guess that this was what Khrushchev was plotting. But his intuition may also have been guided by the persistent tune being played from one of the CIA's most significant sources of intelligence. In his debriefings, Penkovsky had repeatedly expressed the view that Khrushchev was a maniac, and during the Berlin crisis had said that he could try to launch an attack if he felt he had 'sufficient strength to knock out the USA and England'. In his very first meeting with the team in London in April 1961, he had claimed that the Soviet leader was 'patiently awaiting the time when we can begin a war' and that he wanted to bring a 'rain of rockets' down on the West. In the same meeting, he had also suggested that Khrushchev might later send more arms to Cuba, including missiles. 'In fact, there was talk about this with Castro and possibly a few rockets are already there.'

Eighteen months later, the CIA's director insisted, without any proof of it and speaking as a lone voice, that Khrushchev was placing offensive missiles in Cuba. If he had other sources for the assumption, he didn't reveal it to his subordinates. So was this merely coincidence? Perhaps, but the CIA's July 1962 report, 'Soviet Strategic Doctrine for Start of War', had made repeated mention that the Soviets had now placed the concept of preemptive attack on the table, and that report had drawn heavily on material provided by Penkovsky.

Kennedy had also used Penkovsky's intelligence, and had followed the trial with interest. Two days after the sentence was handed down, he sent a memorandum to John McCone asking what had happened to the CIA's greatest asset behind the Iron Curtain. 'I would like to get a report of our estimate of how Penkovsky was caught,' he wrote. 'Was it due, do we think, to his own mistakes, was it ours, or was it almost inevitable.'

The CIA's Soviet division swiftly wrote a report, which McCone handed to Kennedy at a private meeting on 15 May. The document stated that the agency had no proof of how Penkovsky had been compromised, but speculated that it may have been 'due to a combination of circumstances, including the ever-present possibility of a Soviet penetration of either the British or American official government circles'. Conducting the operation in partnership with MI6, the report noted, had 'multiplied the number of possible security leaks'.

The issue was to become a major preoccupation. In May 1963, Howard Osborn sent Dick Helms a report to guide him if he were asked about Penkovsky's bona fides by the House Armed Services Committee, which was examining in the aftermath of the missile crisis the intelligence community's performance. Osborn noted that there had been speculation that Penkovsky might have been a triple agent, working for the Soviets all along. The attached report stated that the CIA had no reason to believe this was the case, or that 'any information he supplied us was wittingly provided to him as deception material by the Soviet authorities'. It also noted that throughout the 'extraordinary operation', the possibility of disinformation or deception had been constantly analysed, and that Penkovsky had been subjected to 'subtle and varied tests' during his debriefings, and had passed them all. The report concluded that there was no evidence of 'planned deception, build-up for deception, fabrication, or double-agent activity', and that the operation represented 'the most serious penetration of Soviet officialdom ever accomplished and one that will hurt them for years to come'.

Helms drew on this for a document he sent to McCone and twenty-one other senior figures in the US intelligence community a week later, in which he set out Penkovsky's career, character and achievements, and stated that he had provided 'more than 8,000 pages of translated reporting, most of which constituted highly classified Soviet Ministry of Defense documents'.

The next month, McCone told the President's Foreign Intelligence Advisory Board that the agency suspected that a security leak had compromised the operation: 'We think that the case was blown because of a penetration in the British government who saw Wynn [*sic*] and Penkovskiy together.' It added that Penkovsky himself may have grown careless.

This was subtly but significantly distinct from the CIA's report to Kennedy of the previous month, which had speculated that the compromise might have been due to 'a Soviet penetration of either the British or American official government circles'. McCone didn't reveal the identity of the British government official now suspected of compromising Penkovsky, nor the source for the supposition that the official had done so.

Despite the operation's unprecedented success, some in the CIA were turning against MI6. Joe Bulik felt that the British had worked Penkovsky too hard and that this had led to his exposure. In July, the British government admitted that Kim Philby had defected to Moscow and had been a Soviet agent. Philby had been one of MI6's most senior officers and had at one point headed its Soviet counter-intelligence section. He had also been under suspicion for years. How, wondered the Americans, could the British have been so stupid? And could Oleg Penkovsky also have been betrayed by a Soviet agent in the West?

The spat soon leaked into the public arena. *Newsweek* asked, 'Should the CIA amend its close working relationship with Britain's MI5 and MI6?' The accompanying article relayed US intelligence's distrust of the 'treacle-footed' way British governments had handled information about possible moles and bemoaned 'the chummy reluctance of one Harrovian or Etonian to doubt the integrity of any other Old Boy'.

*

While the CIA waged a war of words with MI6, Greville Wynne was serving his sentence in a Soviet prison cell. As a foreigner, he was a potential candidate for a spy exchange, and so was not ill-treated to any extent that would endanger that. But he was nevertheless in the Lubyanka, and after several months was moved to an even grimmer prison in Vladimir, 150 miles from Moscow. He lost a lot of weight, and was questioned repeatedly about his role in the operation and his contacts in London and behind the Iron Curtain – he appears to have successfully stuck to his story that he was an unwitting accomplice, and knew nothing of what was in the packages Penkovsky gave him. To keep his sanity, he took to designing kitchen interiors on scraps of paper.

★

Soon the news was dominated by another story. Britain's Secretary of State for War, John Profumo, resigned after admitting he had misled the House of Commons about his relationship with call-girl Christine Keeler. Keeler had also slept with Yevgeni Ivanov, a naval attaché at the Soviet Embassy in London. Profumo admitted to the affair with Keeler but denied any breach of security. However, shortly after his resignation a source in Soviet intelligence reported to the West that he had overheard claims by a KGB officer that Ivanov had obtained information from Profumo via Keeler, and that recording equipment had been used to do it. According to MI5's authorised history, this is unlikely, as Ivanov worked for the GRU, not the KGB. But true or not, MI5 knew that Ivanov was an intelligence officer: Penkovsky had revealed it two years earlier. In 1962, the Foreign Office had even informed MI5 that they had provided Ivanov with 'suitably tailored' material.

Could a Soviet agent have persuaded a prostitute to reveal her pillow talk with the Secretary of State for War? The suggestion of espionage was enough. In October Harold Macmillan resigned as a result of ill health. The government staggered on until the following year, when it lost the general election to Labour and Harold Wilson became Prime Minister.

On 22 November 1963, the United States also lost its leader, and the man who had led it through the Cuban missile crisis, with the assassination of John F. Kennedy. The previous year, Pete Bagley at the CIA had been appointed head of SR's counter-intelligence section, shortly before Penkovsky had been taken into custody. It was part of his job to re-examine the Penkovsky case, over which one question loomed more than any other: how had the KGB detected him?

But with Kennedy's death Bagley, like millions of others, had different questions on his mind. Bagley didn't believe that the KGB were involved in Kennedy's death, but the day after the assassination he sent a memo to James Angleton in which he outlined why the possibility couldn't be overlooked. He called attention to reports from the head of SR, now David Murphy: one was that the FBI had received information that the KGB *rezidentura* in New York contained officers of the agency's 13th Department of the First Chief Directorate (Foreign Intelligence). This department, Bagley noted, was responsible for "'liquid affairs", sabotage and assassination'. The CIA had also received intelligence that Lee Harvey Oswald had been in contact with a KGB 13th Department representative in Mexico City.

It has since become clear that the KGB were *not* responsible for Kennedy's assassination: they were utterly baffled by it. In December 1963, the deputy chairman of the KGB reported to the Central Committee in Moscow that a lead from Polish intelligence suggested that the most likely instigators of the assassination were three American oil magnates 'who have long been connected to pro-fascist and racist organizations' in the Deep South. One could no doubt construct conspiracy theories about why the KGB would lie to the Central Committee, of course, but that way lies the wilderness of mirrors.

But this was not known then, and for the time being, as a result of the Kennedy assassination the Penkovsky operation was not on many people's radar, let alone Pete Bagley's.

★

That changed in early 1964. On 9 January, the British Embassy in Moscow sent a secret memorandum to the Foreign Office in London. Just before Christmas, the *Daily Express*'s Moscow correspondent Martin Page had reported a rumour that Greville Wynne might be exchanged with 'Gordon Lonsdale'. Page had since asked his Soviet source about this, who had admitted he had been told to 'float' the idea of an exchange 'to see what reaction it produced'.

This first whispering would lead to negotiations between the British government and the Soviet Union. With both sides keen for an agreement, the deal was soon done. On a cold day in April, Wynne was ordered from his cell and driven to the Lubyanka, where to his surprise he was taken to an airport. He landed in East Germany and, very early on the morning of 22 April, was pushed into a yellow Mercedes and driven through the fog towards Berlin. He was told that if he spoke or misbehaved he would be shot, and then the car pulled up at the Heerstrasse checkpoint. Police on both sides had tempo- rarily stopped all traffic within 200 yards of the border.

Wynne could see a small stretch of no man's land, and then, on the other side of a set of gates, the West. Two black Mercedes were already parked there. In one of them sat Konon Trofimovich Molody, alias Gordon Lonsdale, accompanied by three British officials. The second car kept radio contact with British headquarters.

With everyone in position, an official from each side got out and slowly walked to the centre. After conferring, each walked on to check that the other had brought along the right man. At 5.35 a.m., Wynne and Lonsdale were marched into the middle of the no man's land, and then kept walking until they reached the other side. It was one of the Cold War's best-known 'spy swaps', and made headlines around the world. The exchange took just twelve minutes – and after sixteen months' imprisonment, Greville Wynne was finally on his way home.

*

In January, Yuri Nosenko – BARMAN – had arrived back in Geneva, where he sent a pre-arranged signal to the CIA. Pete Bagley and George Kisevalter, who had interviewed him in the city two years earlier, flew to Switzerland to meet him again.

To their surprise, Nosenko announced that he no longer felt he could act as an agent-in-place, and that he wanted to defect to the United States immediately. Even more startlingly, he said he had detailed and crucial information about the assassination of John F. Kennedy, and claimed that he had personally reviewed Lee Harvey Oswald's KGB file and as a result he knew for certain that the Soviet Union had not played any part in it.

Bagley and Kisevalter were stunned: less than two months after the most famous murder in the modern era, this agent-in-place apparently had crucial intelligence about it.

The surprises didn't end there. At his debriefings in Geneva two years earlier, Nosenko had claimed that Pyotr Popov had been detected by the KGB in Moscow not thanks to any Soviet penetration of the CIA – as Golitsyn had claimed – but due to the routine surveillance of Western diplomats. He had also claimed that he had overseen the surveillance in the city of the American Embassy's security officer John Abidian, which he said had led to the discovery of a CIA dead drop in December 1960. Now Nosenko told Bagley and Kisevalter that he also knew how Oleg Penkovsky had been caught.

Over the years, he would give several different sources for how he obtained this information, at one point claiming he had heard it from General Gribanov.

This was big news: despite the trial, neither the CIA nor MI6 had any idea of how their greatest agent had been detected by the KGB, and as a result some had started wondering whether he might have been betrayed by a Soviet agent at work in the West.

The CIA's operational files on Nosenko remain classified, but in 1992 George Kisevalter recalled Nosenko's account to journalist David Wise. Nosenko, Kisevalter said, had claimed that Penkovsky's downfall had begun almost by chance. As a matter of routine, the KGB conducted 'light surveillance' on foreigners in Moscow, and one of these was Janet Chisholm, the wife of MI6's Station Chief in the city. One day, a KGB officer following her had noticed that she had appeared to react strangely to a Russian man in the street. As a result, they had increased their surveillance of Janet Chisholm, following her from her ballet class at Spaso House to a shop in the Arbat. When the Russian passed by, she would leave the shop and follow him to an arcade, where for a few moments they would be out of sight. She also often visited a small, triangular park, and the Russian would walk into it from any of three streets.

The KGB brought in an artist to draw a picture of the mystery man. A KGB officer was then dressed like him and told to walk in front of Janet Chisholm in the park, but not to turn his head, so she would not be able to make out his features. Janet Chisholm fell for the trick, turning to follow the KGB officer.

Now they were certain that Janet Chisholm was in contact with the unidentified Russian. They followed him relentlessly, until they identified him as Oleg Penkovsky of the GRU. But they needed proof of what he was up to. Unfortunately, his apartment was on an island, making surveillance difficult. So they hatched a scheme. While Penkovsky was out at lunch one day at a fast-food restaurant he frequented in Gorky Street, he suddenly suffered stomach pangs – they had poisoned him. An old gentleman in the restaurant rushed up to help, saying he was a doctor, and Penkovsky was rushed to the Kremlin Polyclinic. The KGB team immediately moved into his apartment and searched it – but found nothing, because Penkovsky had hidden his one-time pads, Minox cassettes and other spy paraphernalia in a trick drawer in his desk.

With Penkovsky still hospitalised, the KGB then investigated his upstairs neighbour, who worked as a steel trust executive. The man's boss was persuaded to grant him a holiday in the Caucasus, and once he was safely away the KGB moved two officers into the apartment. They drilled a hole in the floor and installed a peephole camera so they could watch Penkovsky in his living room. They set up an observation post across the river, and the officers in the apartment also used a camera attached to a pot of geraniums that could be extended via cable from the balcony to take photographs of Penkovsky at work. Once enough evidence had been gathered, they poisoned Penkovsky again, using a wax smeared on his chair in his office at the State Committee that caused a skin rash, and this time a search of his apartment uncovered his equipment.

So according to Nosenko, Oleg Penkovsky had been detected, just like Popov before him, 'almost by chance' as the result of the routine surveillance of diplomats in Moscow.

Despite all this astonishing new information, Bagley wasn't keen on Nosenko defecting. It's usually far more advantageous to have an agent remain in place with access to classified information: once they defect all they can do is mine memories that become increasingly unreliable and are eventually made obsolete. For various reasons, Bagley also didn't trust Nosenko's account of why he had to defect.

But there was no real choice. Nosenko claimed to have intelligence about Kennedy's assassination, and the CIA couldn't afford to pass up that opportunity – or for it ever to become known that they had turned it down on mere suspicions. Bagley and a team of CIA officers drove Yuri Nosenko to Frankfurt, where a few days later he was placed on a plane bound for the United States.

The Iceberg War

Greville Wynne, crew-cut and gaunt, arrived at Northolt airport in London on 22 April 1964 to a waiting press. 'WYNNE HOME' declared the front page of the *Evening Times*, and most British newspapers ran similar headlines. The *Express*, which had covered his arrest, trial and imprisonment in exhaustive detail, had the first interview with the 'man who came in from the cold'. He revealed over a cup of tea, scones and seed cake in his Chelsea home that he had celebrated his first night of freedom with a small celebration, a bath and then 'late to bed'.

After treatment at a hospital in Westminster, Wynne went on a Caribbean cruise with his wife. But memories of the Lubyanka preyed on his mind, and he found it difficult to adjust to life after the Penkovsky operation. His name had repeatedly appeared in the world's press as a spy, and he had been imprisoned for it: as a result, his business career was essentially over, as nobody would believe he was genuine. His own company dropped him, and he and Sheila eventually divorced. A second marriage also failed, amid allegations of cruelty in the press.

But Wynne had been involved in one of the most famous espionage operations of the era, and realised he had something to sell. In 1964, his story was serialised in the *Sunday Telegraph*

in Britain and in the US by the *Chicago Tribune*. It told much
the same story as he had done at the trial, of a plucky innocent
unknowingly sucked into a sordid espionage operation.

He wasn't the only one to tell his story. The idea that history
is written by the victors doesn't apply in the world of espionage: there are rarely clear-cut winners in the spy game, and
the defeated usually write books claiming that, secretly, they
won all along. Even massive operational failures can be
presented as ingenious double bluffs, triple crosses or deception operations, and in presenting such theories the hope is
that at least some doubts will be sown. Such attempts sometimes succeed in muddying the waters enough to become
more believed than the truth.

Journalist Chapman Pincher called it 'the Iceberg War': the
submerged battle of disinformation between East and West.
The Soviets' main attempt to influence public perception of
the operation was the trial, which was covered by newspapers
and television around the world. It was remarkably effective.
Many newspapers in the West condemned the Russians' decision to stage a 'show trial', yet reported every sensationalistic
claim made in it. When the prosecutor wheeled out a witness
to testify he'd once seen Penkovsky sipping wine from a
woman's shoe at a restaurant in order to demonstrate how
degraded he had become by his lust for the capitalistic lifestyle,
instead of disregarding this as obvious anti-Western propaganda the press lapped it up. The result was that in the West
Penkovsky was not regarded as having been a major agent
who had provided crucial intelligence, but as a venal Russian
sneaking through the back alleys and lining his own pockets.

Irritated that such a triumph had been undermined by Soviet
propaganda, the CIA, after much discussion with MI6, decided
to hit back by producing a book about the operation. Just as
the KGB had its 'Department D', the CIA had a clandestine
hand in publishing, through the Congress for Cultural

Freedom, which sponsored the magazine *Encounter*, and via other arm's-length means. Using the transcripts of Penkovsky's debriefings as a basis, a narrative was crafted that was broadly accurate, but which sanitised, sensationalised, omitted and altered various elements of the story.

The Penkovsky Papers was published in 1965, and was presented as Penkovsky's secret diaries, smuggled out of the Soviet Union shortly before his execution. It quickly became an international bestseller. In Britain, the *Observer* serialised it with a grim illustration of a firing squad by Raymond Hawkey, who had designed jackets for several of Len Deighton and Ian Fleming's novels: it was the height of 1960s spy fever.

The book was hugely controversial. As Chapman Pincher pointed out in the *Express*, it broke 'the only rule of espionage': with the exception of trials and exchanges, both sides avoided publicising the names of opposition agents whenever possible. The Russians had named several British and American intelligence officers at the trial, but in retaliation *The Penkovsky Papers* named 700 Soviets involved in intelligence work, including senior KGB and GRU officers. It also, somewhat bizarrely, published the names of CIA and MI6 officers, including the Chisholms, the Cowells, Felicity Stuart, William Jones, Hugh Montgomery, Dick Jacob and Alexis Davison. This may have been to avoid accusations that the book was CIA propaganda, but instead it caused further embarrassment, and some in MI6 were furious that the book revealed so much about its own agents and techniques.

The strategy also backfired. Claims that the book was a CIA forgery emerged at once. The *Guardian*, not then a sister paper of the *Observer*, launched an investigation into the book's authenticity, and other newspapers soon joined the fray. The *Express* obtained an interview in Moscow with Penkovsky's wife Vera, who said the book couldn't possibly be her husband's diaries and even posed for a photograph opening the secret compartment in his desk. She said he was vain, conceited, and had grown colder over the years of their marriage. One day, he had left for the office, 'and he never came back' – she had not attended the trial. All of this was no doubt true – the book wasn't his diary, and Penkovsky was vain and conceited – but the wife of a recently executed Soviet traitor was in no position to say anything else: the KGB wouldn't have looked kindly on her or her children had she told the foreign press that the diaries were genuine, let alone presented her husband in a positive light.

The Soviets denounced the book as a hoax at every opportunity, and also took retaliatory measures: the *Washington Post*'s Moscow correspondent was given a week to leave the Soviet Union as a result of his newspaper having serialised the book, the *Observer* faced repeated problems with visas to the Soviet Union, and British and American military attachés in the city had travel privileges revoked.

*

Despite its sales, *The Penkovsky Papers* was in many ways a propaganda disaster: the controversy over the book's authenticity overshadowed its story of the operation's success.

To make matters worse, some within British and American intelligence had themselves changed their minds about the worth of the operation. It was becoming increasingly obvious that the Russians had several agents-in-place in Britain, France and the United States. KGB defector Anatoli Golitsyn, emboldened by the trust senior CIA officers had in him, now declared that Penkovsky must have been under Soviet control all along. He pointed out that the American Embassy in Moscow was littered with bugs, which he claimed meant the KGB would have been able to monitor Penkovsky's debriefings there. Penkovsky had in fact never entered the American Embassy in Moscow – he had even warned the team that the

embassy was bugged, and told them that all Soviet staff working in foreign embassies were KGB informers. But Golitsyn's
insistence that Penkovsky must have been forced by the Soviets
to deliver selected documents to the West gathered support
within British and American counter-intelligence circles.

One element about the operation was particularly troubling:
there was no firm evidence for when and how Penkovsky had
been detected. The only explanation for it had been provided
by Yuri Nosenko, who had claimed the KGB had spotted him
accidentally while conducting routine surveillance of Janet
Chisholm. This chimed with Penkovsky's report that he had
seen surveillance after a meeting with Janet in January 1962 –
the man in the black overcoat – but was that really the first the
KGB had known about the operation?

The fact that Nosenko was the source for this didn't help.
On his arrival in the United States in 1964, BARMAN's
responses to the CIA's questions about Lee Harvey Oswald
and other matters had proven 'evasive and inconsistent', and
Pete Bagley had concluded he was a plant, perhaps sent to feed
false information about the Kennedy assassination. In what
remains one of the CIA's most controversial decisions,
Nosenko was imprisoned, first in an attic in a safe house in
Washington, and then in a purpose-built cell at the CIA's
training facility, Camp Peary, in Virginia. But Nosenko didn't
crack, and maintained that he was a genuine defector.

In 1967, the CIA released Nosenko and tried again.
Questioned in gentler environs, he continued to insist he was
genuine, but admitted he had made a 'false statement' relating
to his defection. But was it his only lie? What if he had also
lied about the way Penkovsky had been caught?

The inconsistencies in Nosenko's story looked all the more
troubling when set against other events. In May 1963, Jack
Dunlap, a clerk at the National Security Agency, had his security clearance revoked under suspicion he was a Soviet agent.

He committed suicide two months later. A subsequent search of his home revealed some of the lower-level documents that had emanated from Penkovsky, attributed to 'a reliable Soviet source'. The following year it was discovered that Robert Lee Johnson, a guard at a courier centre for US Army and Air Force bases near Paris, was also working for the KGB. A third American discovered to be working for the Soviets in this period was William Whalen, a retired lieutenant-colonel in the Joint Chiefs of Staff who had access to the Pentagon as late as 1963.

The situation was no better in Britain. In 1962, an Admiralty clerk, John Vassall, had been arrested and charged with espionage, but while he admitted to having worked with Soviet intelligence his confession didn't seem to account for all the documents that had been stolen. Three years later, Frank Bossard, an engineer at the Ministry of Aviation's Guided Weapons Research and Development Division, was arrested in London. Bossard had a drinking problem and heavy debts, and had been easily recruited by the Russians. In return for payment, Bossard regularly placed classified documents in dead drops around London. He was arrested with a suitcase containing four secret Ministry of Aviation files about guided missiles, but it was impossible to know what other documents he had given the Soviets, or even precisely when he had started working for them – he claimed it had been July 1961, but it could have been earlier.

Any of these men might have tipped off the Soviets that intelligence was being leaked from Moscow. None of them could have known the identity of the source, but as soon as the KGB realised there was a mole, officers would have been assigned to try to narrow the field of suspects, just as Harry Shergold had done with the information from Michael Goleniewski to find Blake.

Within the intelligence community – and in MI5 in particular – some became intensely concerned about the extent of

Soviet penetration: had all or almost all of the spies now been discovered, or was it possible that this was the tip of an iceberg, and that the Russians had dozens, or perhaps even hundreds, of agents and assets buried within the West? In this climate, the Penkovsky operation suddenly looked too good to be true, especially the remarkable coincidence of a Soviet source appearing with such an unprecedented amount of high-grade military intelligence about Berlin and Cuba just as both were needed.

MI5 officer Peter Wright, who had played an incidental role in the Penkovsky operation in fitting the microphones in the Mount Royal Hotel, became one of the leading proponents of the theory that British intelligence was the target of massive Soviet penetration and disinformation attempts. MI5's molehunt eventually led to the surveillance of Roger Hollis, the head of the agency, and Graham Mitchell, its deputy head. But if either Hollis or Mitchell had been a traitor, why had they not informed the KGB about Oleg Penkovsky much earlier? Both had been told his identity in May 1961. The answer, according to Wright and others within MI5, must have been that they – or someone else – *did* tell the KGB, and that Penkovsky had been under Soviet control for almost all of the operation.

In 1987, Wright, angry with MI5 in a dispute over his pension, found an Australian publisher for his memoir, titled *Spycatcher*. Written with ITV reporter Paul Greengrass – now better known as a director of Hollywood films – the book was explosive. Initially banned in England, it quickly became an international bestseller.

One of Wright's claims in *Spycatcher*, which he'd also made in a pamphlet a few years earlier and via interviews with Chapman Pincher as well as during his time at MI5, was that Penkovsky could have been a 'disinformation agent', sent by the Russians to feed specific messages to the West. Wright's theory was that the Soviets were desperate to convince the West that they lagged behind in missile strength and development, and that once Penkovsky had provided this information Khrushchev had achieved his 'major aim': forcing Kennedy into an assurance he wouldn't invade Cuba.

Wright's theories hadn't been well received by his peers: he revealed that when he had suggested at a meeting with MI6 that Penkovsky had been a plant, Harry Shergold had gone for him: '"What the hell do you know about running agents?" he snarled. "You come in here and insult a brave man's memory, and expect us to believe this?"'

Spycatcher has sold over two million copies, and many of Wright's claims have appeared in subsequent books, articles and documentaries. But it is now clear that many of his claims about Penkovsky were based on incomplete knowledge of the operation. He stated, for example, that some of Penkovsky's most important documents were shown to him by his uncle, and that he was debriefed within the American Embassy in Moscow, neither of which is the case. He also claimed that there were suspicious gaps in Penkovsky's material, but in 1992 the CIA granted two authors, Jerrold Schecter and Peter Deriabin, access to thousands of files about the operation for a book, *The Spy Who Saved the World*, and shortly after its publication declassified almost all of these documents. The scope and quality of the material Penkovsky handed over make it undeniable that this was the West's greatest intelligence haul of the Cold War. It also came at a crucial time, and played a key role during the missile crisis: Sidney Graybeal, the chief of the CIA's Guided Missile Division, has said that in answering questions from President Kennedy and his advisers about the missiles he had relied 'primarily on the combination of intelligence sources, but mainly Penkovsky's information, which told us how these missiles operated in the field' – this included precise details of how the missiles were moved, erected and fuelled, and explained that such preparations took several hours. The CIA's chief analyst during the missile crisis, Ray Cline, has stated that Penkovsky's intelligence was vital, as it allowed the agency to 'follow the progress of Soviet missile emplacement in Cuba by the hour'. Dick Helms has also said that without Penkovsky's intelligence the photographs could not have been evaluated in such detail, and that the 'precise capabilities of the SS-4 MRBM and other missiles could not have been made known to the President'.

Wright's theory that Penkovsky could have been part of a ploy by Khrushchev to take the world to the brink of nuclear war to stop the Americans from invading Cuba doesn't hold water, either. A mass of evidence testifies to the fact that the Soviets *were* significantly behind in missile strength, and choosing to reveal this to the West would have been extremely foolhardy on their part, not least because hawks in the US might have ordered a preemptive strike as a result. The GRU had even told Khrushchev that the Pentagon had abandoned a planned nuclear attack in the autumn of 1961 because of their fears that the Soviet nuclear arsenal was more powerful than they had thought – this wasn't in fact the case, but if the Russians had wanted to dissuade the US from considering a nuclear strike, it would have made much more sense for a disinformation agent to claim that their missile strength was greater than they believed, not weaker. A plan to use Penkovsky to trigger a retreat over Cuba would also have been illogical: in fact, General Curtis LeMay argued vociferously for invading the island, but was overruled by Kennedy.

In the feverish interest surrounding the British government's banning of *Spycatcher*, many swallowed Peter Wright's conspiracy theories whole – ironically, all the triumphs of the Penkovsky operation were undermined, not by the KGB, but by one embittered British intelligence officer who clearly hadn't even read the debriefs.

PART III

Walking Back the Cat

Beneath the Smoke

So what really happened? When intelligence agencies want to assess the worth of an operation with the benefit of hindsight, they put together a 'murder board', a committee of officers whose job it is to review all the angles. This is called, in spy jargon, 'walking back the cat'. It's now over half a century since the operation, so what if we walk back the cat on it in light of what we know today?

Many questions about the operation have been answered, but one mystery remains: how Penkovsky was detected. Apart from a few snippets of information about his interrogation and execution, the Russians haven't declassified any of their files about Penkovsky. Over the years, Yuri Nosenko's claim that the KGB discovered Penkovsky accidentally by surveillance has been repeated in many Russian sources, and today is widely accepted as the truth in the West. The date of his detection has repeatedly been given as January 1962, but there are fundamental problems with that story. One is that the KGB didn't arrest Penkovsky until ten months later. With the rate of meetings he was having, gathering evidence shouldn't have taken nearly that long and, even if it did, what information was Penkovsky allowed access to during that time? It beggars belief that the KGB would have simply sat by and watched a suspected agent photographing documents and handing over valuable secrets to their enemies for so long, especially as the Berlin crisis was going on and the Cuban crisis was heating up, unless they had a very good reason to do so.

In 1992, a senior KGB officer from the Second Chief Directorate, who didn't reveal his name, claimed to the American author Jerrold Schecter that the KGB had known that Ruari Chisholm was an MI6 officer when he arrived in Moscow, as they knew about his previous work for the agency in West Berlin. The same officer also erroneously claimed that they had known that Ruari's wife had acted as an agent prior to her arrival in Moscow. However, the officer repeatedly referred to Janet Chisholm, as other Russian sources had done during and after the trial, as Anne Chisholm. ANNE was the codename she was given for the Penkovsky operation, and it was only given to her after she arrived in Moscow.

The officer stated that the KGB had placed Ruari under surveillance in 1960. In 1961, he said, they had started following his wife − no explanation was given for why this had happened the following year if they had known both were MI6 officers on their arrival in the city. In December 1961, the KGB officer claimed, 'we noted for the first time that Penkovsky or someone had a meeting with Anne Chisholm'. By January 1962, they had identified him for certain.

The rest of the account broadly followed the one given by Yuri Nosenko: after Penkovsky was hospitalised for a skin condition − in this telling this was entirely coincidental and not as a result of any poisoning on their part − the KGB moved into his flat and installed cameras, allowing them to monitor and photograph precisely what Penkovsky had been doing.

On the afternoon of 22 October 1962, the KGB had enough evidence, and finally made their move. They prepared a simple ruse, telling Penkovsky that his request for a passport to travel abroad had been approved: a KGB officer came to pick him up from the State Committee offices and drove him to KGB headquarters in Dzerzhinsky Square, where he was arrested and placed in a cell. The KGB then showed Schecter what purported to be grainy surveillance footage of Penkovsky and Janet Chisholm in the Arbat, four stills of which were reproduced in the book.

Asked whether the KGB had allowed Penkovsky to continue passing secrets to the West for the ten months between December 1961 and October 1962, and if this had been because they had been 'protecting a mole in the American or British services who had fingered him', the KGB officer denied it, saying this was 'sheer imagination' and that: 'Americans are good enough to make up such things.' They hadn't needed a mole, he said, because 'it was Mrs Chisholm that led us to the Penkovsky case'. However, later in the conversation, he mentioned that 'the case file on Penkovsky was kept a tightly held secret', adding: 'Counterintelligence even now cannot disclose how Penkovsky was uncovered.' This totally contradicted his previous statements, in which he had claimed he was finally telling the full story of how Penkovsky had been uncovered, and that it had been solely through surveillance of Janet Chisholm.

New light was shed on the operation in 1995, when MI6 told its side of the story for the first time in *The Perfect English Spy*, British author Tom Bower's biography of the former head of MI5 and MI6, Dick White. White and others from MI6 gave on-the-record interviews, as did several former CIA and KGB officers. One of the most intriguing claims from the Russian side was that the KGB had *not* spotted Penkovsky meeting Janet Chisholm. According to former general Oleg Gribanov, who had led the investigation, and Nikolai Chistyakov, who had assisted him, the footage of Penkovsky and Janet Chisholm that had been shown to Jerrold Schecter three years earlier was part of a longer film the KGB had made to train its officers, and those scenes had in fact been reconstructed for it. 'Our officers never saw those meetings,' Chistyakov said.

But if this were so, when had the KGB realised Penkovsky was a traitor – and how? Gribanov and Chistyakov didn't answer that.

*

Two years later, a Russian documentary, produced in coop-eration with the KGB successor agency the FSB, revisited the operation. It has not been remarked on, but this programme unwittingly provided proof that the Russians' long-standing 'accidental discovery' story is false. *Penkovsky: Agent of Three Powers* features excerpts of a black-and-white film about the operation made by the KGB. As stated by Gribanov and Chistyakov, several scenes in it are reconstructions, some of them apparently done with Penkovsky himself. One sequence shows a man who looks like him wearing a dressing gown saying goodbye to his wife at the door of their flat, almost as though it were a soap opera. If it is him, the ramifications are chilling: to add to the enormous stress of having been arrested and facing certain death, the idea of having to re-enact scenes of domestic bliss for the KGB's camera crew with his soon-to-be-widow must have been agonising.

The KGB film shows how the surveillance against Penkovsky was conducted, including footage of officers entering and searching his flat. We see Penkovsky photographing docu-ments, with cutaways to the team watching him through long-lens cameras from their post across the river and from the apartment above. The scenes with the officers are clearly reconstructions: intelligence agencies don't generally film themselves while conducting searches or carrying out surveil-lance, and for the early 1960s in the Soviet Union the film has high production values, resembling spy thrillers of the day, with a dramatic soundtrack and handsome, well-groomed and smartly tailored KGB officers. The footage of Penkovsky, on the other hand, is grainy and at times shaky. We see him standing by his window, but it is unclear if he is shaving using a mirror or holding up a document – in another shot, he is hunched over, seemingly photographing documents with a Minox. It would seem, then, that the KGB film is a mix of genuine surveillance footage and reconstruction after the fact.

The documentary also shows the purported surveillance footage in the Arbat of Penkovsky and 'Anne Chisholm'. The camera follows a woman, her face not clearly visible under a hood, as she walks through an archway. She then walks directly into the view of the camera, and down the street. We see, from another camera angle, a man in a black overcoat arriving at the same location. So there are two cameras – or two separately filmed sequences. The woman then enters a building, and we cut away as she is watched, again from another angle, by the man we saw earlier, whom the documentary identifies as KGB Major Boris Nikolaev. It is already clear that this footage is at least partially a reconstruction, because it is implausible that the KGB would film themselves watching their quarry in this way, especially as Nikolaev throws an absurdly hammy sidelong glance in the direction of Janet Chisholm. The cutaways, again, resemble Soviet spy thrillers of the era, not surveillance footage.

The programme then interviews Nikolaev in the present day about the events, and he reveals that the black-and-white footage dated from 19 January 1962. It was filmed, he claims, because on 30 December he had spotted Janet Chisholm acting unusually. There was already light surveillance on her because she was the wife of a foreign diplomat, but Nikolaev's attention had been drawn by the fact that she had bought a kilo of apples in the market and then revisited somewhere she had been only a few minutes earlier, for no apparent reason. He had decided to follow her. She had taken a side street, and he had then spotted a man nearby who he thought might be connected with her in some way. But before he could act on this, the man vanished.

The KGB, Nikolaev went on, had decided to investigate further. Instead of systematically following everyone over Moscow with cameras, he said, they had a grid system in place, with certain areas checked every once in a while, and fixed cameras available at some locations. On 19 January 1962, the areas Janet Chisholm was known to visit were set up to be filmed.

The black-and-white footage then resumes, and we see the camera pan from the door of the building Janet Chisholm has just entered to a telephone booth across the street. A man is standing in the booth with the receiver to his ear. The camera reaches him, and as though on cue he replaces the receiver, opens the door of the booth, strides over to the building, opens the door and enters it.

This moment proves that the Russian version of how they detected Oleg Penkovsky is false: the cameraman *knew* that the man in the telephone booth would leave it, and that he would cross the street to enter the building.

One possible interpretation of this is that Oleg Gribanov and Nikolai Chistyakov were telling the truth in 1995: the film is a reconstruction, either with lookalike actors or with Penkovsky being forced to act a part, and the KGB never witnessed any contact he had with Janet Chisholm. There is another interpretation. The footage of Penkovsky taking photographs looks to be genuine, and he had reported that he was being watched on 19 January 1962, by a man in a black overcoat. But the camera swinging towards Penkovsky only makes sense if the KGB knew in advance that he was to contact Janet Chisholm in this way. Nikolaev's previous sighting of her acting suspiciously on 30 December doesn't explain how the cameraman could be certain that in a different location the

Janet Chisholm – codenamed ANNE by MI6 – with her children in a Moscow park in 1961. Penkovsky would approach her and place microfilm hidden in a box of sweets in her youngest child's pram. (Janie Chisholm)

Ruari Chisholm, MI6's head of station in Moscow, Janet Chisholm (right) and their daughter Janie in Moscow, 1961. (Janie Chisholm)

2 July 1962 – KGB surveillance cameras capture Greville Wynne arriving in Moscow. The man picking him up, seen bending down in the centre image, is Oleg Penkovsky. By now the KGB had known Penkovsky was a traitor for at least six months, and yet he was still photographing highly classified documents and passing them to MI6 and the CIA. (KGB)

A KGB surveillance still of Greville Wynne, right, on 12 April 1961, as he prepared to fly back to London from Moscow. The KGB probably photographed everyone coming in and out of the country systematically. (KGB)

KGB surveillance photograph of Richard Jacob unloading Penkovsky's dead drop, 3 November 1962. (KGB)

Cool head: MI6 officer Gervase Cowell received the emergency signal that a nuclear strike was imminent, but decided to ignore it. (KGB)

This image is from KGB surveillance footage of Gervase Cowell having his passport checked at Moscow airport. The Cowells were expelled from the Soviet Union in May 1963. (KGB)

A KGB film shows Alexander Zagvozdin, who was one of the KGB officers investigating Penkovsky. (KGB)

This illustration, created after the operation with the input of a member of the KGB's surveillance team, shows how they watched Penkovsky's flat in Moscow: an observation post across the river, a camera in the balcony outside his window, and a peephole camera looking down on him from the flat above. (H. Keith Melton)

Sergei Kondrashev was George Blake's controller in London; on becoming chief of the KGB's disinformation division in 1968, he was apparently informed that Oleg Penkovsky had been betrayed by an agent in the West. (KGB)

Felicity Stuart, Ruari Chisholm's assistant in Moscow during the early stages of the operation. She was named in the trial. (KGB)

Purported KGB still of Penkovsky operating his radio transmitter to receive coded messages. This image seems to have been filmed from within Penkovsky's flat, suggesting the scene was reconstructed after his arrest. (KGB)

A photograph of Kutuzovsky Prospekt in Moscow taken by Felicity Stuart from her flat during the Penkovsky operation: Penkovsky would mark telephone pole 35 in the street to tell his handlers they should clear his dead drop on Pushkinskaya Street. (Felicity Stuart)

Purported KGB surveillance footage of Penkovsky photographing a document with a Minox camera, taken from the command post across the river from his flat. (KGB)

Espionage paraphernalia used by Oleg Penkovsky and shown at his trial in Moscow. Pictured are three Minox cameras, their cases, several rolls of microfilm and a fake pack of cigarettes, which Penkovsky used to pass material to Janet Chisholm. (Bettmann CORBIS/SCANPIX)

High treason: Greville Wynne, top, and Oleg Penkovsky, below, both in centre of frame, on trial in Moscow, May 1963. (Bettmann CORBIS/SCANPIX)

'Don't forget the fruit gums, Mum!': Giles's cartoon in the *Daily Express*. (Daily Express)

The funeral of British traitor Guy Burgess, September 1963, Moscow. From left, Reuters correspondent John Miller; British Communist George Hanna; *Daily Telegraph* correspondent Jeremy Wolfenden; Donald Maclean (partially obscured); and Burgess's brother Nigel (in glasses in front). (John Miller)

Jeremy Wolfenden, left, hands over as *Daily Telegraph* correspondent in Moscow to John Miller, previously with Reuters, on the steps of the British Embassy, 1964. Wolfenden drank himself to death a year later, aged 31. (John Miller)

Journalist, drinker and spy: Jeremy Wolfenden. (Daily Telegraph)

man in the telephone booth would leave it at that precise moment in order to enter a building after her.

It may be that they had already seen Penkovsky do this, but were now hoping to get it on film – or it may be that the surveillance was an ambush. The KGB could have already discovered that Penkovsky was in contact with Janet Chisholm, and Nikolaev and other officers assigned to light surveillance of her could have been told to keep a closer watch in the hope that they would then 'accidentally' spot Penkovsky trying to contact her. Once they had caught him doing so on camera, it could then be claimed that Penkovsky had been detected in this way without officers such as Boris Nikolaev even being aware that it was a cover story.

This would explain the curious comments by the KGB official to Jerrold Schecter in 1992, when he had said that 'the case file on Penkovsky was kept a tightly held secret' and that 'Counterintelligence even now cannot disclose how Penkovsky was uncovered.'

The 'accidental discovery' story cannot be true, but why are the Russians hiding what really happened? The answer may be an old one: in 2002, Jerrold Schecter claimed at a talk in Washington that a week earlier someone claiming to be a former KGB officer now living in England had called him and claimed that 'a mole inside the CIA had given Penkovsky away'.

Could it be that, just as Peter Wright and others had feared, an agent in the West informed the KGB about Penkovsky? If so, it would seem the KGB decided it was worth sacrificing a certain amount of intelligence in order to protect their source, before finally stepping in and 'accidentally' discovering the truth.

The Russian intelligence services did not respond to requests for information for this book, and are unlikely to reveal the answer any time soon. However, interest in the operation has been reignited in Russia, ironically by a claim first suggested by defector Anatoli Golitsyn: that Oleg Penkovsky was a loyal Soviet agent all along. The leading proponent of this idea in recent years has been a former KGB officer going by the name of Anatoli Maximov, who has added an ingenious twist: he claims that Penkovsky was not executed, but instead his name and appearance were changed and he was spirited away to a secret location, where he continued his secret work. Maximov has not provided any hard evidence for this, but it forms the basis for his 2010 book, *The GRU's Greatest Mystery*.

In Putin's Russia, the idea that the most notorious traitor of the Cold War was not an imperialist wretch after all but secretly a loyal and brilliant Soviet agent carrying out an incredible deception operation against the West is an attractive one, even if the record clearly shows it cannot be the case. Articles featuring Maximov's theories have been reproduced on the official website of the revamped foreign wing of the KGB, the SVR. This is roughly akin to MI6's website republishing articles from newspapers proposing that Kim Philby was, after all, a British hero.

Maximov appeared in two high-profile Russian TV documentaries about the Penkovsky operation in 2011. One of the documentaries, *Dark Deeds: The Chief Traitor of the Soviet Union*, posed the dramatic question: 'Was Penkovsky really the downfall of Soviet intelligence – or was he in fact part of an ingenious operation organised by them?' Maximov suggested that Penkovsky had played a key role in a GRU deception operation masterminded by Serov and Varentsov, together with Varentsov's aide Buzinov, because they were worried that Khrushchev was blundering towards a nuclear war. Penkovsky had acted a role all along, handing over doctored information. Maximov claimed that top-secret versions of the military journals Penkovsky had passed to the West had been prepared just for him, and had contained disinformation about missiles and rockets. After Penkovsky had photographed them, the same journals had been published anew, with similar titles and names of authors but with the content of the articles replaced with genuine information. The idea was to give the West false intelligence that the Soviet Union was weaker than it claimed regarding its missiles, so that the West would 'relax'. This theory strongly resembles Peter Wright's in *Spycatcher* – and is implausible for all the same reasons.

★

Beneath all the smoke and mirrors, it is now clear that the Russians have lied about how they detected Oleg Penkovsky. The first clue is the silent phone calls to Felicity Stuart and the Davisons' house, none of which quite corresponded with the pre-arranged procedures. Penkovsky was a professional intelligence officer, and his life was on the line. He had his procedures written down for him, and so is very unlikely to have made such basic mistakes. He also had no reason to make the calls – he was not about to travel to the West, and the Soviets weren't planning to launch a nuclear strike – and never mentioned having done so to Janet or in any of his reports. Finally, when the CIA checked his dead drop after the calls to the Davisons' house they found it empty. If Penkovsky had wanted to provoke the West into launching a nuclear attack against the Soviet Union in this way, he would not simply have made the calls but would also have left material in the drop that would have convinced the CIA and MI6 to act on them.

So who did make them? They might all have been wrong numbers, but if so that's a huge coincidence, and one presumes also a very rare one, or Stuart would have been sending a lot of telegrams to London and Abidian would have checked the dead drop more than once. It seems likely that someone else knew something about Penkovsky's signals, and was testing them in some way.

The obvious instigator is the KGB, but all of these calls came *before* 30 December 1961, which is when they claim they first detected Penkovsky. The calls to Stuart alone might be dismissed as coincidence, but whoever called the Davisons evidently didn't know that they were activating a signal that was to be used in the event of an imminent nuclear strike. The chances of such an emergency signal, which was known to only a handful of people in the world, being activated just five days before the KGB accidentally discovered Penkovsky seems astronomically unlikely.

The next aspect of the Russians' version of events that falls apart under scrutiny is their claims about Janet Chisholm. If the KGB had a dossier on her before she arrived in Moscow, it must have been very thin indeed for them not to have even known her first name, especially as it was on her visa to enter the country. Russians often confuse Western names, just as Westerners confuse Russian ones – for example, *Newsweek* mistakenly referred to *Igor* Penkovsky in its reporting in 1963. But this usually happens when one is new to a name, not familiar with it, let alone having investigated the minutiae of a person's espionage career. The repeated use of 'Anne' suggests that the KGB's knowledge of Janet Chisholm came *after* she arrived in Moscow, when she was given that codename.

The claim that they decided to follow her because of her prior experience as an intelligence officer is also very hard to credit. It's a plausible assumption to have made retrospectively, but in fact she had simply been Ruari's secretary, and had left MI6 when they married in 1954. The only time she ever acted as an intelligence officer was as Penkovsky's contact. General Gribanov, who ran the investigation, also stated that the KGB never saw Janet Chisholm and Penkovsky together, and that the purported surveillance footage showing this is an after-the-fact reconstruction: the footage itself suggests this.

As Penkovsky's identity was closely protected by MI6 and the CIA, it may be that someone knew that there was a highly placed agent in Moscow, and knew a few details about how they were contacted, but no more. Such a source could have pointed the KGB in Janet Chisholm's direction, and suggested that following her could lead them to identifying the traitor. Once arrested, Penkovsky would no doubt have disclosed all the details of his contacts with her under interrogation – but he would have referred to her as Anne, as that was the only name he knew her by.

*

Some evidence for this theory came in 2007, when Pete Bagley published his memoir, *Spy Wars*. The book is mainly about the Yuri Nosenko case, but also has a bearing on the Penkovsky operation. According to Bagley, the Soviets could have known about Penkovsky as early as May 1961 – within just a month of his first meeting with MI6 and the CIA, and well over a year before his eventual arrest.

Bagley cited two sources for this startling claim. The first was a British intelligence officer, whom he didn't name in his book but gave the alias 'James Garth'. After tracking Bagley down and exchanging several calls and emails, I flew to Brussels to meet him. 'Garth', he told me as we sat in his darkened study surrounded by books and box files on the Cold War, was Michael McCaul, who had been a senior MI5 officer in the 1960s.

According to Bagley, in 1965 he had attended a party in Washington given by Yuri Rastvorov, a former KGB colonel who had defected to the US in the 1950s. At the party, McCaul told Bagley that he had been part of the team who had debriefed Greville Wynne on his return from imprisonment in Moscow

the previous spring. And Wynne had revealed the most curious thing: he had claimed that at one point he had been
dragged in front of a KGB interrogator, who had repeatedly
asked him which other agents he had been running in Eastern
Europe. Wynne had replied that he hadn't run any agents, in
Eastern Europe or anywhere else.

The interrogator had then asked him if he recognised the
name 'Zepp'. Having no idea who he meant, Wynne had said
he didn't. He was then played a recording of a conversation
between him and Penkovsky in which Penkovsky asked him
about someone of that name. Wynne remembered the conversation: it was in fact about *Zeph*, the prostitute Penkovsky had
slept with in London and had developed something of an
obsession with – he had been asking after her. The KGB had
slightly misheard the name on the tape. McCaul had established with Wynne that the conversation about Zeph had
taken place in a restaurant in Moscow in May 1961.

On hearing this, Bagley was stunned. He remembered that
in 1962, Yuri Nosenko had told him, seemingly in passing,
that he had once tapped the conversations of an Indonesian
intelligence officer called Zepp. What were the chances of
Greville Wynne being asked about someone with the same
highly unusual name? Added to his other reasons for suspect-
ing that Nosenko was a false defector, Bagley now wondered
whether the KGB had primed him to mention the name Zepp,
knowing that one of Penkovsky's case officers, George
Kisevalter, would hear it and might react: a fishing expedition.
If so, it hadn't worked, because unknown to the KGB Zepp
was not part of any spy ring at all.

For Bagley, McCaul's information was significant because
of what it suggested about Nosenko, who he suspected was a
plant. But the information also sheds new light on the
Penkovsky operation, as it suggests that the KGB were
conducting surveillance on Penkovsky and Wynne as early as

May 1961. In 1959, George Blake had worked for MI6 in London, where he had reported directly to Dickie Franks in DP4. He had left that position just two months before Franks had lunch with Greville Wynne at The Ivy and asked him to travel to Moscow – if Wynne had been recruited for intelligence work before that lunch, as he later claimed, Blake would almost certainly have known about it and passed his name to the KGB. The Russians kept visiting foreigners under observation anyway, but if they had been given Wynne's name as an MI6 asset by Blake they would have ordered much closer surveillance of him. Even if Wynne hadn't been blown by Blake, Penkovsky had himself told the team that surveillance on foreigners in Moscow was especially heavy in restaurants.

But this would mean that Penkovsky was blown from a *very* early stage, within just a few weeks of the operation getting underway, and that the Russians have successfully concealed this fact for half a century. Why?

Bagley also referred in his memoir to a Russian source on the Penkovsky operation. He wrote that during the 1990s, after the Wall had fallen, a 'retired KGB colonel' had confided to him that the line peddled about the Penkovsky operation was a ruse: 'Don't believe for a minute that old story that we detected Penkovsky by surveillance,' he had said. This, Bagley tells me, was Mikhail Lyubimov, who in 1961 had been head of the KGB *rezidentura* in London.

Lyubimov had never publicly stated his belief that the official Russian line on the detection of Penkovsky was false before Bagley informed me of it, but by coincidence he repeated the claim in a French television documentary a few months after my conversation with Bagley. *Penkovsky: espion pour la paix* showed many of the same excerpts of the KGB's film about the operation that had been seen previously, as well as some that hadn't. One scene shows Penkovsky using his radio to receive and decipher signals. It is shot not from above, or from across the road, but seemingly from inside his flat, and from three different angles. In a post–Cold War interview, KGB investigator Alexander Zagvozdin said that after arresting Penkovsky they had made him listen to one of the CIA transmissions on his transmitter, and he had shown them how it worked. All this points to some reconstruction, but it doesn't mean that genuine surveillance was not also conducted on Penkovsky, or even filmed, merely that he was filmed recreating some of his actions after his arrest.

Lyubimov told the documentary that he had known several officers in the KGB's Second Chief Directorate, which had been responsible for the surveillance and arrest of Penkovsky, and that he felt that the KGB had misrepresented events: 'It is clear that in the film they tell the story as it suits them,' he said. 'Everything is invented in it. Everything is false. Everything is explained and justified in such minute detail that it suggests to me the KGB was disguising the main point: the informer who had allowed them to discover Penkovsky. They have invented the whole story as a smokescreen.'

For Lyubimov, it was not just the footage that was suspect, but Penkovsky's behaviour throughout the operation. He operated so openly, he said, 'as though somebody was protecting him', that it was no wonder that some felt that the entire operation had been controlled by the KGB.

Former KGB investigator Alexander Zagvozdin professed himself perplexed. 'We have not invented the Penkovsky history,' he said, claiming that it would be impossible to stage such a massive deception operation, including the trial, and that there would be no purpose in having done so. However, he didn't respond to Lyubimov's suggestion that Penkovsky was genuine but that the KGB had hidden the real manner in which they had detected him. Zagvozdin, who has recited the 'accidental discovery' line repeatedly in the last two decades, was probably thinking of Maximov's theories, currently gaining a lot of publicity in Russia.

★

Before I met Pete Bagley, he told me on the phone that shortly before publication of his memoir in 2007, he had received confirmation from a *second* former KGB officer that Penkovsky had been detected earlier than believed. 'This,' he tells me in Brussels, 'was Kondrashev.'

Lieutenant-General Sergei Kondrashev was George Blake's case officer. He went on to head the KGB's German department and then served as deputy chief of the disinformation section Department D before becoming chief in 1968. After retiring from the KGB in 1992, he and an American journalist, George Bailey, co-wrote the book *Battleground Berlin* with David Murphy, who had been the CIA's Station Chief in Berlin. Kondrashev wrote extensively about his role in the Blake operation, and rebutted the idea that had been considered by some in the West that the KGB had used the opportunity of the tunnel to plant disinformation. *Battleground Berlin* was a groundbreaking Cold War history, particularly as it cited several KGB files. With the advent of *glasnost*, the KGB had decided it was time to shine a positive light on the organisation's history, and to allow access to selected archival material on some of its more successful operations.

Also taking advantage of the new era of openness in Russia was Pete Bagley. Following the disintegration of the Soviet Union, he travelled to Russia and met several former KGB officers who had been his adversaries a few decades earlier: he became close with some of them, especially Kondrashev, who would often visit him in Brussels. Eventually, Bagley started writing a biography of Kondrashev with his help, and the two men were working on this when Kondrashev died in September 2007.

Bagley claims that Kondrashev told him in that year that, on becoming chief of Department D in 1968, he had been informed that Oleg Penkovsky had been betrayed by an agent in the West. However, he had not been told the agent's identity: that had been totally compartmentalised by the KGB's Foreign Intelligence department. The KGB, Kondrashev said, had allowed Penkovsky continued access to secrets in order to protect this agent: if they had arrested him too early, that source would have come under suspicion for having leaked it to them.

In addition, Bagley says, Kondrashev told him that the KGB had known about at least some of Penkovsky's signals to the CIA–MI6 team, including one that involved leaving a light on in the window of his apartment, before they had started rejecting his requests to travel abroad, which was in October 1961. They had set up surveillance on Penkovsky's apartment partly to try to monitor these signals: 'Even before they stopped him going abroad,' Kondrashev had told Bagley, 'they had this covered.'

Bagley says he didn't want to reveal when Kondrashev was alive that he had told him this, as it might have affected his friend's pension and the standing of both he and members of his family in the new Russia, where even now discussion of Cold War operations is a highly sensitive matter. He also says that it took him months of discussion with Kondrashev before he opened up about the Penkovsky operation.

*

If Bagley's information is right, and the KGB detected Penkovsky following information from a Western source, events start to make more sense. If the source was well placed enough, they could have known that there was an MI6–CIA agent-in-place in Moscow, and some details about the operation, but perhaps not Penkovsky's identity, which was only known to very few people. But they might have had other information that led to their identifying the agent. The KGB would then have needed a cover story – as with the Berlin tunnel, they had to find a way to appear to have accidentally discovered the operation in order to protect their source.

According to George Kisevalter, in the spring of 1962 Yuri Nosenko claimed that the KGB knew about the CIA's drop in Moscow because they had seen John Abidian visit it in December 1960. Nosenko's date has to be wrong, but the fact he knew about the drop at all meant that the KGB must have already discovered one aspect of the Penkovsky operation. Abidian visited Penkovsky's dead drop after the call to the Davisons' house on Christmas Day 1961, so it may be that the KGB were trying to draw someone out – just as they did eleven months later, when the CIA took the bait and Dick Jacob was arrested as a result. Perhaps the KGB were not fully prepared to arrest Abidian in 1961, or had second thoughts: arresting him straight after the phone calls might not have been believed as accidental discovery. They may also have decided to continue to monitor the situation: now they knew where the drop was, perhaps the next time they could empty it themselves, or ensure that they had officers very close by ready to pounce (as happened with Jacob). They now had confirmation that there was a drop, which pointed to an agent. Five days later, perhaps now guided by their source to follow the wife of the local MI6 officer, they had identified the agent. This surveillance then gave them their cover story to protect the fact that they had been tipped off in advance.

If something like this did happen, the KGB's source would have been extremely closely guarded – and would remain so today. The protection of highly placed intelligence sources even from very senior figures is not unique to the KGB: after all, the CIA's General Carter didn't reveal Penkovsky's identity to John F. Kennedy's advisers during the Cuban missile crisis, instead claiming that intelligence about Soviet MRBMs had come from 'our IRONBARK sources'.

The Blake case is not the only known example of the Soviets using ingenious methods of source protection. According to Victor Cherkashin, an officer in the English department of the KGB's Second Chief Directorate who was involved in the surveillance of Janet Chisholm, in 1987 the directorate sent one of its officers, Alexander Zhomov, to the CIA with an offer to spy for them. The CIA took the bait, and Zhomov then concluded his true mission, which was to provide false leads on the KGB's arrest of agents two years earlier: 'In each case,' Cherkashin wrote, 'the KGB was shown to have found the moles through sheer luck and hard work.' That sounds familiar.

*

Pete Bagley has a theory, which he summarises as: 'It takes a mole to catch a mole.' He says that traitors are never discovered by chance or simply because an agency is looking out for them, but from a source deep within the enemy camp who steps forward. There was a lot of suspicion about the charming, clever Kim Philby after Burgess and Maclean fled to Moscow, but he was only finally exposed when Anatoli Golitsyn defected to the West and stated that the KGB had a ring of five high-ranking agents within British intelligence. If Polish intelligence officer Michael Goleniewski had not defected and provided a list of documents he had seen, George Blake could have continued his career undetected until retirement, and the current accepted history of the Berlin tunnel operation would be completely different as a result. How many events in the twentieth century might not be what they are thought to be as a result of the actions of still-undetected Soviet agents?

This might explain the curious chronology of the end of the Penkovsky operation. Penkovsky was arrested on 22 October:

the same day Kennedy made the missile crisis public via a televised address, and on which US forces were placed at DEFCON-3. It may be that the KGB felt that the stakes were getting too high and, as they had done with the Berlin tunnel, decided to stage an 'accidental discovery' that put paid to any further intelligence emanating from that source.

In 1964, a CIA post-mortem on the missile crisis speculated that if Penkovsky had been arrested on 22 October, as it seemed, this would have given Khrushchev an additional factor to consider in his response to Kennedy's speech that day, as he would have realised that there was a strong likelihood that Penkovsky had given the West intelligence about Soviet capabilities and targets, weakening his position in the event of war. The CIA report speculated that the knowledge of Penkovsky's treason might have strengthened Khrushchev's sense that if the Americans looked 'willing to fight' he would have to back down.

It may be that Khrushchev did see it in these terms, but a more rational reading of Penkovsky's arrest would have been that the Americans now almost certainly knew he was bluffing and that the Soviet Union would *lose* a war, and so rather than continue the charade and risk further humiliation and perhaps annihilation, he should find a way to climb down at once before the worst happened. An immediate interrogation of Penkovsky – perhaps using a room with rats in the Lubyanka, which he had told the team about – would have soon established precisely what he had told the West about Soviet capabilities and targets, and should then have led to Khrushchev rapidly capitulating.

However, it was in fact another three days before Khrushchev finally suggested to the Presidium that they strike a deal with the Americans, and it is clear that Penkovsky was neither harshly interrogated or tortured, or at least not to the degree that he revealed the full extent of his activities – the KGB didn't even manage to coax from him the names of his four case officers.

Perhaps Khrushchev was too distracted by the crisis to pay enough attention to Penkovsky's arrest. But if there *was* a faction of doves within the Kremlin – or simply some sane people who didn't want a nuclear holocaust – the idea of arresting him might also have been to try to rein Khrushchev in, because it should have made it clear that to continue to try to bluff the Americans would be futile when they had been obtaining highly classified material from a GRU officer. If so, the tactic didn't work.

★

So who has this 'accidental' cover story been protecting? And why continue to hide the truth after so long?

The Russians often ran deception operations, or *maskirovka*, during the Cold War, with the protection of Blake being just one example of many. An advantage of them is that people often find it difficult to believe that anyone would go to the lengths to stage them. One reason Kim Philby remained at large for so long is that the idea that such a senior and well-liked MI6 officer could be a long-term Soviet agent had seemed impossibly far-fetched to some, and so had been filed away in the category of conspiracy theory despite the evidence. Ironically, the same blindness afflicted some members of Soviet intelligence, who for a time during the Second World War believed that Philby and the rest of the Cambridge Ring were 'known to the British intelligence organs' and worked 'with their knowledge and on their instructions'.

If Penkovsky was betrayed by a Western source, it would have made sense at the time and in the immediate years following the operation to claim he had been detected another way. And yet this version of events is still claimed as the truth today, half a century later, when such a source is most likely dead.

That may simply be down to bureaucratic procedure: intelligence agencies rarely correct their own untruths unless they have to. Most reveal as little as possible about their workings, and this is especially the case in Russia. Revealing that they lied about Penkovsky would probably not gain the Russian intelligence services any advantage at this stage, and might even backfire, leading to doubts being sown over other carefully nurtured propaganda lines, and perhaps over true statements, too.

Conspiracy theories about Cold War moles are legion, and tore the CIA and MI6 apart for years, but this is partly because there was in fact a conspiracy: the Soviets *did* penetrate Western intelligence services extremely successfully, particularly in France and Britain. While the histories of Philby, Guy Burgess, Donald Maclean, Anthony Blunt and John Cairncross are well known, a commitment to Communism among the British intelligentsia was not limited to five young men from Cambridge. In the last few decades, several people have been exposed as having worked with Soviet intelligence, and while this book was being written the BBC revealed that the former Conservative MP Raymond Mawby was a Czech intelligence asset in the 1960s.

Some British and Americans living in the Soviet Union appreciated that the country was a police state, and that virtually everyone they came into contact with was in some way connected to the security services. Others seem to have only partially grasped this, and felt that instead there were many KGB spies and informants, but that it was foolish to suspect everyone one met. The Russians exploited the Western tendency to extend the benefit of the doubt, and many KGB and GRU informers made close friendships with Westerners who refused to believe they could be so charming and yet report on their every move. A few were more naïve, or foolish, and stepped into much deeper water.

In 1996, Sebastian Faulks wrote a non-fiction book, *The Fatal Englishman*, which comprised three short biographies of minor British figures. One of them was the journalist Jeremy Wolfenden, who Faulks revealed was compromised by the KGB in a honey trap when he was living in the Ukraina Hotel in Moscow. He mentioned several different versions of the story – it was a waiter from the Praga restaurant, it was his barber, it was a Polish boy called Jan, two men sprung from a cupboard – and wrote that it was not clear which really happened, when exactly it happened or if there was even only one incident.

Faulks also speculated that Wolfenden could have been compromised by the KGB long before he arrived in Moscow to work for the *Daily Telegraph*. In 1956, during his second year at Oxford, he visited the Soviet Union with a group from the National Union of Students. The group's minder had been 'Yuri Krutikov', and Faulks speculates that either he or someone else could have compromised and recruited Wolfenden then. 'The nature of any entrapment would not in the first instance be practical,' Faulks wrote, 'it would be mechanical: it would be done because it *could* be done. But if Wolfenden's career flourished as everyone expected then there could be long-term benefits. To have as editor of *The Times* a KGB agent of influence would be more than a coup; it could be useful.'

Wolfenden also appears to have been sexually active on the trip: before he returned to Moscow in 1961 he told a friend that he remembered where all the pick-up places were from his earlier visit and that he expected to be caught and blackmailed within his first fortnight in the city. This airy comment is in keeping with Wolfenden's devil-may-care attitude, but is also something he might have said had he already been compromised on his previous journey.

According to Faulks, Wolfenden was compromised by the KGB on his return to Moscow, and reluctantly reported it to

MI6. This would most plausibly have been to the Head of Station in Moscow, especially if it happened before June 1962, when that was his friend Ruari Chisholm. MI6 apparently advised Wolfenden to do nothing, 'to go along with what the KGB asked him', and when he was on leave in London to call in at an address in Whitehall to 'have a chat with MI5'.

In the autumn of 1962, Wolfenden appears to have done just that, telling a girlfriend – at that time his fiancée, but they later broke it off – while on leave in London that he was 'debriefed by the Foreign Office' while there. In the early autumn of 1962, Oleg Penkovsky was still a free man. This suggests that the KGB could have compromised Wolfenden while the operation was still going on.

As he had been advised by MI6, Wolfenden cooperated with the KGB in Moscow, among other things informing on his colleagues in the press pack. But by now he was drinking enormous amounts, and visibly under pressure. He warned the *Daily Express* correspondent Martin Page never to tell him 'anything that he would not want the KGB to know'. Another British journalist, Douglas Botting, discovered that Wolfenden had been reading his post, and even saw payment he had received for his activities from the KGB. Wolfenden loudly proclaimed over lunch with colleagues who would be appointed to the Politburo in advance of the information being published. In 1964, he wrote an article for the *Daily Telegraph* in which he claimed that the Soviets would blacklist eleven British firms that had been associated with Greville Wynne – he later told colleagues that the story was untrue, but that the Russians had forced him to file it. In the article, Wolfenden named the firms, claiming his source was 'a hastily-compiled list, hand-written in Russian' – presumably given to him by his KGB contact. A brief article a few weeks later reported that the Soviets had decided not to blacklist the firms after all, but by then the damage had already been done: the companies Wolfenden named had all been tainted by their association with a compromised spy, dealing a blow to British businesses, and Wynne's relationship with them was soured as a result, dealing a personal blow to him: his career as a consultant was over.

Several other articles by Wolfenden also point to his covert activities. In December 1962, TASS had reported that Penkovsky had been arrested and that an American Embassy official, Richard Jacob, had been apprehended after being caught red-handed retrieving intelligence material. Several British newspapers mentioned this, but Wolfenden noted in his article that the building TASS claimed was used as Penkovsky's dead drop, 5/6 Pushkinskaya Street, had 'already become famous as the place where Mr Jacob is alleged to have collected secrets'. This suggests Wolfenden knew the details of Jacob's detention before TASS reported it, an unusual level of knowledge even for a well-connected correspondent. And if he was able to pick up such hints about espionage activity in 1962, it's possible he could have done so a year earlier.

Two years later, when the *Sunday Telegraph* serialised Greville Wynne's account of his involvement in the operation, Wolfenden wrote an article claiming that the Soviets were considering releasing 'their own version of what Mr. Wynne said under interrogation'. The implication was that Wynne had something to hide, and that if too much propaganda hay was made of his account the KGB would reveal some embarrassing secrets. They never followed up on this threat, but Wolfenden's article left the impression that crucial information was being omitted, and that the Russians had a hold on British intelligence.

Jeremy Wolfenden never became editor of *The Times*. He died in 1965, having drunk himself to death. He was just thirty-one. Faulks speculates he drank to relieve the pressure he was under to please both MI6 and the KGB – but perhaps it was also to blot out the guilt at having betrayed his colleagues and his closest friends. Faulks suggests the *Telegraph* knew that their brilliant young correspondent was homosexual, but posted him to Moscow despite the risk of him being caught in a honey trap. And once he had been compromised, MI6 decided that he could still be of use: 'they gambled that any information he gave to the Soviets could only be of trifling use because he had no access to military or other secrets – unless they gave him some for the purpose of disinformation'.

Former Reuters correspondent John Miller finds it hard to believe that his old Moscow friend might have acted as a spy for the British in this way. 'Nobody in MI6 would have trusted him to that degree,' he says. 'He was too much of a piss artist – and he was homosexual. I just don't think it would have happened.'

Janie Chisholm also doubts such involvement, and finds the idea that Wolfenden was a double agent equally implausible. 'The truth could have been less sensational – that he was a highly intelligent, restless and troubled character, intellectually and sexually complex, who flirted with all kinds of things and lived on the edge.'

However, Faulks's book makes it very clear that Wolfenden was a KGB asset. The question is not whether he worked for the Soviets, but precisely what he told them. He would have been under pressure to provide any information he could about British intelligence activities in Moscow, especially as it can't have escaped the KGB's notice that he had informal MI6 links. He could easily have revealed that both the Chisholms were working for MI6, thinking that this was something the Russians would already have known.

Someone else who was highly intelligent, restless, troubled and extrovertly gay at a time when that was illegal was Guy Burgess. If he hadn't defected, thus revealing he was a Soviet agent, an assessment of Burgess today could run along the same lines as Janie Chisholm's of Wolfenden: indeed, one reason he remained undetected for so long was precisely because the idea that the Russians would make use of such an indiscreet 'piss-artist' seemed absurd. Spies often deceive even those closest to them, and do not suddenly become less charming because they happen to be engaged in espionage.

Sebastian Faulks's claims about Jeremy Wolfenden didn't garner much attention in the espionage world, perhaps because he suggested he was a small-time asset who could only have handed over 'trifling' snippets of intelligence to the Russians. Faulks didn't discuss the possibility that Wolfenden may have betrayed Penkovsky, but the young *Telegraph* correspondent was almost absurdly qualified to have done so. It is an extraordinary coincidence that a British KGB asset was not only in Moscow at the time of the operation, but was a close friend of the head of MI6 there and his wife, who was Penkovsky's key contact in the city, and a frequent visitor to their home. Wolfenden later married their nanny, Martina Browne, and in a letter to her in August 1963 claimed he had sat through the trial and asked if the press had picked up 'all the bits about us', such as Ruari Chisholm saying to Wynne when he had handed material to him: 'You mustn't talk because we have an English girl sleeping in the next room, and we don't want the press to hear all about it.' But the press *had* picked up on that – the *Express* reported it, which is evidently where Wolfenden learned of it, as he hadn't in fact attended the trial. But he put a much stronger emphasis on it than the *Express* had, and together with the lie about his having watched the trial it suggests a ploy: by falsely suggesting that Ruari had implicated her as a potential leak Wolfenden may have hoped to stir the pot, making Browne resentful enough of her previous employers to tell him about genuine incidents she had seen in the Chisholms' home. He would also have read this brief article about her in the *Express* with a particularly sensitive eye, and may have been probing to find out if she was also a KGB asset.

There are other candidates who might have betrayed Penkovsky, directly or indirectly, but none of them were anywhere near as close to the operation. Having studied all the available files, memoirs and articles, and interviewed several people who were involved in the operation or aspects of it, my conclusion is that the answer to this final mystery has been hiding in plain sight, and that Jeremy Wolfenden gave the KGB information that led to the discovery of Oleg Penkovksy. There are countless ways in which he could have done this, but in the next few pages I present an imagined scenario of one way it could have happened . . .

★

'It's so good to see you again, Greville.'

Wynne smiled. 'And you, Alex.'

They were in a restaurant in Gorky Street – Wynne had just passed Penkovsky the instructions from Chisholm under the table, and both were feeling a little more relaxed.

'How's Zeph?' said Penkovsky, grinning.

Wynne laughed. 'Oh, Alex!' he said. 'Fine, I'm sure.'

A waitress arrived to take their orders. Penkovsky chose for them both, teasing Wynne that Russian food was much better than the slop he had forced him to eat in England.

Across the street, in a small cabin on the roof of a block of flats, a spool of audio tape was slowly turning.

★

1 MARCH 1956.
TOP SECRET

REPORT ON ENGLISH STUDENTS

I ACCOMPANIED THE ENGLISH STUDENTS AS REQUESTED: THE ITINERARY IS ATTACHED. IN MY ASSESSMENT, ONE OF THEM IS SUITABLE FOR RECRUITMENT: JEREMY WOLFENDEN. HE IS EXCEPTIONALLY CLEVER, SOCIABLE, AND WELL PLACED IN ENGLISH

SOCIETY. HIS FATHER, SIR JOHN, IS A WELL-KNOWN ACADEMIC
AND HEADS AN IMPORTANT GOVERNMENT COMMITTEE INVESTI-
GATING THE LEGALISATION OF HOMOSEXUALITY. THE SON'S
SPOKEN RUSSIAN IS GOOD – HE IS A GRADUATE OF THE BRITISH
NAVAL INTELLIGENCE COURSE – AND HE IS ALREADY WORKING
AS A CORRESPONDENT FOR THE LONDON TIMES DURING HOLI-
DAYS FROM OXFORD UNIVERSITY. HE HOPES TO BECOME A
CORRESPONDENT IN MOSCOW. HE IS NOT A BELIEVER IN OUR
CAUSE – HOWEVER, HE IS HOMOSEXUAL, WHICH IS ESPECIALLY
SIGNIFICANT CONSIDERING HIS FATHER'S POSITION (IT COULD
SERIOUSLY DAMAGE HIS CAREER IF PUBLICISED). WITH YOUR
PERMISSION, I WILL USE ORLOV AND THE PHOTOGRAPHER.
  KRUTIKOV

Gribanov smiled as he read the report. Yuri Krotkov, alias Krutikov, alias agent SULIKO, was himself homosexual, a playwright he had recruited expressly for the task of compromising foreign visitors. Gribanov found Krotkov's sexuality repellent, but he had discovered that homosexuals often made exceptional spies, and Krotkov had exceeded expectations. He had a flair that made him stand out among his drab colleagues. It made him a risky prospect, but it was also his chief talent. He spoke English, German, a smattering of French, and was amusing, perceptive and sophisticated. He was extraordinarily adept at gaining the trust of Westerners: they seemed incapable of understanding that someone with a deep appreciation of the arts and who criticised aspects of Soviet life could also be a dedicated KGB operative. Westerners were so complacent, Gribanov thought: they were not attuned to the arts of deception, and almost always dismissed anything but its crudest forms as implausible. 'Absurd! Nobody would go to such trouble!' – he had seen it a hundred times.

Once Yuri had spotted a potential recruit, he would assess the best way to entrap them. If they were not ideologically committed, as in this case, sex usually provided the easiest and most reliable means. He had been involved with the snaring of the French and Canadian ambassadors, the *latter in a homosexual trap. The directorate had a pool of actors and actresses for these operations, and their methods had been honed to a fine art: Krotkov would simply indicate which of the scenarios was the most suitable: the girl in the park, the angry husband, the boy hiding in the wardrobe. After the photographs had been developed, he would arrange a meeting with the victim to smooth the way to cooperation.*

Gribanov took out his fountain pen and scribbled his approval to trap the English student. Perhaps it would be worthwhile, perhaps not, but Gribanov seized such opportunities as a matter of routine. Counter-intelligence was an enormous chessboard, and he wanted as many pieces on his side as he could find, even if they were only pawns. Sometimes pawns could be used to draw out powerful opposing pieces, and were well worth the sacrifice. And sometimes pawns became powerful themselves: if you had enough of them, the law of averages meant that a few would manage to plod, one step at a time, until they reached the other side of the board and became queens, after which they could roam wherever he wished.

*

Jeremy Wolfenden looked down at the photographs, his face ashen. The young barber he had met in the toilet behind the Metropole, his jacket hanging on the chair in his room, their pale bodies twisted on the bed . . .

'Don't worry,' said Yuri gently. 'We don't want to use you yet. In ten years, perhaps, we'll be back in touch. Just continue with your career. You want to be a journalist, don't you?'

Wolfenden nodded numbly. He felt like a humiliated child, and hated himself for it. But a part of him was – what? Yes, excited. So this was a Russian honey trap, and it had been sprung on him. Wolfenden was a prodigy, but he was also the boy most likely to be rusticated, to disgrace his family, to wind up involved in some awful scandal. But the secret scandal, the scandal that was only his . . . there was something to savour there. A holdover from his adolescence was his fondness for thriller novels, and he especially enjoyed Ian Fleming's books, with their atmosphere of world-weary hedonism. But here he was in the real world of espionage, with a real Soviet agent. Despite the humiliation, there was something undeniably thrilling about it: to be recruited by SMERSH, or its real-life counterpart at any rate. Something had happened to him, at least, something dangerous. Finally, his life contained real drama.

Krotkov watched the young man in silence. Although he was simply another mark, another gullible foreigner, he felt for him. He vividly remembered how he had himself been compromised a decade earlier, after which he had been taken to the flat in Chapligin Street and asked if he would be interested in helping out the organs of the state from time to time. Now his livelihood, and indeed his life, depended on his ability to trap others. He had done so many times, and no doubt would do so many more, and this arrogant and naïve young man had only himself to blame. He had all the advantages of the West – wealth, freedom, a life without cares – but despite all he knew of Russia he had thrown it away on a cheap encounter. And yet Krotkov felt sorry for him. There had been a spark in him, a spark of brilliance, and he had deliberately extinguished it and dragged him into his own world of coercion and fear. What was he doing this for? Why was he here? Was this truly life?

Krotkov blinked. Idiotic questions all, the instinctive cries of an overly sensitive soul in the face of cold reality. He was here because he had been born Russian, and he was doing this because the alternative was a camp. He had no choice in the matter, and neither would Wolfenden. Yes, this was life – and no amount of sympathy or reverie could change it.

★

November 1961, Moscow.

General Oleg Gribanov placed the report on his desk and sat back in his armchair. So. One of his pawns had taken a step closer to the other side of the board – he had returned to Moscow.

He wondered for a moment if he should call Yuri in, but then decided not to: this one was too risky, and he wanted it to go without a hitch. He would handle this himself. It would be fun, too, he thought, to go back out in the field again: he had left it too long. Gribanov knew he wasn't as charming as Yuri: he was stout, balding, a middle-aged man in baggy trousers. But that could also be disarming. He now looked so much like a mid-ranking government official that no Westerner would have ever dreamed he was head of the KGB's Second Chief Directorate. Indeed, what did they think such a person would look like? They didn't really believe spies existed outside fiction.

It was time to push the pawn a few steps closer to the edge of the board.

★

It was mid-afternoon when the knock came on the door of Room 865 of the Ukraina Hotel. Jeremy Wolfenden scrambled out of bed and opened the door to two unsmiling faces.

'Come with us, sir.'

It wasn't a request. Wolfenden followed them down the corridor, past the old crone whose job it was to inform on everyone's movements on the floor. The men indicated that he step into the iron-cased lift. Wolfenden's mind was racing. Potatoes and onions, he thought, as the men took up position either side of him and he inhaled their stale body odour. Goulash. Stew. And he was in one.

The lift seemed to descend further than he thought possible, then jolted to a standstill. One of the men pushed the doors open, and he was bustled out. They walked down a corridor identical to the one they had just walked above, although now it seemed somehow narrower.

They reached an unmarked grey door, and one of the men rapped on it with his knuckles three times. It opened, and Wolfenden saw a small room with a large oak desk, its top inlaid with baize that was fraying at the corners. A balding man with rimless spectacles sat behind it, and in his hands he held a slim blue folder.

'Hello, Mr Wolfenden,' said the man, standing up and offering his hand. 'So nice to meet you. Please take a seat. I'm an old friend of Yuri Krutikov.'

Wolfenden sat down dumbly, his stomach cramping at the name that confirmed his fears. The incident in 1956 had followed him around for months like a second shadow, but eventually the lurking anxiety had faded and he had almost forgotten the debt. Even being posted to Moscow had not been enough to rouse him from his insouciance. What a fool. What a damn fool. As if the Russians wouldn't pounce for their pound of flesh. He'd stupidly believed Yuri's assurance of being left alone for a decade, as though he could mature like a fine wine – worse, he had finessed that assurance into a promise in his mind, and had never really believed that a decade would ever be over.

'Where's Yuri?' he said, despite himself. 'He said I wouldn't be contacted for ten years.'

Gribanov sat down again. 'It got cut short,' he said bluntly, then gave a small pretence at a smile. 'You've done even better than we hoped. The Moscow correspondent for the Daily Telegraph at twenty-six is quite an achievement. It also means you are close to the centre of the action here – presumably you are reporting to British intelligence?'

Wolfenden hesitated for a moment, then nodded. It was hardly worth denying, as all correspondents were instructed to inform Six of anything unusual they came across, and it was clear that the KGB would know this.

'So,' said Gribanov. 'What can you tell me?'

'Nothing.'

Gribanov stared at him, his eyes very still, and Wolfenden held his gaze with difficulty.

'Really,' he said. 'I'm not given any information.'

'I'm disappointed, Mr Wolfenden. I had such high hopes from what Yuri told me of your talents, but we have only just met and already you are lying. You're a friend of Ruari Chisholm. Do you *want me to show you photographs of you leaving his home? You must know he is the MI6 man here and yet you don't even tell me this?'*

Wolfenden blushed. 'Yes, well . . . I thought you knew that.'

'Don't presume I know anything. Tell me all you know. All you have discussed. Anything that may be useful.' As he spoke, Gribanov placed one hand gently on the blue folder.

Wolfenden started talking.

*

Half an hour later, Gribanov remembered why he had been so pleased to leave field work: it mostly consisted of chasing dead ends. He had questioned the young man thoroughly on his dealings with other foreigners, but it seemed there was little to learn: he'd been instructed before leaving London to report anything he came across of an intelligence nature to Chisholm. On arrival in the city he had met Chisholm once formally at the British Embassy, since when the two had become friendly, but other than a few pieces of insignificant chatter he hadn't given him anything. Wolfenden claimed to have no knowledge of how British intelligence operated in Moscow beyond that there was a secure room in the embassy, a fact of which Gribanov was already keenly aware. He decided to try a new tack.

'What about socially?' he said. 'Has anyone in the British circle ever said or done anything in your presence that you found unusual? Has Chisholm ever mentioned running an agent in Moscow, for example?'

Wolfenden laughed despite himself. 'He'd hardly be likely to tell me that!'

The Russian stared back impassively.

'You don't understand,' said Wolfenden. 'I sometimes have a drink with Ruari in the embassy bar, or visit him at home, and I've given him information when I've had it – but it never happens the other way around.'

'I understand. But you are a professional journalist: a trained observer. It's very difficult to keep one's personal life entirely separate *from the professional. Has he never revealed anything at all related to his work, however minor or unwitting?'*

'Never. I saw Janet standing close to a chap in the Praga once, but that's it, sorry.'

Gribanov lifted his chin slightly.

'Janet?'

Wolfenden blinked. 'Ruari's wife – she was his secretary originally.'

Gribanov nodded as though he had already known this and had simply been checking Wolfenden was aware of it himself.

'And who was the man?'

'I don't know. A Russian. It wasn't anything, really. It was just . . .'

'Just what?'

'Just . . . odd.'

Wolfenden took a breath and tried to think. Why had he blurted that out? It was true he had thought it a little furtive at the time, but surely it had just been his imagination playing tricks on him, a fantasy fed by too many novels. Gribanov was looking at him, waiting for him to explain.

'It may be nothing,' he said. 'I'd just had lunch and went to their delicatessen counter to buy some rolled ham when I spotted her standing very close to this chap. I can't put my finger on it, but they were a little too close, somehow. It was only for a moment, but they were looking at each other, and then suddenly the man turned and left. She acted like nothing had happened, but I had the feeling that something had.'

'Something like what?' Gribanov pushed.

'You tell me! I don't know how you spooks operate. I just presumed the man was passing a message to Ruari through her or something. Isn't that how it's done?'

Gribanov picked up the glass of water from the desk in front of him, and considered the Englishman's reply as he drank from it. On the face of it, the idea was absurd: there were a thousand other possible interpretations. But it was possible. Mikhailov had managed to identify the American commercial attaché in Nairobi as a CIA officer simply because his wife had spotted him outside a church talking a little too intently to a local. And then there were the messages. A couple of months ago, the radio experts in the Eighth Chief Directorate had intercepted repeated bursts of figures being read aloud from the Americans' base in Frankfurt. They hadn't been able to decipher the code, but Zagvozdin was convinced they were running an agent in the city using one-time pads and a portable receiver. Could this be related to that – or to another agent entirely? It would be clever of the British to use one of their officer's wives as a courier, as the surveillance on family members was much lighter. It was unlikely. But it was possible.

'The man – what did he look like?'

Wolfenden removed his spectacles and fidgeted with the arms.

'Middle-aged, I think. Let me see . . . He was wearing a coat.'

'He was wearing a coat,' *Gribanov repeated heavily.* 'How very helpful of you, Mr Wolfenden. After all, there can't be too many middle-aged Russians wearing coats in Moscow at this time of year.'

'I'm sorry, but this happened weeks ago, and it was over in a couple of seconds. He was there, and then he was gone.'

'Did you mention the man to Janet, or did she mention him to you?'

'No. I just said "Hullo!", and she looked up and said "Hullo!" back, and we had a chat about her ballet lessons, I think . . . yes, that was it. And then she hurried off and I queued up for my rolled ham.'

'What time of day was this?'

'Let me think. About one o'clock – I'd just had lunch.'

'Perhaps you had a little too much to drink at lunch and imagined you saw something that wasn't there? Perhaps he was simply a stranger who had picked up a glove she had dropped.'

Wolfenden gave a wan smile – he could hold his drink all too well, and he had a feeling the man in the rimless spectacles knew it. He wondered if he also knew about his brief dalliance with one of the Praga's waiters.

'*I wasn't drunk, but yes, I could be mistaken. I thought I'd mention it anyway. You said even the tiniest thing—*'

'*Yes. Thank you very much.*' Gribanov took another sip of water and thought for a moment. '*I would like you to find out more about this man. Talk to Ruari Chisholm discreetly, and ask him if he is using his wife at all.*'

Wolfenden shook his head. '*I can't do that. He's got no reason to tell me anything about his work. He'd smell a rat at once.*'

Gribanov decided this was probably true. He didn't reveal information about his work to friends, either. He didn't even discuss operational details with colleagues unless it was absolutely necessary that they know them: outside Semichastny, nobody else in the agency knew he was running Wolfenden. And he was right: Chisholm had no reason to tell him anything . . . But what if he gave him a reason?

'*You are of no use to me if you can't obtain intelligence,*' he said, '*and as it stands this is of little more use than a laundry woman's gossip. So here is what I propose. If it doesn't work, you can consider our relationship over – but it will also mean your career is over, and your father's, too, so I think you would be advised to make sure it succeeds.*'

*

'*They've trapped me,*' said Wolfenden, wishing he had downed another glass of vodka before his arrival – his stomach was clenching and he could feel a trickle of sweat running down the back of his neck.

The men peered at him, and he wondered if they had heard what he had said in the acoustics of the peculiar room.

'*Who's trapped you?*' said Chisholm, his tone sharp. Not the old Ruari now, not his friend from the embassy bar.

'*The Russians, of course! They burst into my hotel room the other night. I was with someone, a barber . . . I'd met him earlier in the hotel. They showed me photographs and said I had to cooperate with them or they would tell the world, ship me out, ruin my career. I didn't know what else to do. I am so, so sorry.*'

That much was true. If necessary, the KGB would send the photographs to the British, and nobody would be able to tell that they had been taken five years earlier. But even without the photographs, simply admitting this could lead to his being sacked and perhaps even prosecuted: if that happened his career would be in tatters, and so would his father's. But it was also possible that the British would decide not to prosecute him, and then he would be in even greater hock to the harmless-looking man in the rimless glasses who sometimes worked out of an office in the basement of the Ukraina Hotel. And he didn't know which fate he feared more.

'This is very serious, Jeremy. Very serious indeed.'

They conferred among themselves, and Wolfenden found his mind wandering again: he thought back to his schooldays, when he had memorised great chunks of encyclopedias, and repeated them to himself internally to shut out the world. Quotations, proverbs, collective nouns . . . What was the collective noun for spies? A gaggle, a flock? A conspiracy, of course. A conspiracy of spies.

Finally they turned to him again.

'Did they give any indication of how you were to cooperate?' said one of the men, a first secretary, wearing a vile knitted yellow-and-maroon tie. Assistant spook attaché.

'Yes,' he replied. 'They asked me to find out if you have any agents.'

'What sort of agents?'

'I don't know, they didn't say, they just—'

'Did they specify where these agents were based?'

Wolfenden shook his head. 'They just said I should try to find out the identities of any agents you had.'

There was silence, but Wolfenden could feel the electricity between the men standing before him.

'Did they mention anyone by name in connection with this?' asked the man with the tie.

Wolfenden shook his head. 'No.'

Silence again, and now the electricity almost felt like a physical presence. They told him to wait in an ante-room on a hard plastic chair, where he bit his nails and recited Byron poems in his head to make the time pass more quickly and keep his thoughts from turning elsewhere. Finally they summoned him back into the Tank.

'Here's what we've been thinking,' said Vile Tie Man. 'We want you to do as they say.'

Wolfenden looked up, now unsure if the acoustics were playing tricks on him.

'That's right. We want you to cooperate with the Russkies — within certain very carefully circumscribed limits. And if you fuck it up in any way, we'll cut your balls off and feed them to the lions. Understood?'

Wolfenden nodded. 'Understood. Thank you.' Was it better, or was it worse? He didn't know. Who did he fear more?

'This is the situation,' the man went on. 'We do have an agent working for us at the moment. One of theirs. That's all we're telling you, now or ever. But we're worried that they may be on to him. We want you to find out.'

★

'Is he in the KGB?'

'I don't know,' said Wolfenden. 'I told you: "One of theirs." That was all.'

'And they said "him", yes — it's definitely a man?' A man was expected, of course, but he wanted to be clear, especially as a woman would have been easier to trace.

'Yes, "him". Listen, do you have anything to drink?'

Wolfenden felt like a corpse being played with by vultures. Collective noun? A parliament of owls, a murder of crows . . . a committee of vultures? He couldn't remember, but it sounded right. He was being picked at by a committee of bespectacled, badly dressed vultures. He'd told the Russians as much as he dared about the British, and the British as much as he dared about the Russians. But both still wanted more and he was caught between the two, living in continual fear that the whole house of cards would collapse on his head. He was no longer

*a double agent, or a triple agent – he had no idea who was winning
with his information, and detested both masters equally. Almost as
much as he detested himself.*

*

*Gribanov had spent a couple of days wrestling with the problem, and
had finally settled on Nikolaev. He was an officer in the Seventh
Directorate, which was responsible for surveillance: his blandly handsome features made him ideal for street work but he was a doer, not a
questioner, and that was what he was after. Gribanov called Nikolaev
in and assigned him and three of his men to follow the Chisholm
woman for a fortnight: a routine check, he had said. At the same time
he had put a few men on Ruari Chisholm and a couple of the American
diplomats they knew had CIA connections, but that had been more to
cover tracks. He had a hunch that Wolfenden was right, and that
Chisholm's wife was somehow involved in running an agent. And if
that were the case, he wanted to make sure he alone knew she had been
deliberately placed under surveillance. Even Nikolaev would go to his
death thinking it had been a matter of routine, and that was just the
sort of cover story he liked. Nothing would lead back to his source.*

*Gribanov smiled as he thought of the young man, the pawn unex-
pectedly emerging from the pack. He was a neurotic, of course, as all
homosexuals were – but one day he might be the editor of a great
English newspaper. Gribanov hoped it would be* The Times. *He had
always wanted an agent on* The Times.

*

It was snowing outside the dacha *by the time Gribanov arrived.
Semichastny was waiting for him in his armchair by the fireplace, the
bottle of vodka already open.*

'We have a lead,' Gribanov said.

'From your English asset, the reporter?'

*Gribanov nodded. 'There's a colonel in the GRU, Penkovsky. He
works for the science committee under Levin. It looks like he is giving*

*the British and Americans intelligence – precisely what, I don't yet
know. We searched his flat and found a couple of scraps of paper with
the telephone numbers of a few diplomats, but nothing conclusive to
prove espionage.'*

'Why did he have their numbers written down?'

*'Some sort of signal, it looks like, based on the number of rings, but
we don't know what they mean yet. We called a couple of them to see
if anyone would come out to check a drop, but as far as we know
nobody did.'*

'As far as you know?'

*Gribanov gave a sorrowful nod. 'The surveillance coverage wasn't
ideal. You know the problems with getting too close in such situations.
We can try again.'*

*'No.' Semichastny spoke softly but firmly. 'You've done enough.
Leave it alone.'*

*Gribanov tried not to look surprised, and failed. 'But what if he is
giving them—'*

*'I said bury it. Watch from a distance, by all means, but leave this
Penkovsky to continue with whatever he is doing until I say otherwise.' He lifted his glass and took a swig, swilling the fiery liquid
around his mouth before swallowing. 'I will see you tomorrow, Oleg.'*

*Gribanov nodded, and trudged back out to the Chaika. His chauf-
feur had only just lit a cigarette, and quickly stamped it out and
opened the door.*

*Semichastny sat by the fire, wondering if he had acted too impul-
sively. He decided he had played it just right. He didn't want to get
involved in the GRU's mess. He would drag his heels on it and wait
to see what happened. If this Penkovsky were giving the British tittle-
tattle there would be no real harm or consequences. If he were handing
over major secrets, well, that was Serov's lookout, and Serov would pay
for it. But he wasn't giving up their asset to protect that little bastard's
neck. He'd lost Burgess, Maclean and Blake, and right now he wanted
to know what the British were thinking. The reporter had the trust of
MI6, and in particular MI6 in Moscow. If a situation like Berlin flared*

again, he might be able to find out what the Brits were planning, and through them the Americans. When the chips were really down, you always told your friends what you would do. The young Englishman might end up being the Soviet Union's early warning system.

★

'This Wynne is a slippery customer — he plays the role of innocent businessman very well.'

'You think he was more than a courier?'

'Perhaps. He certainly spent a lot of time here, most of it with Penkovsky. Remind me — when did we first place him under surveillance?'

'Last May.'

'I want the tapes on my desk. All of them, from the very beginning. Before I leave today.'

★

Gribanov listened through the headphones, his eyes closed in concentration. The voices were irritatingly muffled, and he made a mental note to ask the technical department if they could upgrade the miniature microphones placed in ashtrays in restaurants. But he could hear them, just about. They were speaking English:

"'It's good to see you again, Greville.'" That was Penkovsky.

"'And you, Alex.'" And that was Wynne.

"'How's Zeph?'"

Gribanov looked up, startled.

Who?

He rewound the spool, and pressed his finger down on the button again.

★

Gribanov placed the dossier to one side and smiled. It was all over — and it had run like clockwork. The traitor had been found, arrested, tried and executed. The British and Americans had been humiliated. And his source had been protected. Wolfenden could now be used as a conduit to place information in the British press. As for retrieving more intelligence, well, you never knew. He had led them to Penkovsky by a combination of coincidence and being in the right place at the right time: if he hadn't been in Moscow, and hadn't known the Chisholms, the moment he had seen her next to Penkovsky at the Praga would have been meaningless. Such a coup was very unlikely to happen again, he knew, but life was unpredictable and it helped to be prepared. Especially as the British believed Wolfenden was working for them: if the pressure on him were exerted carefully, his usefulness could increase significantly in the years to come. It was the same game they'd played with Burgess, Maclean and Blake. They were out of play now, but a new pawn was working his way across the board . . .

EPILOGUE

Many of those involved in the Penkovsky operation never shook themselves free of it. In 1966, the CIA paid Greville Wynne a $213,700 'resettlement' package, but he nevertheless continued to have financial difficulties. He sued the *Daily Mirror* for their 1962 article, which had suggested he had staged his arrest as a practical joke, and was awarded 'substantial' damages. He also published two ghost-written memoirs in which he claimed, in contradiction to his testimony at the trial, that he had worked for British intelligence for years before the operation.

He moved to Malta, and in 1969 approached British screen-writer Jack Whittingham to write a film about his experiences. Whittingham flew out to meet him several times, but although the script was finished it was never filmed. His experiences did eventually become the basis for a BBC TV series, *Wynne and Penkovsky*, broadcast in 1985.

Wynne finally settled in Majorca, where he had a business exporting roses, and he occasionally appeared in the British press to comment on other spy cases, sometimes revisiting his own. In 1990, he died of throat cancer in London, a few weeks short of his seventy-first birthday.

After leaving Moscow, the Chisholms moved to the Sussex countryside. Close by was a mansion that had belonged to an aristocrat who had died in the 1920s, and which had not been cared for much since. They discovered shortly after moving in that the house was used by Soviet diplomats for weekend retreats. The Chisholm children were delighted. 'We thought it was very exciting that it was the Russians' place,' says Janie, 'and we used to run around, and every now and again we would see a face at the window.'

The Chisholm children presumed that their father was simply a diplomat and their mother a housewife: Janie, who as a seven-year-old had been given sweets by Penkovsky in the park off Tsvetnoy Boulevard, had no memory of those occasions, and assumed that her parents' involvement with Penkovsky had been a fabrication by the Soviet authorities. In 1963, Ruari and Janet had told the *Daily Express* that they had never spied on anyone, and they stuck to that story: once the newspapers had left their front door, Ruari didn't speak about the affair. 'My father was one of these people who came back from the office at six o'clock in the evening and would switch off and be a country type, chopping logs,' says Janie. 'He didn't bring his work home with him. After the Penkovsky case, he was obviously blown for any posting, and so his attitude to MI6 was a little bit, "Oh well, it's the day job." The only posting he got after that was South Africa, presumably because the South Africans didn't mind having someone who had blotted his copybook in the Soviet Union.'

When she was eighteen, Janie wandered into her parents' bedroom and rummaged through one of her father's drawers looking for a pair of socks to wear. She found some socks, but also a passport with his photograph in it, and someone else's name. 'I was completely terrified,' she says, 'and thought, "My God, my father's an international criminal or something – what is going on?"' After telling her mother of her discovery, she was summoned by her father to his garden shed, where he explained that he worked for MI6 – which in those days officially didn't even exist. He never spoke about it again, but she remembers being most surprised by the fact that diplomats didn't use their roles to engage in a little espionage on the side, but that MI6 was an entirely separate organisation and that, in effect, her father's entire career had been a cover for something else: 'Suddenly to think he *wasn't* a diplomat, and he was never going to become an ambassador because he didn't have that career path, that was a surprise.'

In later life, Ruari Chisholm pursued an interest in military history. He wrote a book on the Boer War, and started work on a second about General von Lettow-Vorbeck. Stopping off in Tanzania to carry out some research for it, he caught cerebral malaria and died in Scotland in 1979, aged just fifty-four. His memorial mass was held at Westminster Cathedral.

Janet Chisholm died in 2004, aged seventy-five, a talented garden designer and a keen hiker and traveller. Shortly after the disintegration of the Soviet Union, she and her three sisters had tried to visit Russia, but her visa was turned down by the authorities at the last moment: perhaps even then, the name Chisholm was stored in a black book somewhere. 'She was always very quiet about the Penkovsky case,' says Janie, 'even after the fall of the USSR when she no longer had to deny it. When friends tried to encourage her to speak proudly of her achievement, she used to say that it was all very sad because in the end a man had died. And that wasn't false modesty.'

Janie describes her mother as 'a classic colonel's daughter' who had a strong sense of loyalty to her country. 'I think doing what she did was the last thing that would have come naturally to her – had it not been for the fact that she felt she had a duty to do it. She smoked in those days, and smoked even more as a result of the pressures of the case. And although I'm not sure exactly how the dates coincide, she had a miscarriage in Moscow (and a particularly gruelling time in a Soviet hospital) and I think it was very much taken for granted that it was as a result of the stress.'

Like his predecessor in Moscow, Gervase Cowell also became involved in military history. After being expelled from Moscow, and despite being mentioned by name in the trial, he went on to serve with MI6 in Bonn, Paris and Tel Aviv. He was later awarded the CMG Moscow for his part in the Penkovsky operation. He was an accomplished painter and sculptor, and exhibitions of his work were held in several cities he was posted to while he was in MI6.

He retired from MI6 in 1981, and translated the work of several Russian authors, including Vladimir Tendryakov and Ivan Valeriy. In 1988, he was appointed the Foreign Office's adviser on the wartime work of the Special Operations Executive, despite not having served with that agency; he was widely admired as a tireless defender of its memory. He later became chairman of the Special Forces Club Historical Sub-Committee, a role he elegantly explained to the Queen on receiving his MBE shortly before his death: 'I help the old to remember and the young to understand.' He died in 2000. His name lives on in the acknowledgements pages of dozens of books on SOE, but his own role in the secret world, in running Oleg Penkovsky, and not passing that phone call on, is less appreciated. After his death, one of his friends was quoted as saying that Gerry Cowell would probably have been as happy to have been remembered for being 'the only MI6 officer who had a set of verses in Japanese haiku format published in *The Jerusalem Post*'.

George Kisevalter, despite the trouble in Paris, was fêted by the CIA, who in April 1999 opened the Kisevalter Center for Advanced Studies. It is the only CIA facility named after an individual apart from the headquarters building, which was renamed the George Bush Center for Intelligence on the same day. He was also honoured as one of the agency's 'Trailblazers'.

After leaving the CIA, Kisevalter became a real-estate agent near CIA headquarters in McLean, where many former officers live and work. He died in 1996, after dictating most of his life story to another former CIA officer, and real-estate colleague, Clarence Ashley. It was published as *CIA SpyMaster* in 2004.

Joe Bulik retired in 1976 and became a rancher in Colorado. At a dinner in Washington, he was given a medal, which he had to return at the end of the meal because it would have linked him with the agency. After a near-death experience in 1986, he wrote a memoir about his life, but the CIA censored it. They later allowed him to discuss the operation on the record, but he never forgave the 'high-ups' in the CIA who had left Penkovsky to his fate without intervening. He died in 1999, aged eighty-three.

Paul Garbler, the CIA's first Station Chief in Moscow, fell victim to James Angleton's paranoia. In 1963, Angleton set up an operation with the FBI, MI6 and MI5 codenamed HONETOL to find Soviet moles within Western intelligence agencies. Anatoli Golitsyn's claims that there was a KGB mole in the CIA codenamed SASHA led to Garbler falling under suspicion, and his career stalled as a result. He was eventually cleared, and given a six-figure sum in compensation for the false allegations. He settled in Arizona, where he wrote self-published spy novels, one of which speculated that Golitsyn had himself been part of a KGB deception operation, designed to stir up Angleton and others in the CIA into a rabid mole-hunt. Garbler died in 2006, aged eighty-eight.

Harold Shergold died in 2000. He trained guide dogs as a hobby and lived a quiet life with his wife in Richmond. Shortly before his death, he maintained that despite the story ending in capture and execution, there had been little choice but to run the operation at the speed Penkovsky had wanted – anything else wouldn't have worked.

One result of the Penkovsky operation was a revision of some of the tradecraft used on the streets of Moscow and a concerted attempt to better the technology and techniques. However, the basics of how the operation was run have not changed, and the need for human intelligence has not disappeared with improvements in technology. Case officers continue to run agents and gather intelligence using dead drops and face-to-face conversations, even if the dead drops are now often electronic and the conversations take place via encrypted video conferencing. The analysis of intelligence from these sources also still requires the astute assessment of human psychology. All intelligence is human in the end, dictated by the same motivations as have always existed: better and more reliable technology doesn't make someone a better or more reliable source.

Espionage doesn't have as high a profile as it did during the Cold War, but it continues all the same, and always will. Espionage is in itself a cold war: it is waged in secret against one's enemies and has far fewer fatalities than a hot war, but it's a war nevertheless.

Neither have the risks faded since the end of the Cold War. The threat of nuclear extinction has never been more vivid than it was in 1961 and 1962, and it would have been constantly on the minds of all those involved in this operation. But the odds of nuclear war have, if anything, increased as a result of the disintegration of the Soviet Union and the emergence of volatile rogue states, even if the possibility is no longer as prevalent in our minds. Sources like Oleg Penkovsky are currently desperately needed in Iran, North Korea and elsewhere.

AUTHOR'S NOTE

British, American and Soviet intelligence agencies were all involved in the Penkovsky operation, and have all taken different approaches to releasing material about it. The Americans have been the most open by far: in 1992, the CIA declassified over 2400 pages about the operation, albeit with many pages still containing redactions. It declassified further documents related to the operation in 2001, 2004, 2006 and 2007, and information relating to it appeared in several documents declassified in 2011.

Those files have been my primary source for this book, but I have also drawn on documents from the National Security Agency, Britain's National Archives and NATO, as well as memoirs written (or ghost-written) by former intelligence officers. Since 1992, a wealth of new information about the operation has emerged, some of it incidental, some shedding substantial new light.

Joe Bulik, Sidney Graybeal and several others discussed both the operation and its wider implications in the joint CNN–BBC documentary series *Cold War* in 1998. For permission to quote from the full transcript of the interview with Alexander Zagvozdin, I'm indebted to the Trustees of the Liddell Hart Centre for Military Archives. Shortly before his death, George Kisevalter, perhaps the most important member of the team that ran Penkovsky, finally gave his account of the operation to Clarence Ashley, which was published in 2004 in *CIA SpyMaster*. Harry Shergold and Mike Stokes also gave some limited information for that book. Many former CIA officers have spoken on and off the record to journalists about the operation, or written about it themselves.

I am very grateful to Leonard McCoy, one of the last surviving CIA officers who worked directly on the operation, for his detailed responses to me about it, which fleshed out a great deal that I could not discover elsewhere and revealed new aspects of the operation. He didn't answer all my questions, but he answered a great many of them.

For MI6, it seems that, despite a wealth of material about its involvement in this operation being in the public domain (largely thanks to the CIA), half a century on it is still a state secret. MI6 has yet to release any of its files about this operation; indeed, with the exception of a few brief excerpts in Keith Jeffery's authorised history of the agency, published in 2010, MI6 has never released material about *any* of its operations, and only admitted to its own existence in 1980. Many former MI6 officers have gone on record about their work in the Second World War, and Jeffery's history concluded in 1949. But although the operation described in this book began just twelve years after that, the gap between the 'war period' and the Cold War could not be more striking in terms of declassification.

This is a long-standing British policy, but the fact it remains in place may partly be because there has yet to be a definitive ceasefire in the Cold War. The Berlin Wall fell and the Soviet Union collapsed, but while Russia is no longer an outright enemy, it is not quite a trusted ally either. The 2006 assassination of Alexander Litvinenko in London caused a wound in diplomatic relations between Britain and Russia that has not yet fully healed, but even without this, the nature of the intelligence apparatus in Russia has not fundamentally changed since the Soviet era. In 1991, the KGB was nominally split in two and renamed the Federal Security Service (FSB) and Foreign Intelligence Service (SVR), but in 2005 these two organisations celebrated their eighty-eighth birthday, proving that they are essentially the same as what has variously been called the Cheka, the NKVD, the MGB and the KGB. Vladimir Putin is a former KGB officer who headed the FSB before becoming president, and parts of the FSB still operate out of the Lubyanka.

My sources for British aspects of the operation – outside of the information given in CIA files, of which there is a surprising amount – were chiefly biographies, memoirs, newspaper archives and interviews. MI6 documents are cited and quoted in both *The Spy Who Saved the World* and John Hart's *The CIA's Russians*. John Miller, who covered the trial as a Reuters correspondent and who was a close friend of the Chisholms in Moscow, generously explored his memories with me over a long lunch and further discussion in his home. Janie Chisholm also very kindly rummaged through her family's vaults and shared many fascinating details of her parents' lives. I am also indebted to Felicity Stuart, who went on record about the operation for the first time, providing some crucial new information about it. MI6 vetted her responses, as the CIA did Leonard McCoy's, but I have interpreted all information as I have seen fit and have not shown either agency the manuscript of this book, sought approval from either or discussed its contents with them at all.

For the Russian intelligence services, this operation is more secret still. Very few documents about it have been released, and I received no response to my requests to declassify further files. Some material from the Russian side has come to light in 'unofficial sources' (itself something of a misnomer in Russia), in memoirs, biographies, articles, documentaries and even novels, but some of it has been highly speculative and contradictory.

As well as additional CIA releases of material about the operation, many documents relating to broader events that took place during the same period have also recently been declassified, some of which alter perceptions of the importance of the operation, and much of which adds to our knowledge of this period of history. For the chapters on the Berlin crisis, I have drawn on several documents declassified by NATO in June 2011 and by the CIA in October 2011. For events relating to Cuba, I have relied on a mass of documents released in recent years, including material declassified by the National Security Agency in June 2011 and by the CIA in August (on the Bay of Pigs), and November 2011 (on the 'missile gap'). I have also drawn on British government files dealing with preparations for a nuclear war, and Cabinet papers on the Berlin situation and Cuban crisis.

However, no source can ever tell the whole story or, when it comes to matters of espionage, be entirely 'clean'. Memoirs can be self-serving or even state-serving narratives: spies are professional deceivers, so gauging the information produced by them can be especially problematic. Declassified files can also mask the truth, through omission, error, deliberate deception or bias: a report might be slanted a particular way to impress a superior, to belittle a colleague or to hide fault. Documents do not generally relate the conversations being whispered in the corridors, and can be mired in unseen politicking. There have also been several sensationalistic accounts of this operation, and aspects related to it. In a few cases I have used sources that are problematic when I felt there could be little doubt that the information in question was true. An example of this is *The Penkovsky Papers*, which despite some rearranging and cleaning up of language consists primarily, as many of the CIA's own files show, of Penkovsky's own words – with some notable exceptions. However, some of the information in that book stems from CIA files that have not yet been declassified.

Similarly, CIA files are quoted in Jerrold Schecter and Peter Deriabin's *The Spy Who Saved the World*, including some information that was redacted from the same files when they were declassified by the CIA following that book's publication in 1992. Although I have a fundamentally different interpretation of some aspects of the operation from Schecter and Deriabin, I thank those authors both for their scholarship and for the fact that it was through their efforts that so many files were declassified by the CIA.

Many thanks also to Lena Konovalenko, Guy Walters, Steven Savile, Charles Buxton, Mike Kenner for sharing with me the fruits of British National Archives documents he has accessed via FOIA requests, David Foster, Gordon Corera, Rupert Allason, Katherine Stanton, Mike Jones, Kathryn Court, Antony Topping and my family for their help and support.

Jeremy Duns
February 2013

APPENDIX A

CIA translation of Penkovsky's instructions for his signals and dead drop, August 1960

PLAN (DIAGRAM) FOR MARKING SIGNALS

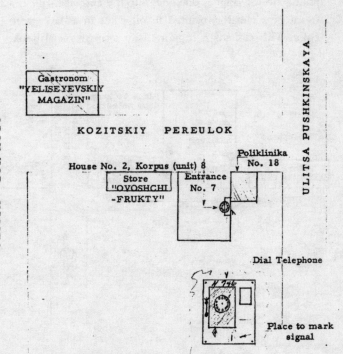

Description of Dead Drop Number 1

<u>Address and Location:</u>

Moscow, corner of Proezd Khudozhestvennogo Teatra and Pushkinskaya ulitsa. The dead drop is located in the main entrance (foyer) of Number 2, located on Pushkinskaya ulitsa – between the store Number 19 "Myaso" and the store "Zhenskaya obuv'."

The main entrance is open 24 hours a day. The entrance is not guarded, there is no elevator.

In the entrance (foyer) – to the left /upon entering therein/ a dial telephone, No. 28, is located. Opposite the dial telephone /to the right as one goes into the entrance hall/ is a steam heat radiator, painted in oil paint in a dark green color. This radiator is supported by a single metal hook,

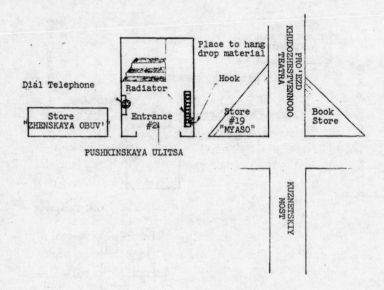

fastened into the wall. /If one stands facing the radiator, then the metal hook will be to the right, at the level of one's hand hanging from the arm./

Between the wall, to which the hook is attached, and the radiator there is a space of two-three centimeters.

For the dead drop, it is proposed to use the hook and the space /open space/ between the wall and the radiator.

Method of Using the Dead Drop:

It is necessary to place and camouflage any written material, for example, in a match box, then the box should be wrapped with soft wire /of a green color/, and the end of the wire bent hook-shaped, which will permit the small box to hang from the hook (or bracket) of the radiator between the wall and the radiator.

The location of the dead drop is on the unlighted right-hand corner of the entrance hall. In the entrance hall it is convenient to make a call on the dial telephone and it is very simple and easy to hang some type of small object on the indicated hook.

The site for placing the signal indicating that material has been placed in the drop, is located at a five minutes' ride from the dead drop /or a fifteen minutes' walk/. Thus the time that the material is in the dead drop can be held to a minimum.

I will await the signal indicating placing of the material in the dead drop after 12.00 and after 21.00 each day, beginning with 15.8.60.

APPENDIX B

Checklist for British nuclear deputies in the event of war, 18 October 1961

<u>TOP SECRET</u>

<u>ANNEX II</u>

<u>MATTERS TO BE COVERED IN CONSULTATIONS RELATING TO NUCLEAR RETALIATION</u>

A. <u>Conversation with the President</u>

1. A general decision whether to launch strategic nuclear forces, British and American (Macmillan–Kennedy general understanding).
2. Operational use by United States forces of bases in the United Kingdom.
   (a) S.A.C. air bases (Atlee–Truman agreement for "joint decision").
   (b) Polaris submarine bases (Holy Loch) (Holy Loch agreement, 1969, for "joint consultation").
3. Use of Bomber Command Thors. (1958 agreement – Command 366).
4. Clearance for launching of:-

(a) United States tactical nuclear aircraft in United Kingdom assigned to SACEUR (Murphy–Dean agreement).

(b) United Kingdom tactical nuclear aircraft in United Kingdom assigned to SACEUR and carrying United States warheads. (Murphy–Dean agreement.)

5. Clearance for SACLANT to launch British nuclear striking forces in his command (arrangements not yet complete).

6. Declaration of R-hour by SACEUR and SACLANT. May they declare it at discretion? If not, when?

B. Conversation with SACEUR

1. Declaration of R-hour (see A.6 above).

2. Launching of his tactical aircraft based in United Kingdom (see A.4 above).

'The Essential Facts of The Penkovskiy Case', CIA memo, 1963

SECRET

May 31 1963

MEMORANDUM FOR: The Director of Central Intelligence
SUBJECT: Essential Facts of the Penkovskiy Case

1. In view of the recent publicity given the Penkovskiy case, much of which is garbled or misleading, we are presenting in the attached paper essential facts about Penkovskiy and his associates for the background information of those who have followed his reporting and those who are studying possible ramifications of the case in the sphere of Soviet politics.

[REDACTED PASSAGE]

Richard Helms
Deputy Director (Plans)

The Essential Facts of the Penkovskiy Case

1. The Penkovskiy case covered the period August 1960 through August 1962 and provided more than 8,000 pages of translated reporting, most of which constituted highly classified Soviet Ministry of Defense documents. Penkovskiy was strongly motivated to work against the present regime. On the basis of checks and counterchecks, together with our familiarity with the methods and purposes of Soviet deception operations, we have concluded that there is no evidence that this case represents planned deception, build-up for deception, fabrication, or double-agent activity. Rather it represents a most serious penetration of Soviet officialdom and one that will hurt them for years to come. We present below essential facts about Penkovskiy and his associates for the background information of those who have followed his reporting and those who are studying possible ramifications of the case in the sphere of Soviet politics.

2. Colonel Oleg Vladimirovich Penkovskiy served with distinction as a Soviet artillery officer throughout World War II. After the war he attended the Frunze Academy for two years, followed by four years at the Military-Diplomatic Academy. He then entered the Chief Intelligence Directorate (GRU) of the General Staff, serving as a headquarters desk officer and subsequently as assistant military attache in Turkey in 1955 and 1956. Because of differences with his superior in Ankara, he was reassigned to the Near Eastern and Far Eastern desks in Moscow. Subsequently he attended the 1958–1959 missile refresher course for artillery officers at the Dzerzhinskiy Artillery Academy, serving as class leader. In 1960 he was placed by the GRU in the State Scientific-Technical Committee (GNTK) to perform intelligence collection functions. By the time of his arrest in September 1962, he had risen

to the position of Deputy Chief of the Foreign Liaison Department of the External Relations Directorate of the GKKNR (the State Committee for Coordination of Scientific Research Work, successor organization to the GNTK).

3. By nature Col. Penkovskiy was highly intelligent, very imaginative, and supremely, perhaps even fatally, self-confident. He could never be satisfied with a merely adequate grasp of the skills required of him, or perfunctory performance of duties assigned him. He was devoted to his wife, a daughter of the late General D. A. Gaponovich, and two daughters (one still an infant). He also maintained a liaison with a younger woman in Moscow and indulged in broadminded enjoyment of the pleasures of London and Paris. A longstanding feeling that his talents were not recognized by the Soviet regime after he reached the rank of colonel (at age 31) had embittered him and doubtless contributed to his willingness to work against the Soviet regime.

4. Col. Penkovskiy came from a capable and respected family. The commander of the Belorussian Military District, General of the Army V. A. Penkovskiy, was his great uncle; the two officers seldom met however. The colonel's father cast a shadow over his son's career by having served with the White Army during the Revolution. This background may well have been one of the reasons that Col. Penkovskiy was not further promoted.

5. Col. Penkovskiy provided the West with intelligence from August 1960 to August 1962. During this period, three series of lengthy debriefing and briefing sessions were held with him outside the Soviet Union. Every Western intelligence requirement of any priority was covered with him during this time, and all aspects of his knowledgeability and access were explored.

Over 90 percent of the approximately 5,000 pages of Russian language documentary information provided by him concerned military subjects. Roughly half of this information came from the GRU Library, while the remainder was acquired by him unofficially either in the missile and artillery headquarters of Marshal Varentsov or at the Dzerzhinskiy Academy. Documentary information on other subjects, such as Party letters and economic matters, came from the GKKNR. Col. Penkovskiy responded in some manner to every intelligence requirement levied on him.

6. Many high-ranking Soviet personalities were included in Col. Penkovskiy's social and official contacts but, contrary to accounts in the press, there is no apparent basis for associating him with Marshal Zakharov or Party Secretary Kozlov. The following are the most important Soviet officials with whom he was closely associated:

a. General of the Army Serov. On one of Col. Penkovskiy's trips in 1961, Serov charged him to look after Mrs. Serov and a daughter, who happened to be departing Vnukovo on the same plane with the colonel. Col. Penkovskiy became quite friendly with Serov's daughter, while Western intelligence officers filled the Serov shopping list as part of the colonel's job; a small gift was added for Serov. When Col. Penkovskiy returned to Moscow, he was invited to the Serov home to receive the general's thanks, and spent some time talking with Serov.

b. Chief Marshal of Artillery Varentsov has been a close friend to Col. Penkovskiy since early in World War II, when they served together. Col. Penkovskiy was in the Varentsov home several times weekly, and had the run of Varentsov's office.

c. Col. Penkovskiy had a large number of friends among senior artillery officers, such as Col.-Gen. G. S. Kariofilli, Varentsov's Chief of Staff; Col. V. M. Buzinov, Varentsov's aide-de-camp; Major General I. V. Kupin, first in the GSFG and now Artillery Commander of the Moscow Military District; Col. I. A. Gryzlov, in the GSFG Artillery Directorate; Col, V. I. Fedorov, commander of a missile and free rocket brigade in the GSFG and formerly Varentsov's aide-de-camp; Major-General A. R. Pozovnyy, Chief of the PVO Strany Political Directorate; and other generals, colonels, and lesser officers with whom he had served or studied.

d. Col. Penkovskiy's friends and close associates in the GKKNR included D. M. Gvishiani, who was his immediate superior and is the son-in-law of First Deputy Premier Kosygin. Gvishiani moved up in the Committee during August 1962 and was replaced by V. V. Petrochenko.

e. Within the GRU, Col. Penkovskiy was closely associated with the branch chiefs responsible for several Near Eastern countries, and contacts in the Military-Diplomatic Academy, including librarian Dolgikh.

f. Among other, important individuals with whom Col. Penkovskiy briefly came into contact socially were Marshal Malinovskiy and Central Committee Candidate Member V. M. Churayev.

APPENDIX D

Article by Jeremy Wolfenden in the *Daily Telegraph*, 10 September 1964

RUSSIA DELAYS ARTICLES ON WYNNE

JEREMY WOLFENDEN
Daily Telegraph Staff Correspondent

MOSCOW, Wednesday.

Russian officials told me that they are holding off publication of their material on Mr. Greville Wynne until they see the rest of his memoirs, which are being serialized in The Sunday Telegraph.

"We don't want to use our big guns on sparrows," they said. So far, they added, Mr. Wynne's account of what had happened to him had been "objective", or satisfactorily so to them. Their chief objection had been to his strictures on Russian prison food.

For most of his imprisonment he had been given the same food as Russian officers of the K.G.B., the Committee for State Security, or secret police, in their head office at Lubianka in the centre of Moscow.

If he complained about that, they said, the Russian officers had an equal complaint.

Material prepared

But they are awaiting the succeeding articles. If these contain more serious complaints, they will publish their own version of what Mr. Wynne said under interrogation.

They are not prepared to disclose for public consumption what they have against Mr. Wynne. Material has already been delivered to Russian newspapers, including *Izvestia*, the official organ of the Soviet Government. Their editors are awaiting the "green light" to publish it.

This will be given if the Russians consider that Mr. Wynne's memoirs contain material that they must either deny or discredit. But, for the moment, they are holding their fire.

APPENDIX E

Article by Jeremy Wolfenden in the *Daily Telegraph*, 26 September 1964

WYNNE REPRISAL BY RUSSIA

11 British firms put on blacklist

PASSAGE IN ARTICLE "INCITEMENT TO SPY"

JEREMY WOLFENDEN
Daily Telegraph Staff Correspondent

MOSCOW, Friday.

Eleven British companies are to be blacklisted by the Russians because they are said to have had dealings with Mr. Greville Wynne, the London businessman who was gaoled on an espionage charge in Moscow in 1963 and released after 13 months.

The Russian Ministry of Foreign Trade has taken exception to some sentences in Mr. Wynne's article in The Sunday Telegraph of September 13. He is accused of inciting British businessmen to work for "English intelligence services".

I have been given the impression that, strange as it may seem, the initiative for this ban came from the Trade Ministry, not from any of the other departments involved.

Orders have apparently gone out to the Soviet commercial commission in London. The firms involved may expect to be told about the ban on Monday or Tuesday.

They are all companies which, the Russians say, have been represented at one time or another by Mr. Wynne.

HAND-WRITTEN LIST
Hastily compiled

According to a hastily-compiled list, hand-written in Russian, they are:

PLESSEY INTERNATIONAL LTD., a subsidiary of the Plessey Company Ltd., of Ilford, manufacturers of components for the radio, electrical, aircraft and mechanical engineering trades; EDGAR ALLEN AND CO., of Sheffield, manufacturers of plant machinery, tools, &c.

RICHARDSONS WESTGARTH AND CO., of Wallsend, Northumberland, marines, turbine, electrical and general engineers; FERRANTI LTD., of Hollinwood, Lancs, electrical and general engineers.

LEO COMPUTERS LTD., of Bayswater; WESTOOL LTD., electrical engineers; JONES AND SHIPMAN; MARSHALL RICHARDS MACHINE CO., a subsidiary of Marshall Sons and Co., engineers, of Gainsborough, Lincs.

TURNER MACHINERY; JOHN THOMPSON LTD., of Wolverhampton, a manufacturing group of companies with 18 subsidiaries in Britain and 11 overseas; UNICAM INSTRUMENTS LTD., a subsidiary of Pye Ltd., of Cambridge.

OFFENDING PASSAGE
Translation difficulties

Allowing for the difficulties of translation from English into Russian and back again this seems to have been the passage that caused the trouble:

'I happened to be the right person in the right place at the right time. And I believe that most British businessmen would have done the same.'

This is regarded by the Russians as open incitement to espionage. A Russian contact said: "The impression is created that this attitude of Mr. Wynne sounds like an appeal to co-operate with the Government's intelligence service."

DEALINGS SUSPENDED
Business "used"

"It is possibly inspired by the English intelligence service in order to use business relations for its special interests. In connection with this, we have suspended business dealings with the following firms." Then he showed me his hand-written list.

The Russians have been anxiously watching the whole series of articles in The Sunday Telegraph by Mr. Wynne. But until now they have been somewhat relieved by what they have found.

The day before the series started I was asked by a Soviet official what it would contain. After he had read the first article he told me: "We had expected big guns but this is just small arms fire."

UNPUBLISHED MATERIAL
Article factual

Russians said the article was factual, indeed almost "objective", but the official warned me then that they had a good deal of unpublished material, much of it from the interrogation that Wynne went through before his trial.

This material remains in the hands of Soviet newspapers for use "when the green light is given". Each instalment of Mr. Wynne's memoirs has been carefully studied.

His second, which has caused the present boycott, appears to have been tolerated without too much difficulty by the Soviet Foreign Ministry. However, the Ministry of Foreign Trade, with whom Mr. Wynne was chiefly dealing, has raised objections.

As the result of a discussion which may have even reached the Central Committee of the Communist party, the British firms which, it is claimed, dealt with or through Mr. Wynne have been blacklisted.

When the decision to do this was taken to-day, it was not even known whether all or any of these firms were doing business with Russia.

The intention is clearly not to punish individuals. It is to dissuade businessmen from working for British intelligence and to persuade British companies to give their employees strict orders not to do so.

NOTES

Part I: Spy of the Century
Chapter 1: The Tallest Building in Moscow
It reminded him of his idea: see Chapter 3.

According to several Russian accounts: the KGB 'training film' showing a reconstruction of the arrest can be seen in *Penkovsky, espion pour la paix* (Betula Productions/France Télévisions, 2011). See also *Lubyanka 2*, an official history of KGB operations published in 1999 in collaboration with the Moscow City Archives, p. 279; *Inside Story*: 'Fatal Encounter' (BBC/Novosti Press Agency, 1991); and the unnamed senior KGB official quoted in *The Spy Who Saved the World* by Schecter and Deriabin, p. 412. No account specifies precisely when Penkovsky was arrested, and it may be that it happened on 22 October, Washington time, i.e. the morning of 23 October in Moscow, after Kennedy's speech. But as most sources say 22 October and it seems most likely that this would refer to Moscow time I have placed it before the speech.

'the tallest building in Moscow' on account of its floors of cellars: it was also called this because 'you can see Siberia from it'.

a special room filled with transparent plastic pipes: Penkovsky described this to his case officers; see 'Meeting 7, Birmingham', 27 April 1971, paragraph 12, CIA.

the previous winter: *Molehunt* by Wise, pp. 132–4.

offered to turn triple agent: 'Interrogations of Oleg Penkovsky', Central Archive, FSB, cited in *Khrushchev's Cold War* by Fursenko and Naftali, p. 477 and corresponding note. See Chapter 13.

inspired one of his best-known books: In *The Russia House*, le Carré updated the Penkovsky operation to the *glasnost* era, but retained the basic thrust of events. It contains many astute insights into the operation, particularly regarding the frictions between the CIA and MI6 and the problem of doubting one's best sources. Le Carré acknowledged that Penkovsky was an inspiration for the character 'Goethe' in an interview with *Der Spiegel*, 7 August 1989; quoted in *Conversations with John le Carré*, edited by Matthew J. Bruccoli and Judith S. Baughman (University Press of Mississippi, 2004), p. 120. Le Carré was also a close friend of MI6 officer (and later head of MI6) Dickie Franks for many years, and may have had first-hand information about the operation from him: Franks recruited Greville Wynne, and several telling details in the novel were not known at the time. Echoes of the operation can also be found in *Tinker Tailor Soldier Spy*, for example the way in which the MERLIN material is guarded and revered by a few MI6 officers, and later comes under suspicion of being disinformation (although there were different reasons for that with Penkovsky's material). For his friendship with Franks, see 'Sir Dick Franks: Wartime SOE officer who became Chief of the Secret Intelligence Service in the Cold War' by Alastair Rellie, *Independent*, 30 October 2008.

'the spy of the century': *The Perfect English Spy* by Bower, p. 271.

Chapter 2: The Man on the Bridge
It was eleven o'clock . . . tinged with grey: 'Memorandum for the record, Contact and Debriefing of Henry Lee COBB on his meeting with [REDACTED] in the USSR', 28 September 1960, CIA; American 'embassy memorandum' quoted in *The CIA's Russians* by Hart, p. 61; transcript of interview with Joe Bulik on 31 January 1998 for *Cold War*, episode 21: 'Spies', CNN–BBC, National Security Archive, George Washington University.

Neither of the students . . . give them a letter: 'Memorandum for the record: Contact and Debriefing of Henry Lee COBB on his meeting with [REDACTED] in the USSR', 28 September 1960, CIA.

'*Byl*': 'Joe Bulik interview with Eldon Ray Cox', 6 September 1960, CIA.

the downing of a U-2 over Sverdlovsk: for contemporary reports of the incident, see 'Soviet Downs American Plane: U.S. Says It Was Weather Craft: Khrushchev Sees Summit Blow' by Jack Raymond, *New York Times*, 6 May 1960; and 'U.S. Concedes Flight Over Soviet, Defends Search For Intelligence, Russians Hold Downed Pilot As Spy' by Drew Middleton, *New York Times*, 8 May 1960.

'an officer friend' . . . by the time he had landed: 'Joe Bulik interview with Eldon Ray Cox', CIA; and 'Memorandum for the record: Contact and Debriefing of Henry Lee COBB on his meeting with [REDACTED] in the USSR', 28 September 1960, CIA. Gary Powers wrote in his memoir that he had not lost consciousness after his plane was hit, although his head had ached on landing. See *Operation Overflight*, pp. 82–9.

thrust two sealed envelopes . . . vanished into the night: 'Joe Bulik interview with Eldon Ray Cox', CIA; Interview with Eldon Ray Cox on 'Going Public', KRCU, Southeast Missouri State University, 26 April 2009; 'Memorandum for the record: Debriefing of Vladimir I. Toumanoff re [REDACTED]', 5 October 1960, CIA; and Schecter and Deriabin, p. 41.

The two students had very different reactions . . . fuming at the scolding: ibid.

a large transparent box of double-wall Plexiglas . . . nicknamed 'the Tank': *Tchaikovsky 19* by Ober Jr., Kindle location 2319.

an electronic sweep: with the embarrassment of Gary Powers's capture dominating the news, on 26 May 1960 Henry Cabot Lodge, the American ambassador to the UN, showed the Great Seal and its microphone to the Security Council. See Wise, p. 14; and *Spycraft* by Wallace, Melton and Schlesinger, p. 162.

some staff had taken to communicating: see *Undiscovered Ends* by Kent, p. 104, which mentions this technique being used by a British diplomat in Moscow in 1964; and 'Rep. Podell Followed, Spied Upon In Moscow', Associated Press, *Palm Beach Post*, 4 June 1971, which discusses its use by Jewish dissidents. When this practice was reported in the American media in 1987, President Reagan referred to it in his White House Correspondents' Association Dinner speech: 'And we've still got that spying problem at our Embassy in Moscow. You have to use a child's magic slate to communicate. I don't know why everyone thinks that's such a big deal. The Democrats have been doing the budget on one of those for years.' Remarks at the White House Correspondents' Association Annual Dinner, 22 April 1987, Ronald Reagan Presidential Library.

stationed in neighbouring buildings: *Tchaikovsky 19* by Ober Jr., Kindle location 4694.

Joining Abidian: 'Memorandum for the record: Debriefing of Vladimir I. Toumanoff re [REDACTED]', 5 October 1960, CIA; Schecter and Deriabin, p. 10.

'My dear Sir!': 'Letter in Russian Regarding Penkovsky'; and 'Doc Is Letter Translated From Russian And To Be Passed To Appropriate Authorities', both CIA.

a detailed description of the location of the dead drop: 'Plan (diagram) for marking signals and of dead drop, CIA'. See Appendix A for a reproduction of this.

'The main entrance is open . . .': 'Plan (diagram) for marking signals and of dead drop', CIA.

The writer also left detailed instructions: Schecter and Deriabin, p. 427. It is probably simply an oversight that the CIA has not declassified the original page regarding the signal for the dead drop, as the diagram showing it and other parts of the letter referring to it have both been declassified, and the text of this part of the letter was reproduced by Schecter and Deriabin with CIA approval.

'I know that you have no sound basis . . .': *CIA SpyMaster* by Ashley, p. 144; 'Memorandum for the record: Debriefing of Vladimir I. Toumanoff re [REDACTED]', 5 October 1960, CIA; Wise, p. 55. The list of names has not been declassified.

a photograph of three men: Schecter and Deriabin, p. 12; Ashley, p. 144.

It was raining again . . . walked off into the night: Interview with Eldon Ray Cox on 'Going Public', KRCU, Southeast Missouri State University, 26 April 2009; and 'Man tells about encounter with Russian spy' by C. J. Cassidy, KFVS12, 28 April 2009.

'near-paralysis': Hart, p. 62.

annual quotas: *KGB* by Barron, p. 100.

made wonderful Martinis: Wise, pp. 45–7.

In 1959, the KGB had created 'Department D': Barron, pp. 225–6; *Battleground Berlin* by Murphy, Kondrashev and Bailey, p. 312.

In the 1920s, Soviet intelligence had created: for The Trust, see *The Sword and the Shield* by Andrew and Mitrokhin, pp. 34–5; *MI6* by

Jeffery, pp. 183–4; and *Deception* by Epstein, pp. 21–30. Later examples include the NTS (People's Labour Union) and OUN (Organization of Ukrainian Nationalists) in the Ukraine and WiN (Freedom and Independence) in Poland: see Bower, pp. 202–8; *MI6* by Dorril, pp. 260–6 and 404–24; and Epstein, pp. 34–42. Pavel Sudoplatov has also discussed how Soviet intelligence set up fictitious underground organisations in Germany and Russia: see *Special Tasks*, pp. 155–6.

This had happened with Lieutenant-Colonel Pyotr Popov: Hart, pp. 54–5; Ashley, pp. 132–6; Murphy, Kondrashev and Bailey, pp. 277–81.

smuggling out of the country wheat and rye hybrid seeds: 'Coloradan Recalls Years as Link to Key Soviet Spy' by Greg Lopez, *Rocky Mountain News*, 28 October 1992.

'mortal enemy': transcript of interview with Bulik for *Cold War*, CNN–BBC, National Security Archive, George Washington University.

He now headed SR/9 ... presence in Moscow at all: Wise, p. 46; *Cold Warrior* by Mangold, p. 374, note 15. The CIA had overt and covert sides.

'knew how to keep a secret': Pete Bagley to author, 24 May 2011.

All clues as to the identity: Leonard McCoy to author, 20 November 2011. McCoy distributed the document, but was also not informed of the source's identity. McCoy still works for the CIA, and cleared all the information he provided me with the agency in advance, although neither he nor they have seen this book. In his written responses to me, McCoy referred to 'Penkovskiy', a frequent spelling for his name in the West during the Cold War. I have altered this throughout to the now standard Penkovsky for the sake of consistency, but have not changed anything else in his responses.

'It looks like we've got a live son of a bitch here': Schecter and Deriabin, p. 12.

There were reports: ibid., p. 14.

looked decidedly Latino: transcript of interview with Bulik on 31 January 1998 for *Cold War*, episode 21: 'Spies', CNN–BBC, National Security Archive, George Washington University.

Interviewed in a Washington safe house: 'Memorandum for the record: Contact and Debriefing of Henry Lee COBB on his meeting with [REDACTED] in the USSR', 28 September 1960, CIA.

'That's the man': interview with Cox on 'Going Public', KRCU, Southeast Missouri State University, 26 April 2009.

didn't want any further intelligence headaches: Ashley, p. 147.

became convinced that the KGB: 'Letter No. 1 from COMPASS', 11 October 1960, CIA.

He proposed that Penkovsky: ibid.

'an unmanageable beast': 'Report from COMPASS', 9 January 1961, CIA.

he followed one of the scientists: 'Reported Provocation Attempt', 30 December 1960, CIA.

on returning to London: ibid.

COMPASS fluffed it: Wise, p. 56; 'Memorandum for the record: Conversations with Mr. Helms by CSR, SR/COP and ACSR/9', 25 July 1961, CIA.

a visiting Canadian geologist: 'Office memorandum: Meeting with Mr. Pankovski [sic], State Scientific and Technical Committee', 13 January 1961, CIA; and Hart, pp. 66–7. In April, a new Canadian ambassador was appointed, Arnold Smith, and in reviewing the situation decided it had been handled badly – the Canadians decided to inform MI6 of the earlier approach, but by then MI6 and the CIA had already agreed to run the operation. See 'Canada Spurned Soviet Spy In '61' by John F. Burns, New York Times, 3 March 1991; Wise, p. 56, footnote; and Schecter and Deriabin, pp. 28–33.

'pleasant and well-mannered . . . weak and frightened look': Hart, p. 65. MI6 has yet to declassify this document, or indeed any other associated with this operation, but it is quoted in this former CIA officer's book. Hart stated in his introduction that he had been granted access to the CIA's Penkovsky files, which is presumably where he found the copy of this British report.

without a clear idea: see Mark Frankland's surreal account in his memoir Child of My Time, pp. 79–82.

recruited into this game: an account of this, with names changed, appears in *The Man from Moscow* by Wynne, p. 31; see also obituary of Dickie Franks, *Daily Telegraph*, 20 October 2008; and obituary of Dickie Franks by Alastair Rellie, *Independent*, 30 October 2008.

lunch at The Ivy: *The Man from Moscow* by Wynne, pp. 25–6.

On 6 April, he visited Wynne . . . take them back to London: Hart, p. 67; *The Man from Moscow* by Wynne, pp. 42–3.

drew him to one side: Hart, pp. 67–9; *The Man from Odessa* by Wynne, pp. 217–19.

Chapter 3: Spilling Secrets

shabby maze: see *The Buildings of England* by Nikolaus Pevsner (Penguin, 1951), vol. 41, p. 467; and *England! An uncommon guide* by Lawrence and Sylvia Martin (McGraw-Hill, 1963), p. 80: 'a vast tourist-warren with inadequate staff and elevator service'. In 1940, Donald Maclean and his wife Melinda stayed here after leaving the British Embassy in France, but moved after a near-miss on the building by the Luftwaffe. *A Divided Life* by Cecil, p. 104. It is now part of the Thistle chain.

A Polish intelligence officer . . . Peter and Helen Kroger: Bower, pp. 258–9.

Shergold had been a schoolmaster . . . British Zone of Germany: *The Friends* by West, pp. 17, 21, 124.

During the war he had worked: 'Recommendation for Award for Shergold, Harold Taplin, Temporary Major P/174752, Intelligence Corps, Italy, Member of the Most Excellent Order of the British Empire', 19 April 1945. UK National Archives, WO 373/72.

'best Soviet specialist': Bower, p. 259.

joined during the war . . . life as a traitor had begun: *Encyclopedia of Cold War Espionage, Spies and Secret Operations* by Richard C. S. Trahair (Greenwood Press, 2004), pp. 25–7; *No Other Choice* by Blake, pp. 5–144; Bower, pp. 258–61. According to Nigel West, the seeds of Blake's treason were planted before his captivity by the North Koreans, and he was motivated by what he perceived to be anti-Semitism by Sir Oswald

Peake, the father of an MI6 secretary who he was besotted with during the war, and who had made it clear that marriage between them was out of the question. West to author, 13 January 2013.

Blake had attended an early CIA–MI6 meeting . . . even the Head of Station, the Rezident, was not informed: Murphy, Kondrashev and Bailey, p. 215.

took just one measure: ibid., p. 226.

protecting him was worth the sacrifice: ibid., p. 218. Kondrashev also discussed the KGB's decision to protect Blake in this way during a panel discussion at the Yale Club, New York, broadcast on *About Books*, C-SPAN2, 11 September 1997.

In the spring of 1956: Murphy, Kondrashev and Bailey, p. 227.

'gangster act': cited in *The Berlin Tunnel Operation 1952–1956*, Clandestine Services History, 24 June 1968, CIA, Appendix D, p. 94.

'a penetration of the UK or US agencies concerned' . . . 'purely fortuitous': ibid., Appendix A, 'Discovery by the Soviets of PBJOINTLY', 15 August 1956, CIA, p. 58.

he asked Blake to report . . . as a result of his own beliefs: Bower, pp. 264–6. Nigel West's account suggests that Blake was not accused of having been brainwashed, but that in a break during the interrogation MI5 watchers saw him approach a telephone kiosk twice, evidently considering whether to contact his Soviet handler, and that when questioned about this later he couldn't provide an explanation and confessed. See *A Matter of Trust* by West, p. 92.

off to his cottage in Richmond: Bower, pp. 266 and 268.

two-part ciphered telegram was sent: ibid., p. 268; *The Art of Betrayal* by Corera, p. 143.

'about one year for each agent'. . . 'more likely 400': '40 Agents Betrayed' by Chapman Pincher, *Daily Express*, 20 June 1961; and *No Other Choice*, pp. v–x.

would have resulted in their deaths: *Spymaster* by Kalugin, p. 160.

nearly half a million conversations . . . some 50,000 reels of tape: *The Berlin Tunnel Operation 1952–1956*, Clandestine Services History, 24 June 1968, CIA, p. 51.

'rumpled and roly-poly': Paul Garbler, cited in *The Secret History of the CIA* by Trento, p. 129.

He had been born . . . running this operation himself: Ashley, pp. 31, 44–50, 60–1, 80, 86–97, 151.

handed over a package: ibid., pp. 152–3; Schecter and Deriabin, pp. 46–7.

'soldier'; 'fixed sum': quoted in Hart, pp. 57 and 68–9. Hart appears to have confused the timing, stating that this was the document Penkovsky gave Wynne at the airport in Moscow on 12 April: other accounts make it clear that this was in fact the letter he handed Wynne at Heathrow on 20 April. See Ashley, pp.152–3 and Schecter and Deriabin, pp. 41–2.

at around twenty to ten: 'Meeting 1', 20 April 1961, CIA. All following quotes and information in this chapter are drawn from this document, unless noted.

much to Kisevalter's irritation: Bower, p. 275.

'Here was a man': 'Ex-CIA chief, Russian friend made spy history' by Bill Briggs, *Denver Post*, 18 August 1992.

might overplay his hand: Ashley, p. 189.

had become enraged: *The Penkovsky Papers*, p. 68; Schecter and Deriabin, p. 64.

small suitcases or satchels: 'Meeting 2', 21 April 1961, CIA.

He also suggested disguising them . . . placing them next to the targets: 'Meeting 4', 23 April 1961, CIA; 'Meeting 5', 24 April 1961, CIA.

'real big mess': 'Admiral Burke's conversation with Cdr Wilhide', 18 April 1961, US Department of State, Office of the Historian, Foreign Relations of the United States 1961–1963, vol. X, Cuba, January 1961–September 1962, Document 121 (via the Naval Historical Center).

the difficulty of finding decent food: In June 1962, food shortages would lead to riots in the city of Novocherkassk, during which twenty-two people were killed.

Chapter 4: On Her Majesty's Secret Service
The team also examined: Schecter and Deriabin, p. 93.

'Never fall in love with your agents': transcript of interview with Bulik for *Cold War*, CNN–BBC, National Security Archive, George Washington University.

neurotic, vain and crazy: Bower, pp. 274–5.

That transcript . . . four o'clock sharp every afternoon: McCoy to author, 20 November 2011.

the following evening: 'Meeting 2', 21 April 1961, CIA. All following quotes and information in this chapter are from this document unless noted.

'war now could more or less be taken for granted': *Like It Was* by Muggeridge, p. 299.

'Where one stood in the Kremlin hierarchy': Paul Garbler, quoted by Trento, p. 244.

episode reminiscent of a Laurel and Hardy film: Ashley, pp. 190–1.

the greatest spy in history . . . in Britain's interests: Ashley, p. 227; Bower, p. 275; transcript of interview with Bulik for *Cold War*, CNN– BBC, National Security Archive, George Washington University.

'sweated crocodile drops': transcript of interview with Bulik for *Cold War*, CNN–BBC, National Security Archive, George Washington University.

Penkovsky then returned to the Mount Royal: 'Meetings 11 and 12, London', 1 May 1961, and 'Meeting 16, London', 5 May 1961, CIA.

often eating at a Lyons Corner House: McCoy to author, 20 November 2011.

he would like to meet Audrey Hepburn: Schecter and Deriabin, p. 140.

'She has a pretty name': 'Meeting 13, London', 3 May 1961, CIA. Perhaps to spare potential embarrassment, the name 'Zeph' was redacted in this document when the CIA declassified it in 1992. However, it appears unredacted in Schecter and Deriabin (p. 151), and is important to the story.

women with security clearance . . . meeting with a prostitute: Bower, p. 275; Schecter and Deriabin, pp. 221 and 268; Ashley, p. 211.

'Well, Colonel,' . . . tell the Queen about his work: 'Meeting 14', 3 May 1961, CIA. This meeting is dated 4 May by the CIA in its files, but the transcript shows it took place during the evening of 3 May, eventually ending at five past midnight on 4 May.

'was clearly not impressed': transcript of interview with Bulik for *Cold War*, CNN–BBC, National Security Archive, George Washington University.

'I realised it was not what he wanted to hear': Bower, p. 277.

Also on 4 May, the team rehearsed . . . 'I don't have such a nice one!': 'Meeting 15', 4 May 1961, CIA.

'Arrangements for receiving material from Subject . . .': 'Operational Instructions', 5 May 1961, CIA.

entered a telephone booth . . .: Schecter and Deriabin, p. 175.

Chapter 5: Russian Roulette

Oleg Penkovsky walked into the Ministry of Defence complex . . . leaned the chair against the doorknob and took out his Minox: Schecter and Deriabin, p. 176.

Before he had left London . . . 'Only for Officers, Admirals and Generals of the Soviet Army': Leonard McCoy to author, 20 November 2011.

McCoy knew from a previous operation: ibid. McCoy had analysed the intelligence from Soviet naval officer Nikolay Artamonov, who had defected to the United States in 1959 and taken the name Shadrin. Artamonov/ Shadrin was killed by the KGB in Vienna in December 1975. See *Shadrin* by Hurt and *Spymaster* by Kalugin, pp. 171–9, for more information.

in four frames: George Kisevalter interview: 'Penkovskiy Operation Parts Three and Four, Taped 22 October 1966', CIA.

Wynne arrived in Moscow . . . from the Special Collection library: Schecter and Deriabin, pp. 176–7.

'some no-star hostel in the wilds of Cornwall': *The Man from Moscow* by Wynne, p. 27.

Felicity Stuart sent a ciphered message: Stuart to author, 20 November 2011.

operated out of a warehouse in Alexandria: McCoy to author, 20 November 2011.

He had visited: ibid.

MI6 reassigned their own analyst: ibid.; and George Kisevalter interview: 'Penkovskiy Operation Parts Three and Four, Taped 22 October 1966', CIA.

'There are two hundred and forty people . . .': *The Russia House* by le Carré, p. 151.

In Britain, 1,700 people: *Spycatcher* by Wright with Greengrass, p. 265.

Dick White also gave the go-ahead . . . a further MI5 officer was similarly informed: *The Defence of the Realm* by Andrew, pp. 493–4 and p. 955, note 52.

The CIA gave Penkovsky . . . most classified secrets: transcript of interview with Sidney Graybeal, *Cold War*, episode 21: *Spies*, CNN–BBC, National Security Archive, George Washington University; Schecter and Deriabin, pp. 274–5; Wise, p. 117.

'ultimate achievement': 'Final Report of the Select Committee to Study Governmental Operations with Respect to Intelligence Activities, Supplementary Detailed Staff Reports on Foreign and Military Intelligence (Book IV)', United States Senate (United States Government Printing Office, 1976), p. 58.

'He lies like a grey stallion': 'Meeting 7, Birmingham', 27 April 1971, CIA.

'did not exactly fit the views of anyone at the meeting': 'Memorandum of conversations with Ed Proctor and Jack Smith, Re: The Use of Chickadee Material in NIE 11-8-61', 7 June 1961, CIA.

'a sharp downward revision': 'CIA/DI/ONE National Intelligence Estimate 11-8/1-61, Supplement to NIE 11-8-61, Strength and Deployment of Soviet Long-Range Ballistic Missile Forces', 21 September 1961.

'it tentatively supported . . .': 'Closing the Missile Gap' by Leonard F. Parkinson and Logan H. Potter, 28 May 1975, Center for the Study of Intelligence, CIA.

'It is my view . . . Penkovsky was able to give us.': transcript of interview with Bulik on 31 January 1998 for *Cold War*, episode 21: 'Spies', CNN–BBC, National Security Archive, George Washington University.

'splinter the CIA in a thousand pieces . . .': quoted in 'CIA: Maker of Policy, or Tool?', *New York Times*, 25 April 1966.

'a tough struggle going on in the back alleys . . . no quarter asked and none given': ibid.

'joy juice': *Jack Kennedy* by Barbara Leaming (W. W. Norton, 2006), p. 296.

'the cherubic to the choleric': 'USSR: Vienna meeting: Background documents, 1953–1961: Briefing book, notes on Khrushchev', John F. Kennedy Presidential Library and Museum.

'The important thing is to make the Americans believe that . . .': Sergei Khrushchev revealed this at the Havana Conference in 1992. See 'Transcript of Conference on the Cuban Missile Crisis, Havana, Cuba, January 9–12 1992' in *Cuba on the Brink* by Blight, Alleyn and Welch, p. 130.

Kennedy had expressed surprise: 'Record of a meeting held on President Kennedy's yacht, "Honey Fitz", on Thursday 6th April at 4 p.m., Top Secret'. Records of the Cabinet Office, East–West Relations, UK National Archives, CAB 129/105.

'invoke a war': see Chapter 4.

Kennedy used back-channel communications with Georgi Bolshakov: *Khrushchev's Cold War* by Fursenko and Naftali, pp. 353–4. Some sources say Bolshakov was in the KGB, but most agree he was GRU. See *The Sword and the Shield* by Andrew and Mitrokhin, p. 181, which specifies he was a colonel in the GRU, like Penkovsky.

'the torch has been passed . . .': 'Inaugural address by John F. Kennedy', 20 January 1961, John F. Kennedy Presidential Library and Museum.

'the greatest detonation . . . 95% probability that there will be no war':
'Minutes of Soviet party presidium meeting', 26 May 1961, edited and
annotated by Timothy Naftali, translation by Rivkin and Naftali,
Kremlin Decision Making Project, Miller Center of Public Affairs,
University of Virginia. See *A Cardboard Castle?* edited by Mastny and
Byrne pp. 16–17.

privately estimated that there was a one in five chance: *With Kennedy* by
Pierre Salinger (Doubleday, 1966), p. 190.

'the Soviet Union will do so and nothing will stop it'; 'let it be so':
'Memorandum of Conversation, Vienna, 3 June 1961, 3 p.m.', *Foreign
Relations of the United States, 1961–1963*, vol. XXIV, Laos Crisis; and
'Talking Points Reviewing Conversations between President Kennedy
and Chairman Khrushchev', 3–4 June 1961, *Foreign Relations of the United
States, 1961–1963*, vol. V, Soviet Union, Department of State,
Washington, DC.

'negotiated solution': 'Current Intelligence Memorandum, Khrushchev's
Conversation with Ambassador Thompson on Berlin', 25 May 1961, CIA.

'The thought, though, of women and children perishing . . .'; 'My
impression was that he just didn't give a damn . . .': *The Dark Side of
Camelot* by Hersh, pp. 253–4.

'would perhaps envy the dead': 'Mr Khrushchev Ready for Test Ban',
The Times, 20 July 1963.

Newsweek claimed: 'Showdown on Berlin' by Lloyd Norman, *Newsweek*,
3 July 1961. See also *Anatomy of Mistrust* by Welch Larson, p. 127; and
'Berlin Crisis Chronology', CIA.

'and were perhaps shooting each other instead of elk'; 'ten of which
could destroy . . .'; 'ridiculous': 'Report by Her Majesty's Ambassador
In Moscow of His Private Conversation With Mr. Khrushchev on 2nd
July, Annex G to Cabinet East–West Relations Memorandum by the
Secretary of State for Foreign Affairs', UK National Archives,
CAB/129/105.

'the last president of the United States of America': translated excerpts
of speech by Khrushchev in *Cold War International History Project Bulletin*,
3, (Autumn 1993), p. 59, Woodrow Wilson International Center for
Scholars, Washington DC.

'an isle of freedom in a Communist sea' . . . capacity for sea and airlift: unofficial transcript of President Kennedy's report to the nation on Tuesday, 25 July 1961, US Delegation, NATO.

a 112,544-square-foot bunker . . .: *This Is Only a Test* by Krugler, p. 167.

In February . . . one 'Doomsday Plane' was in the air at all times: 'Fact Sheet: E-6B Airborne Command Post (ABNCP)', United States Strategic Command.

the Joint Intelligence Committee had noted with alarm: 'Confidential Annex to minutes of J.I.C. meeting', 29 September 1960, Joint Intelligence Committee, UK National Archives, CAB 159/34.

the telescope at Jodrell Bank in Cheshire was adapted: 'Early warning by Jodrell Bank', *The Times*, 22 September 1961; 'Jodrell Bank telescope "was secret nuclear missile warning system"' by John Bingham, *Daily Telegraph*, 21 November 2008.

The 'Four Minute Warning' would also trigger: I also used some of this research in my novel *The Moscow Option* – see pp. 27–9.

'the National Programme': BBC War Book 1965, p. 130.

In late 1961, £72,000 . . . 'impracticable': 'Equipment of Central and Regional Seats of Government, Appendix II to letter from F.G. Betts, BBC, to W.W. Norris, Radio Services Department, General Post Office, Secret', 10 August 1961; 'Equipment of Reserve Seats & Regional Commissioners' Headquarters: Stockpiling of Records and Recorded Programmes, 222 Committee; letter from T.G. Mead, Civil Defence Department, Home Office, to Miss M.M. Randall, Radio Services Department, General Post Office, Secret', 31 October 1961. BBC Written Archives Centre, E/56/31. Courtesy of Mike Kenner.

My Word!: 'Broadcasts from the Bunker': *Document*, BBC Radio 4, 28 January 2008.

two secret reports . . . one third of the population: 'Machinery of government in war: Report of working party and related papers', 1955, UK National Archives, CAB 21/4135; and 'Thermonuclear weapons fallout: Report by a group of senior officials under chairmanship of W. Strath', Records of the Cabinet Office, Minutes and Papers, 1955, UK National Archives, CAB 134/940. Both courtesy Mike Kenner.

'The kind of person we want': 'Central Government Headquarters in time of war: General Papers', unsigned letter, 28 June 1961, UK National Archives, T199/924.

The Gray Ghost, The Fisherman and The Scarecrow: Wise, p. 32.

'wilderness of mirrors' . . . disastrous consequences: Mangold, pp. 18, 20 and 47–8. The phrase 'wilderness of mirrors' is from T. S. Eliot's *Gerontion*.

'undoubtedly the most important case that we had for years . . . regarding the Berlin crisis': 'John M. Maury memo for the record on conversation with Mr. Angleton re CHICKADEE material', 30 June 1961, CIA, quoted in Schecter and Deriabin, pp. 204–5.

Chapter 6: Sunday in the Park with Oleg
'fit of intelligence lunacy': Trento, p. 245.

the most dangerous city for espionage in the world: in 1994, Gervase Cowell stated that prior to the Penkovsky operation MI6 had never run an agent in Moscow – see 'The Role of the Intelligence Services in the Second World War' edited by Christopher Andrew, Richard J. Aldrich, Michael D. Kandiah and Gillian Staerck, Institute of Contemporary British History Witness Seminar, 9 November 1994, p. 45.

'complete order of battle': Bower, p. 278.

Janet Chisholm was no longer in MI6 . . . posted to the Allied Control Commission in Germany: Janie Chisholm to author, 30 August 2011. See also obituaries from *The Times*, 10 August 2004; *Daily Telegraph*, 6 August 2004; and the BBC, 12 August 2004.

'immensely likeable': unpublished manuscript by John Miller, provided to author. Biographical details from Janie Chisholm; *Secret Classrooms* by Elliott and Shukman, p. 23; and *The Foreign Office List and Diplomatic and Consular Year Book for 1965*, vol. 137 (Harrison and Sons, 1965), p. 159.

'I was dying to go there . . . rushing off to burn the paper': Felicity Stuart to author, 3 October 2011. Stuart, who is married, asked me to use her maiden name in this book, which was her name at the time of the operation. She provided me with information after seeking approval from MI6.

'a "portakabin" toilet, bank vault and boardroom': *All Them Cornfields and Ballet in the Evening* by Miller, p. 104.

Ruari grandly proclaimed: ibid., p. 154.

Miller and Stuart were both frequent visitors . . . the children attended the city's Anglo-American school: ibid., pp. 41 and 198; *The Russians* by Hedrick Smith (Sphere, 1976), pp. 26–7; Janie Chisholm to author, 30 August 2011.

Ruari would often dip into the bar . . .: 'Power always has its rough edges but the British would rather not know' by Mark Frankland, *Independent*, 12 May 1996. Frankland was the *Observer*'s correspondent in Moscow during this time.

'He used to tell us children that he was Jeremy Fisher . . .': Janie Chisholm to author, 16 August 2011.

'He wrote as though it were all such a waste of his time': *The Fatal Englishman* by Faulks, p. 238.

'And they don't seem to mind me being homosexual': *A Very Different Country* by Faith, p. 24.

One former correspondent on the paper: Eric Downton, who was the *Telegraph*'s Moscow correspondent in 1953, has called the paper's managing editor at the time, Roy 'Pop' Pawley, a 'servile lackey' of the secret services, and said that he was appalled at 'the widespread use made of British foreign correspondents by Six'. Downton claimed that when the *Telegraph* posted him to Moscow he was ordered to work for MI6's officer there, whose cover was the press attaché of the British Embassy, and that he was briefed by MI6 officers in London in advance. See 'Why spies and scribes have a lot in common' by Phillip Knightley, *Khaleej Times*, 11 August 2006; and *Wars Without End* by Downton, p. 337. Faulks also discussed the links between Pawley and intelligence in *The Fatal Englishman*, pp. 301–2, and Alistair Horne revealed that Pawley was 'very cooperative' with MI6 in his memoir *But What Do You Actually Do?* (Weidenfeld & Nicolson, 2011), p. 140.

it may be that Wolfenden received similar instructions: there is some evidence for this. The *Daily Express*'s Moscow correspondent Martin Page was asked by MI6 if he knew anything about a Soviet diplomat at the United Nations, Yuri Vinogradov. Page refused to be drawn, but

Wolfenden later told him that he had suggested to MI6 that they ask him about Vinogradov, as he knew Page had been in contact with him. See *The Second Oldest Profession* by Knightley, p. 386.

'Everyone knows the private affairs of everyone else': 'The Western Village in Moscow' by Jeremy Wolfenden, *New York Times*, 7 February 1965.

Burgess lived in a flat in the city . . . one of the pallbearers at his funeral: see *Burgess and Maclean* (Secker & Warburg, 1963) by Anthony Purdy and Douglas Sutherland, *A Divided Life* by Cecil and *All Them Cornfields and Ballet in the Evening* by Miller.

Janet was wearing a brown suede jacket: 'YOGA Meetings Second Phase – July–August in London, Meeting 18', CIA.

a box of multi-coloured vitamin C tablets: This has been identified as a box of chocolates in many sources about the operation, but according to Janie Chisholm her mother was 'most emphatic' that they were vitamin tablets eaten as sweets. Janie Chisholm to author, 7 February 2013.

'heroine': 'YOGA Meetings, Second Phase – July–August in London, Meeting 18', CIA.

seven rolls of undeveloped film and two typewritten sheets of paper: this material has still not been fully declassified, but according to former CIA analyst Clarence Ashley it also included intelligence that pointed to the closing of the borders around Berlin. In his 2004 biography of George Kisevalter, *CIA SpyMaster*, Ashley wrote that Penkovsky had quoted Soviet defence minister Rodion Malinovsky as saying that he would put up concertina wire to stem the flood of refugees entering the West: 'The Americans would come with their tanks – rubber treads, no less – just stop and stare, and would do nothing.' Ashley, p. 199. 'George told me that,' Ashley said when I called him at his home near Langley to ask him about this point. 'There's no way to corroborate it,' he added (Kisevalter died in 1997). Ashley to author, 13 August 2011.

'an important statement on Berlin': Schecter and Deriabin, p. 185.

Penkovsky told how he had visited . . . he would back down: 'Memorandum for the Director of Intelligence and Research, Department of State, Subject: Comments of a Senior Soviet General Officer on Soviet Plans Regarding Berlin', CIA.

senior members of the CIA . . . 'an anarchist or crank': 'Memorandum for the record', 13 July 1961, CIA.

Dulles met Kennedy in the Oval Office: Schecter and Deriabin, pp. 188 and 191.

'operational history' of their source . . . 'more than a dozen Soviet Intelligence agents active in the West': Operational History, 18 July 1961, and Evaluation of the Counterintelligence Product, CIA, both quoted in Schecter and Deriabin, pp. 194–5.

'squeezed up to him': 'Meeting 19', 20 July 1961, paragraph 4, CIA.

George Kisevalter later estimated . . . 'Out of this world': 'George Kisevalter interview: Penkovskiy Operation Parts Three and Four, Taped 22 October 1966', CIA. 'Meeting 13, London', 3 May 1961, CIA. 'Meeting 15, London', 4 May 1961, CIA.

From previous experience McCoy felt: the CIA had previously used polygraph tests on agents to establish their bona fides. Eight days before Penkovsky arrived in London, Yuri Gagarin had visited the British capital as part of a tour following his orbiting of the earth. Gagarin had left London on 15 July, but while in the city he had been accompanied by an interpreter, Boris Belitsky. A senior correspondent for Radio Moscow, Belitsky spoke cut-glass English and had managed Gagarin's appearances with aplomb. But when not looking after the cosmonaut, he had been busy meeting with CIA officers in safe houses around London – in 1958, Belitsky had walked into an American Army office during the Brussels World Fair and offered to act as an agent. The CIA had given him the rather unsubtle codename WIRELESS. McCoy had been sent to London to help with Belitsky's debriefings, but when he reviewed the transcripts he was dismayed: it was clear that Belitsky was under the KGB's control, and was acting as a double agent. However, the CIA had fluttered Belitsky, and he had passed with flying colours. McCoy informed Langley of his suspicions, and they replied that he was to send all of Belitsky's intelligence anyway: they would decide his bona fides. McCoy says his reputation was also attacked, and that he was cut out of the Belitsky operation. Penkovsky arrived in London, and McCoy returned to coordinating the translation, evaluation and distribution of his reports, as well as drawing up future intelligence requirements for the operation with MI6, MI5 and the Ministry of Defence. However, McCoy later became involved in the Belitsky operation again, and distributed all his material stamped 'FABRICATION', an assessment that was finally accepted by CIA headquarters. Leonard McCoy to author, 20 November 2011.

McCoy remembers being summoned . . . 'got up and left': ibid.

'a secret opposition': 'Meeting 23', 28 July 1961, CIA.

he had asked to be made a colonel . . . took photographs of the Russian posing proudly in both outfits: transcript of interview with Bulik on 31 January 1998 for *Cold War*, episode 21: 'Spies', CNN–BBC, National Security Archive, George Washington University; Schecter and Deriabin, p. 217.

'For me it is not only your respect . . . That is also an alternative!': 'Meeting 30', CIA.

'even a few hours of a third world war if it is unleashed': 'Nikita Set for Talks on Berlin' by Preston Grover, *Montreal Gazette*, 5 August 1961; see also 'Berlin Crisis Chronology 1961', CIA.

'most enthusiastic': 'Memorandum for the record: Subject: Developments re [REDACTED]', 3 August 1961, paragraphs 7 and 8, CIA.

On the evening of Saturday 12 August 1961 . . . The Iron Curtain had been made physical: *The Great Cold War* by Barrass, p. 133; Murphy, Kondrashev and Bailey, p. 375; 'Remembering 1989' by Brian Moynahan, *The Sunday Times*, 3 May 2009.

Chapter 7: 'Atomic Hitler'
The Aeroflot TU-104 skimmed across the tarmac: 'Meeting 31, Phase III – Paris', 20 September 1961, CIA.

'except with hostility and antagonism' . . . 'Britshits': all quotes are from Leonard McCoy to author, 20 November 2011. Other details here are from Ashley, pp. 205 and 210–12, and Schecter and Deriabin, p. 227.

'I can see now why you need twenty-five days in Paris' . . . 'we are keeping everything in readiness': 'Meeting 31, Phase III – Paris', 20 September 1961, CIA.

'MI6 sent the chiefs of its Soviet and European divisions': McCoy to author, 20 November 2011.

'highly unusual': *On the Front Lines of the Cold War: Documents on the Intelligence War in Berlin, 1946 to 1961* edited by Donald P. Steury, CIA History Staff, Center for the Study of Intelligence, 1999, CIA.

'firm decisions of this kind'; 'construed': 'Soviet Tactics in the Berlin Crisis, SNIE 11-10/1-61', 5 October 1961, CIA.

'Khrushchev today is the new Hitler' . . . 'that is what all Russian people are afraid of': 'Meeting 32', 22 September 1961, CIA.

Janet Chisholm entered the room . . . Penkovsky was impressed: 'Meeting 35', 27 September 1961, CIA.

'at the highest egotistical pitch ever noted': Hart, p. 113.

Bulik had asked him for his help . . . to impress the British with his operational skills: Ashley, p. 211.

After one of the debriefing sessions . . . Bulik was privately awarded the same medal: McCoy to author, 20 November 2011.

'He proposed that I come to London . . . a task force in the Central Building of the original CIA address, 2430 E Street.': ibid.

Kennedy had been given a proposal: See 'JFK's First-Strike Plan' by Fred Kaplan, *Atlantic Monthly*, October 2001; and related documents in *First Strike Options and the Berlin Crisis, September 1961* edited by William Burr, National Security Archive Electronic Briefing Book No. 56, 2001, National Security Archive, George Washington University.

discussed plans with him for how he could contact them: 'Meeting 37', 2 October 1961, CIA.

'from responsible Soviet officials' . . . 'Hello, Mrs Davison speaking': Schecter and Deriabin, pp. 430–1.

In February 1962, Jones was replaced by Hugh Montgomery: see Wise, p. 120 (footnote), and *The Penkovsky Papers*, p. 273.

'blow three times into mouth piece and hang up': Schecter and Deriabin, p. 432.

Harold Macmillan was asked: 'Letter to Prime Minister', 5 October 1961, Cabinet Papers, UK National Archives, CAB 21/6081.

'silenced': '1. Draft letter appointing the Prime Minister's Deputies for purposes of Nuclear Retaliation', Cabinet Papers, UK National Archives, CAB 21/6081.

checklist for nuclear war: 'Macmillan letter to Lloyd and Butler, Annex 2', 18 October 1961, UK National Archives, CAB 21/6081. See Appendix B for the full document.

'full nuclear response': 'Meeting minutes, Eyes Only For The President', 14 October 1968, declassified by the Interagency Security Classifications Appeal Panel. See 'US Had Plans for "Full Nuclear Response" in Event President Killed or Disappeared during an Attack on the United States', National Security Archive Electronic Briefing Book No. 406, 12 December 2012, edited by William Burr, National Security Archive.

'I wasn't a hundred percent certain that it was the signal . . . the following morning I sent a telegram to say I'd received it': Stuart to author, 3 October 2011. The Soviets claimed later that this signal to Stuart was to signify Penkovsky's safe return to Moscow: see TASS's summary of the indictment, which dates the call to 16 October (*Current Soviet Documents*, 1:14, p. 7); and *The Penkovsky Papers*, p. 275, which dates it to 17 October. Stuart says this is wrong: the signal did not mean all was well (as it had when calling the assistant naval attaché John Varley in May), but that he was about to 'go to the West'. It may be that Stuart simply misremembered an operational detail from fifty years ago, and there is no record in the CIA files or elsewhere that Penkovsky was to give such a signal in the event of his being about to travel to the West or defect. However, there is no mention of *any* signal to Stuart in CIA operational files. No MI6 files about the operation have been released, but a call to her on this date was mentioned in Penkovsky's trial. Stuart also told me that the Soviet account of this was wrong without any prompting – I hadn't considered it might be and had presumed it was, as described, to signal he had arrived safely. She also had a very lucid memory of many details of her life and work in Moscow, including deciphering the telegrams about George Blake, the bugging at the embassy and elsewhere, the muddy green Pobeda that followed her and how she avoided it, and so on.

stopped a blue Volkswagen . . . a sigh of relief: *Fragments of Our Time* by Martin J. Hillenbrand (University of Georgia Press, 1998), p. 195; *Berlin 1961* by Frederick Kempe (Putnam, 2011), pp. 451–81.

soon peered through again: unpublished memoir by Felicity Stuart, p. 30.

Paul Garbler arrived in the city . . . it could sometimes take two days: Trento, pp. 226–7; Wise, pp. 50–1.

'Bugging is funny in summer . . .': Stuart to author, 20 November 2011.

Chapter 8: The Man in the Black Overcoat
a top-level meeting in London: Schecter and Deriabin, p. 286; Dorril, p. 707.

telephone rang in the Moscow flat of Alexis Davison: Schecter and Deriabin, pp. 288–9.

Alexis Davison immediately called Spaso House . . . must simply have been a false alarm: see Schecter and Deriabin, pp. 288–9; Wise, pp. 60–1 and pp. 117–21; and *Spy Wars* by Bagley, pp. 148–9. These accounts differ, but I have tried to triangulate what happened from the information in them: the CIA documents about this remain classified. Wise relates two incidents in which Abidian checked the drop, once 'late in 1961', but without having received any signal, and another a year later. He and/ or his interviewees may have conflated the calls to Davison with those received by Montgomery the following year. It's clear from Wise's book that he didn't know that there were two variants of the DISTANT signal, both of which were to be used for an early warning and only one of which signified the checking of the dead drop. Wise cannot have seen the CIA files about the procedures when he wrote his book, as they were only declassified the same month it was published, March 1992. It seems indisputable that two calls were made to the Davisons' apartment on 25 December 1961: Schecter and Deriabin did have access to the CIA files about this and discussed the subsequent reaction to the calls from Harry Shergold, who told the CIA that Penkovsky had given no indication that anything was wrong at his meeting with Janet Chisholm on 23 December, nor mentioned activating the signal at his next rendezvous with her on 30 December 1961.

rang the doorbell at the home: Mangold, p. 50.

'the most important defector in history': *Spytime* by Buckley, p. 86.

He wanted a private jet . . . was eventually introduced to Robert Kennedy: Wise, p. 21; Mangold, pp. 66–7.

Angleton introduced ... anything seemed possible: see Wise, pp. 5–9 and 96–7; and Bower's detailed account of the British mole-hunts in *The Perfect English Spy*, pp. 290–340.

'I tried to urge Shergold to cut down on the meetings . . .': transcript of interview with Bulik on 31 January 1998 for *Cold War*, episode 21: 'Spies', CNN–BBC, National Security Archive, George Washington University. See also Ashley, p. 227.

'heavily surveilled'; 'seldom followed'; 'fairly relaxed about her part in the operation': 'Memo for the record: Discussion between SR/COP, CSR/9, DCSR/9, [REDACTED] re: SR/COP's European trip', 1–5 February 1962; and 'SR/COP conversations with [REDACTED]', 6 February 1962, CIA. The latter redacted name is that of Shergold – see Schecter and Deriabin, p. 294.

'She might have appeared so . . .': Janie Chisholm to author, 16 August 2011.

'handsome present' . . . 'speculated whether George Blake might know of him': 'Memo for the record: Discussion between SR/COP, CSR/9, DCSR/9, [REDACTED] re: SR/COP's European trip', 1–5 February 1962; and 'SR/COP conversations with [REDACTED]', 6 February 1962, CIA.

he spotted a car: 'Translation of letter passed by Penkovsky dated March 28 1962', 10 April 1962, CIA.

'I have just heard from Shergie . . .': 'Letter from Oldfield to Maury', 28 February 1962, CIA, quoted in Schecter and Deriabin, p. 296.

The occasion was a cocktail party . . .: Schecter and Deriabin, p. 300.

'perhaps periodically': 'Translation of letter passed by Penkovsky dated March 28 1962', 10 April 1962, CIA.

'for an initial intelligence collection program only': '"The Cuba Project", Top Secret/Sensitive memorandum, MONGOOSE', 2 March 1962, Department of State, Washington, Department of State, S/S Files: Lot 65 D 438.

'a Communist Cuban terror campaign . . .': 'Annex to Appendix to Enclosure A, Memorandum for the Secretary of Defense, Subject: Justification for US Military Intervention in Cuba (CS)', 13 March

1962, The Joint Chiefs of Staff, available at the website of the National Security Archive, George Washington University.

during an interval . . . aged just thirty: Epstein, pp. 52–3; Bagley, pp. 3–9 and 49; Hart, pp. 128–34.

potential future director: Dick Helms, quoted in Epstein, p. 46.

installed hidden microphones: Wise, p. 67.

codename BARMAN: Bagley, p. 291, note 1.

claimed that the KGB had detected . . . delivering a message via a dead drop: Bagley, p. 9; and Ashley, p. 254.

when he had recalled a lecturer . . .: 'Meeting 2', 21 April 1961, CIA.

Bagley and Kisevalter's accounts of what he said differ . . .: Kisevalter claimed Nosenko mentioned the dead drop in Moscow in the May 1962 debriefings, while Bagley says he only discussed this at a subsequent debriefing with himself and Kisevalter in 1964. Nosenko died in 2008, but in 1991 former CIA officer Donald Jameson asked him to clarify this point. Nosenko said he couldn't remember if he had revealed that he had overseen surveillance of Abidian in 1962 or in 1964, but said 'it was something I knew about before '62, and logically I would have mentioned it, but I don't recall'. So it seems plausible Nosenko knew about the drop while the operation was still running, which would of course mean the KGB also knew about it. Kisevalter later claimed that as soon as Nosenko mentioned this he informed Langley that Penkovsky's drop had been blown. If so, his warning seems to have been ignored, because the CIA later visited that dead drop again. This is doubly strange, because the CIA's own instructions to Penkovsky had specified that the drop could only ever be serviced once, due to the 'emergency nature of its use'. See Wise, pp. 71–2 and 120. Bagley insists Kisevalter muddled the dates, and says it is 'unthinkable' that in May–June 1962 the CIA had any indication that the KGB knew about Penkovsky's Pushkinskaya Street dead drop 'without our noticing or commenting or recording it anywhere, ever'. Bagley to author, 4 October 2012.

located in 225 acres of woods in McLean . . .: *Encyclopedia of the Central Intelligence Agency* edited by Smith, p. 160; and 'Headquarters Tour', CIA website.

Bagley and Kisevalter had both been recalled . . . chief of the Soviet Russia division's counter-intelligence section: Bagley, p. 19; Wise, 130–1.

Maury felt the case had potential . . . was a KGB plant?: Bagley, pp. 19–27; Epstein, p. 74; *Wilderness of Mirrors* by Martin, pp. 110–11.

'The first pressings from a defector . . .': *Their Trade Is Treachery* by Pincher, p. 295.

Khrushchev told his foreign minister . . .: *Khrushchev's Cold War* by Fursenko and Naftali, pp. 434–5.

'tangible and effective deterrent': *Khrushchev Remembers* by Nikita Khrushchev, edited by Strobe Talbot (Little, Brown, 1970), pp. 493–4.

In March, the GRU had produced two reports . . .: *The Sword and the Shield* by Andrew and Mitrokhin, p. 182.

'a doctrine of <u>pre-emptive attack</u>': underlined in original. 'Soviet Strategic Doctrine for Start of War', 3 July 1962, Current Intelligence Staff Study, CAESAR XVI-62, Office of Current Intelligence, CIA, p. 11. The document is stamped IRONBARK, indicating that Penkovsky was a source.

After a Soviet delegation returned . . . over fifty thousand Soviet troops stationed there: *Khrushchev's Cold War* by Fursenko and Naftali, pp. 439–40.

hand-delivered to those in the know: Nikolai Leonov, head of the KGB's department for Cuban affairs in 1962, in *Penkovsky, espion pour la paix* (Betula Productions/France Télévisions, 2011).

In the alcove of a cloakroom . . .: Schecter and Deriabin, pp. 306–8.

'send film and a small pistol . . .'; 'We will continue to work until the last opportunity': ibid., p. 309.

in which his old MI6 contact Dickie Franks was conveniently a sleeping partner, owned England's longest articulated lorry: obituary of Dickie Franks, *Daily Telegraph*, 20 October 2008.

Wynne gave Penkovsky some records . . . if he could get him a gun: *The Man from Moscow* by Wynne, pp. 100 and 194–5; Hart, p. 119.

'too nervy to take the pressure': Faulks, p. 295.

'the Moscow fear': le Carré, p. 148.

The CIA analysed every moment: '[REDACTED] Meeting with [REDACTED] at Fourth of July Reception', 6 July 1962, CIA.

Wynne met Ruari Chisholm: Schecter and Deriabin, p. 315. This account and Hart's both appear to be based on an account Wynne wrote of his movements that remains classified, presumably because it was written for the British.

'You are being followed': Hart, p. 120, *The Man from Moscow* by Wynne, p. 196.

Chapter 9: The World Holds its Breath

'We conclude he is under suspicion . . .': 'Memorandum on Counterintelligence Activities', 20 July 1962, CIA. Around half of this document remains redacted. See also Schecter and Deriabin, p. 318.

'1. Communications with HERO must be maintained . . . and his clandestine communication role will cease.': 'Memo for the record', 26 July 1962, CIA. Only the first page of this document has been officially declassified – the remaining excerpt quoted here is from Schecter and Deriabin, p. 319. As with other discrepancies, this is, in effect, declassification, as the CIA provided those authors with the documents.

'covert agent'; 'one special phase of operations': 'Memorandum for Deputy Director (Plans); Expenditure Authorization', 30 July 1962, CIA. See Schecter and Deriabin, p. 257.

Reliable reports suggested: 'Timetable of Soviet Military Buildup in Cuba, July–October 1962', Document 2 in *CIA Documents on the Cuban Missile Crisis* edited by McAuliffe.

McCone examined intelligence that included: *The Cuban Missile Crisis, 1962* edited by Chang and Kornbluh, p. 365.

'including medium range ballistic missiles': 'Memorandum: Soviet MRBMs In Cuba' by John A. McCone, 31 October 1962, Document 4 in McAuliffe. In this memorandum following the crisis, McCone set out his own chronology of his suspicions.

'The only construction I can put . . .': 'Chronology of John McCone's Suspicions on the Military Build-up in Cuba Prior to Kennedy's

October 22 Speech', CIA memo, 30 November 1962, quoted in *President Kennedy* by Reeves, p. 339; see also *Memoirs* by Krock, p. 352.

his subordinates advised him: 'The "Photo Gap" that Delayed Discovery of Missiles' by Max Holland, *Studies in Intelligence*, 49:4 (2005), CIA; *Memoirs* by Krock, p. 352.

'rocket installations in Cuba': Chang and Kornbluh, p. 366.

'Were it to be otherwise . . .': 'US Reaffirms Policy on Prevention of Aggressive Actions by Cuba: Statement by President Kennedy', 4 September 1962, *Department of State Bulletin*, vol. 47, p. 450.

Penkovsky finally reappeared . . . if he needed to escape suddenly: '[REDACTED] Forwarding Of Material Received 27 August, From Chief of Station Moscow', 29 August 1962, CIA; and '[DOC UNDATED-PUB DATE EST] PASSPORT IX-SA NO. 601266', CIA.

performed in the same production: *Secret Classrooms* by Elliott and Shukman, p. 23.

'happily my career henceforth was quite hairy and turbulent': 'The Role of the Intelligence Services in the Second World War' edited by Andrew, Aldrich, Kandiah and Staerck, Institute of Contemporary British History Witness Seminar, 9 November 1994, p. 44.

All these flats had tins of Harpic . . . 'HERO NO SHOW': Schecter and Deriabin, pp. 327–8.

sent a top-secret message . . . accompanied by a Project 627 nuclear subma-rine: 'Report from General Zakharov and Admiral Fokin to the Defense Council and Premier Khrushchev on Initial Plans for Soviet Navy Activities in Support of Operation Anadyr', 18 September 1962; and 'Report from General Zakharov and Admiral Fokin to the Presidium, Central Committee, Communist Party of the Soviet Union, on the Progress of Operation Anadyr', 25 September 1962. Both in the Volkogonov Collection, Library of Congress, Manuscript Division, Reel 17, Container 26, and both trans-lated by Gary Goldberg for the Cold War International History Project and the National Security Archive.

'Food cannot be provided on the journey . . .': Government War Book, BURLINGTON Manning Orders, Appendix B, First Information Slip, Annex 4, Treasury, UK National Archives.

'used up in the first few hours and days after attack': 'FALLEX 62: Report by the Home Office', May 1963, UK National Archives.

'highest readiness stage since the beginning of the Cold War': *American Cryptology during the Cold War, Book II: Centralization Wins, 1960–1972* by Thomas R. Johnson (National Security Agency), pp. 330–1.

the eponymous villain's plot: an early script treatment was partly inspired by the failed Bay of Pigs invasion. *The James Bond Archives* edited by Paul Duncan (Taschen, 2012), p. 31.

'unwitting deception': *Reflections on the Cuban Missile Crisis* by Garthoff, p. 48 (footnote). The precise wording used at this meeting is unclear. See *Kennedy* by Theodore Sorensen (Konecky & Konecky, 1999), p. 668; *KGB* by Andrew and Gordievsky, p. 474, which dates the meeting to 6 October (and, incidentally, refers to Bolshakov as a KGB rather than a GRU officer, something Andrew corrected in *The Sword and the Shield*); *One Hell of a Gamble* by Fursenko and Naftali, p. 219, which dates the meeting as 5 October using Robert Kennedy's appointment calendar; and the same authors' later and fuller account of this meeting in *Khrushchev's Cold War*, p. 463.

In the early morning of 14 October . . . the same missile as in Heyser's photos: *Eyeball to Eyeball* by Brugioni, pp. 182–99.

The SS-4 had a range of around 1,100 nautical miles . . . around 14,000 tons of TNT: *One Hell of a Gamble* by Fursenko and Naftali, p. 217.

entered Kennedy's bedroom: Brugioni, p. 22.

'This is the result of the photography' . . . 'or even a day or two.': 'Meeting on the Cuban Missile Crisis, October 16 1962', *The Presidential Recordings, John F. Kennedy: The Great Crises* edited by Timothy Naftali, Philip Zelikow and Ernest May, vol. 2 (W. W. Norton, 2001), pp. 397–401.

43,000 Soviet troops on the island . . . escalated to a full-scale conflict: Robert McNamara, foreword to Chang and Kornbluh, p. xi.

On the evening of 16 October . . . 'the play-by-play account.': *The Presidential Recordings, John F. Kennedy: The Great Crises* edited by Timothy Naftali, Philip Zelikow and Ernest May, vol. 2, (W. W. Norton, 2001), pp. 431–2.

'with fixed launchers zeroed in on the Eastern United States': 'McCone, Memorandum for File', 19 October 1962, Document 60 in *CIA Documents on the Cuban Missile Crisis*, CIA, 1992.

'pursued solely the purpose . . .' Blight, Alleyn and Welch, p. 494.

he was called in by the director: McCoy to author, 20 November 2011.

'The magnitude of the total Soviet missile force being deployed . . .' . . . '. . . put into motion last spring': 'Joint Evaluation of Soviet Missile Threat in Cuba, prepared by the Guided Missile and Astronautics Intelligence Committee, the Joint Atomic Energy Intelligence Committee and the National Photographic Interpretation Center', 18 October 1962. Document 61 in *CIA Documents on the Cuban Missile Crisis*, CIA, 1992.

'I think we ought to think of why the Russians did this' . . . '. . . we're going to have the problem of Berlin anyway': 'Joint Chief of Staffs Meeting, October 19 1962', *The Presidential Recordings, John F. Kennedy: The Great Crises* edited by Timothy Naftali, Philip Zelikow and Ernest May, vol. 2 (W. W. Norton, 2001), pp. 581–2.

'something funny in his voice' . . . 'than live without you': *Jacqueline Kennedy: Historic Conversations on Life with John F. Kennedy* by Arthur Schlesinger Jr. (Hyperion, 2011), p. 263.

'21 medium-range ballistic missile sites . . . avoiding the outbreak of a third world war': 'Conclusions of a Meeting of the Cabinet held at Admiralty House, S.W. I. on Tuesday, 23rd October, 1962, at 10.30 a.m., Secret', Records of the Cabinet Office, Cabinet Minutes and Papers, UK National Archives, CAB 128/36.

'speed of decision to be essential': 'Conclusions of a Meeting of the Cabinet, 23rd October, 1962', UK National Archives, CAB 128/36.

informed of the situation at the same time: Draft: Vol. IV, Chap. II: *The Cuban Missile Crisis*, p. 5. CIA Historical Review Program, in the Mary Ferrell Foundation Collection.

a cartoon by Osbert Lancaster: Reproduced in Barrass, p. 120.

placed its military forces at DEFCON-3: *The Cuban Missile Affair and the American Style of Crisis Management* by Dan Caldwell (Rand Corp, 1989), p. 6.

'large, long-range, and clearly offensive weapons of sudden mass destruction' . . . 'transform the history of man': 'Remarks of President John F. Kennedy', 22 October 1962, Office of the White House Press Secretary, Papers of John F. Kennedy, John F. Kennedy Library and Museum, Boston. JFKPOF-041-018.

'My fellow Americans . . . from the soil of Cuba': Reproduced in *The Kennedys and Cuba* by White, pp. 207–8.

'SUGGEST HERO EARLY WARNING PROCEDURE . . .': Schecter and Deriabin, p. 337.

Chapter 10: Nuclear Gun-barrel

'extraordinarily high state of alert'; 'as if to insure that Kennedy understood that the USSR would not launch first': *American Cryptology during the Cold War, Book II: Centralization Wins, 1960–1972* by Thomas R. Johnson (National Security Agency), p. 331.

'piratical acts by American ships on the high seas': *Khrushchev's Cold War* by Fursenko and Naftali, p. 469.

placed the US Strategic Air Command at DEFCON-2: *One Minute to Midnight* by Dobbs, p. 95; *One Hell of a Gamble* by Fursenko and Naftali, p. 263.

'slept with a wooden knife': *Khrushchev's Cold War* by Fursenko and Naftali, p. 469.

'When I arrived he was already sitting at the table . . . ". . . something must be done to save the situation"': Scali in an ABC News special of 13 August 1964, quoted in 'Using KGB Documents: The Scali-Feklisov Channel in the Cuban Missile Crisis' by Fursenko and Naftali, *Cold War International History Project Bulletin*, 5 (Spring 1995), pp. 58 and 60, and in 'John A. Scali, 77, ABC Reporter Who Helped Ease Missile Crisis' by Lawrence Van Gelder, *New York Times*, 10 October, 1995. Also quoted and discussed by Fursenko and Naftali in *One Hell of a Gamble*, p. 264.

'Fomin' now suggested: 'John Scali's notes of first meeting with Soviet embassy counselor and KGB officer Alexander Fomin', 26 October 1962, Document 44 in Chang and Kornbluh.

'horrible conflict' ... perhaps prompted by someone close to Khrushchev: 'Using KGB Documents: The Scali-Feklisov Channel in the Cuban Missile Crisis' by Fursenko and Naftali, *Cold War International History Project Bulletin*, 5 (Spring 1995), pp. 60–2; see also Fursenko and Naftali's *One Hell of a Gamble*, p. 265, and *Khrushchev's Cold War*, p. 616, note 69.

A CIA report from 26 October: 'The Crisis, USSR/Cuba: Information as of 0600, October 26 1962, Prepared for the Executive Committee of the National Security Council, Memorandum, Top Secret', CIA, p. 5.

he was in la Cueva de los Portales: Dobbs, p. 80.

'We're going to blast them now ...': recollections of Vadim Orlov, quoted in 'Cuban Samba of the Foxtrot Quartet: Soviet Submarines during the 1962 Caribbean Crisis' by Aleksandr Mozgovoi, *Voennyi parad*, 2002. The excerpt quoted here is from a translation by Svetlana Savranskaya of the National Security Archive.

'staring at each other down a nuclear gun-barrel': *Counselor: A Life at the Edge of History* by Ted Sorensen (Harper, 2008), p. 325.

'chain reaction' ... 'itching for a fight': translation of telegram from Anatoli Dobrynin to the Soviet Foreign Ministry, 27 October 1962, original source Russian Foreign Ministry archives, quoted in *We All Lost the Cold War* by Lebow and Stein, p. 525.

'We should invade today!': *The Crisis Years: Kennedy and Khrushchev, 1960–1963* by Michael R. Beschloss (HarperCollins, 1991), p. 544.

MI6's Head of Station, Gervase Cowell ... simply sat on the information: *The Secret State: Preparing for the Worst, 1945–2010* by Peter Hennessy (Penguin, 2010), p. 44.

'He did nothing ... real bravery and judgement.' Sir Gerry Warner, interviewed by Peter Hennessy, *Great Spy Books: Fact or Fiction?*, BBC Radio 4, 1 December 2012.

'While we have serious reservations ...': Corera, pp. 171–2.

He set out in his Ford: 'Spies' by Anatoly Agranovsky, *Izvestia*, 16 December 1963.

'dry cleaning': *Spycraft* by Wallace, Melton and Schlesinger, p. 485, note 12.

taken to a nearby *militsiya* station: 'Dick Jacob debrief on his arrest, Tape No 4 – Friday Afternoon – November 9 1962', CIA. Perhaps due to an oversight, the other tapes of this debriefing have not been declassified. In December 1962, an updated version of a propaganda film, *Along the Black Path*, was shown in fourteen cinemas in Moscow and broadcast three times on television, and featured footage of Jacob visiting the dead drop in Pushkinskaya Street, as well as photographs of Ruari and Janet Chisholm, Hugh Montgomery, Felicity Stuart, the Cowells and others involved in the operation. It also showed footage of Gervase Cowell presenting his passport at Moscow airport before leaving the country.

'somewhat indifferently': Schecter and Deriabin, p. 341, quoting the same debriefing by Jacob as above. Schecter and Deriabin note that the KGB were surprised to learn that Jacob was American, perhaps because their surveillance had been on Janet Chisholm. American counter-intelligence specialist David Major elaborated on this in a talk at the International Spy Museum on 15 October 2002, broadcast on C-SPAN, suggesting that the KGB 'only thought they had a British spy' when they arrested Jacob, and that they did not yet know that the CIA were even involved in the operation. But the indifference of an official in a police station may simply have been due to the nature of Soviet bureaucracy, and the KGB must have at least suspected that the CIA were involved: they made the call to Hugh Montgomery that led to Jacob going to the drop in the first place, where they ambushed him. It seems that at this stage they were not certain whether he worked for one, the other, or both: see Zagvozdin's comment to this effect in Chapter 10. I think the likeliest reason for the KGB to have called Montgomery and Cowell is the one I outline in the first chapter: to catch a British or American intelligence officer red-handed visiting Penkovsky's dead drop, so that they had proof of their involvement in the eyes of the world. This idea can also be found in the 1979 novel *TASS Upolnomochen Zaiavit* (*TASS Is Authorized to Announce*) by Julian Semyonov, which was a bestseller in the Soviet Union. The novel draws inspiration from KGB operations to catch three Russians working as CIA agents: Anatoli Filatov, Aleksandr Ogorodnik and Penkovsky. A sequel, *Intercontinental Knot*, also dealt with aspects of the Penkovsky operation, updated to the 1980s (as le Carré did in *The Russia House*).

Semyonov claimed to have been given access to KGB operational files by Yuri Andropov, and to have interviewed a senior KGB officer involved in tracing Penkovsky.

Both novels contain information about the Penkovsky operation that was not in the public domain at the time, but *TASS Is Authorized to Announce* offers several intriguing insights into how the KGB may have been thinking during it. The novel follows a KGB team as they hunt for a traitor, codenamed MASTERMIND by the CIA, at large in Moscow. The CIA transmits coded messages to MASTERMIND, who is the best agent-in-place they have ever had – via radio: one message states they have bought him 'medicine and some gold and silver articles' as he requested, while another says that his intelligence is so valuable that they would prefer him to delay defection for another year, but that they have accumulated over $57,000 in his account. The KGB intercept some of these messages – they know they emanate from the CIA, but can't decipher what they say. But the fact that they are being transmitted regularly makes them suspect that the CIA has an agent-in-place in Moscow. Other clues suggest that the CIA is planning a coup in Nagonia, a fictional African nation under Communist control. The team determines that the CIA's messages could only be picked up by a very powerful radio, 'such as a Philips, Panasonic or Sony'. They investigate several suspects to find out whether they own such radios, and after charting the precise times at which signals are sent, discount several by carrying out surveillance to see whether they were at home at those times.

The team eventually homes in on one man, Sergei Dubov. They break into his apartment when he is out, but find nothing incriminating. They set up surveillance from a flat across the street, and finally spot him removing film from a battery hidden in a torch, so arrest him. Dubov immediately offers to work against the CIA if they can guarantee his life. He starts to write a confession, and then kills himself with a poison capsule hidden in the pen – this is inspired by the Aleksandr Ogorodnik operation.

Dubov's death creates a dilemma one of the team has already raised: 'Unless we catch one of their local CIA agents red-handed, they'll deny it.' The team now has deciphered CIA messages to Dubov, but they refer to rendezvous locations using codenames, and they don't know where these are. Surveillance reveals that CIA officers regularly drive past a certain stretch of road, seeming to check the area – one of these officers is called Jacobs. They eventually figure out that the CIA has a dead drop in a cache on the bridge over the Moskva, and that CIA officers check the drop if they see Dubov placing a lipstick mark on a particular lamp post nearby. The KGB finds one of their officers who looks reasonably like the dead Dubov, dresses him so up he resembles him and sends him to the lamp post to mark it. This leads to a CIA officer being arrested red-handed clearing the dead drop; the plans for the invasion of Nagonia are intercepted, and the KGB saves the day.

There are many very precise similarities here with the Penkovsky operation: like the fictional agent-in-place MASTERMIND, HERO received coded messages from the CIA via portable Sony and Zenith receivers – but he had also told the team that the KGB monitored radio traffic obsessively (Meeting 2, 21 April 1961, CIA). He was given medical items by his case officers, had a dead drop in Moscow that he could signal was loaded by marking a particular lamp post, and according to Nosenko, a lookalike of Penkovsky was also used at one point in the operation to check Janet Chisholm's reactions to him. The novel even features a minor character called Zepp.

It seems Semyonov was granted access to KGB files for several operations, and picked what he found most exciting from them. In doing so, the book offers an explanation for the calls on 2 November that led to the arrest of Dick Jacob: the need for proof of the involvement of Western intelligence agencies before the trial. It also suggests another way in which the KGB could have been alerted to the operation: as radio messages were regularly being sent to him from Frankfurt, they could have deduced that there was an agent-in-place in Moscow from that alone, without any need to decipher the messages. See *TASS Is Authorized to Announce*, pp. 249–322. For more on Semyonov's connections with KGB sources, see the discussion between Semyonov and Graham Greene in which they discuss Andropov (and, fascinatingly, Kim Philby) at http://www.semenov-foundation.org; 'KGB link adds to author's intrigue' by Steve Huntley, *Chicago Sun-Times*, 13 October 1987; 'In Yulian Semyonov's Thrillers the Villains Are CIA Types – and Some Say the Author Works for the KGB' by Montgomery Brower, *People*, 6 April 1987; and *Neizvestnyj Julian Semenov: Razoblačenie* (*Unknown Yulian Semyonov: Exposure*), compiled by Olga Semyonova (Veche, 2008) , p. 108.

'this source will be of no further value': Schecter and Deriabin, p. 347.

'It's just awful' . . . 'Why didn't someone tell him to get out?': *Jacqueline Kennedy: Historic Conversations on Life with John F. Kennedy* by Arthur Schlesinger Jr., pp. 192–3.

'start a game'; utterly terrified: transcript of interview with Alexander Zagvozdin, December 1997 for *Cold War*, episode 21: 'Spies', CNN–BBC, Liddell Hart Military Archives, London, COLDWAR: 28/125.

'but give me my freedom after this': transcript of interrogation with Greville Wynne in *Penkovsky, Facts and Fancy* by Viktor Kutuzov (Novosti, 1965), quoted in *Seven Spies Who Changed the World* by Nigel West (Mandarin, 1992), p. 204.

'Anne Chiskow': transcript of interview with Alexander Zagvozdin, December 1997 for *Cold War*, episode 21: 'Spies', CNN–BBC, Liddell Hart Military Archives, London, COLDWAR: 28/125. The surname may have been misheard for the transcription, but this is more evidence that the KGB story of knowing Janet Chisholm was working for MI6 before they detected Penkovky is implausible, as Zagvozdin still thought she was 'Anne' – from the context, it seems that this was the first he had heard of her. Zagvozdin also says he was only brought into the investigation in October 1962, shortly before Penkovsky's arrest, so it seems his role was more to gather all the evidence than track Penkovsky, and it may be that he was never informed how he had first been detected.

'be useful again to the Soviet Union' Alexander Zagvozdin in *Inside Story*: 'Fatal Encounter' (BBC/Novosti Press Agency, 1991). Zagvozdin has given several interviews about the operation, and it looks as though he was appointed the acceptable public face for it after Gribanov's dismissal. Zagvozdin may also not be his real name: Russian intelligence officers often employ aliases similar to their real names, and in a discussion of the operation in the 1968 book *Front Taynov Voyny* (*Front of the Secret War*) by Sergei Tsybov and Nikolai Chistyakov, his role appears to be taken by an 'Alexander Gvozdilin' – of course it may also be that this was an alias, or that neither of these is his true name. A 2004 interview with Zagvozdin contains a peculiar error: it states that spy novelist Julian Semyonov based the character 'General Gvozdilin' on him in his 1979 novel *TASS Is Authorized to Announce* – but there is no character of that name in that book. The novel does, however, feature a wily and noble KGB investigator, and as discussed in a previous note appears to include disguised information about the Penkovsky operation, so it may be that Zagvozdin confused two hagiographic representations of his career in discussion with his interviewer. See 'General Zagvozdin: 80 years old' by E. Malyshev, *Dvinovazhe*, 19 February 2004.

A rare KGB file: 'Interrogations of Oleg Penkovsky', Central Archive, FSB, cited in *Khrushchev's Cold War* by Fursenko and Naftali, p. 477 and corresponding note.

'I didn't know much, but I used the bits that I knew, and they helped' . . . 'most important thing': transcript of interview with Alexander Zagvozdin, December 1997 for *Cold War*, episode 21: 'Spies', CNN–BBC, Liddell Hart Military Archives, London, COLDWAR: 28/125.

'since he knew he was doomed . . .': transcript of interview with Bulik on 31 January 1998 for *Cold War*, episode 21: 'Spies', CNN–BBC, National Security Archive, George Washington University.

'in case of unexpected danger'; 'blow three times into the mouthpiece': 'Spies' by Anatoly Agranovsky, *Izvestia*, 16 December 1962; English translation: *The Current Digest of the Russian Press*, 14: 51, 16 January 1963, p. 27.

widespread attention in the British press . . . offending some influential people there: 'Reds arrest Briton', *Daily Express*, 6 November 1962; 'Director suspected of spying', Reuter's report in the *Guardian*, 7 November 1962; 'Spy arrest may be due to a prank', *Daily Mirror*, 9 November 1962.

Joe Bulik repeatedly pressed: Bulik was himself accused of complacency regarding the handling of the operation. George Kisevalter was furious at the fact that John Abidian, who was not in the CIA, had serviced a dead drop that Nosenko had told them was blown, and claimed he had complained about it to Bulik. 'I raised hell about it,' he said. Bulik had apparently replied that it had been felt that Abidian, whose tour of duty in Moscow was due to come to an end, was safe to use to service the drop. See Wise, p. 120.

'billions of dollars' . . . 'The only risk was to have some kid . . .': transcript of interview with Joe Bulik on 31 January 1998 for *Cold War*, episode 21: 'Spies', CNN–BBC, National Security Archive, George Washington University.

Angleton forwarded his idea: Schecter and Deriabin, p. 371.

'Quite recently' . . . 'cleared British attorney': 'Memorandum from Osborn to Deputy Director (Plans): Negotiations with SIS Concerning Letter to KGB/GRU', 10 December 1962, CIA.

the TASS news bureau announced Penkovsky's arrest: 'Russian on spy charge in Moscow', *The Times*, 12 December 1962; 'Russians Arrest Science "Spy"' by Jeremy Wolfenden, *Daily Telegraph*, 12 December 1962.

'so far as I know': 'No news yet of Mr. Wynne', *The Times*, 20 November 1962.

'It's not as though he is being kept in Bradford General . . .': unpublished manuscript by John Miller.

'more problems to the Soviets than to us': 'Possible Developments in the Trials of Oleg Penkovskiy and Greville Wynne', 3 May 1963, CIA.

Chapter 11: The Trial
filmed the whole trial: *One Chilly Siberian Morning* by Botting, pp. 16-17; and Hart, p. 123. The court translator was none other than Boris Belitsky, the man the CIA had codenamed WIRELESS.

'haunted': Miller to author, 30 August 2011.

usually referred to in the trial as either 'Ann' or 'Anna' Chisholm: in the indictment, she was referred to initially as 'Janet Ann Chisholm', which was her name, but after that as 'Ann Chisholm'. See *Current Soviet Documents*, 1: 1–14, pp. 5–15. This mistake was repeated throughout the trial and in many subsequent accounts – see later analysis of why this suggests that Penkovsky was the primary source for information about her.

'Don't forget the fruit gums, Mum!': cartoon by Giles, *Daily Express*, 9 May 1963.

'Mata Hari in a woolly skirt and sensible shoes': 'Mata Hari My Foot!', *Daily Express*, 8 May 1963.

Ruari took one precaution: Janie Chisholm to author, 30 August 2011.

'I cannot make any comment,': 'Mata Hari My Foot!', *Daily Express*, 8 May 1963.

'Suddenly friends knew what one did': Stuart to author, 3 October 2011.

not even similar to the cover names: the team's cover names were 'Joseph Welk' (Bulik), 'Harold Hazelwood' (Shergold), 'George McAdam' (Kisevalter, an implausible Scot) and 'Michael Fairfield' (Stokes). Schecter and Deriabin noted in *The Spy Who Saved the World* (p. 354) that the names Penkovsky gave at the trial were 'phonetic approximations' of those he thought he had been told by the team, but even allowing for differences in reporting and the most strangled of accents all are a long way from the cover names, phonetically or otherwise: 'Oslaf', for example, doesn't bear any resemblance to any of them.

'A thousand miles from here there are my own people . . .': 'Wynne "victim of Western espionage"' by 'Monitor', *The Times*, 9 May 1963.

'vague and bullied relationship': 'Why spies stay out in the cold' by 'Pendennis', *Observer*, 26 April 1964.

'That would come with it in our country': 'Threatened by British intelligence contacts, says Wynne', *The Times*, 9 May 1963.

'one of them by submarine': ibid.

Wynne later claimed: *The Man from Moscow* by Wynne, pp. 99–100.

'had all the makings of a fictional spy thriller': 'Pair Admit "Spying" on Moscow', *Boston Globe* (via *UPI*), 8 May 1963.

'the need for other Oleg Penkovskiys'; '. . . a reflection of low moral level': 'Memorandum for: Chief, SR Division, Subject: Oleg V Penkovskiy', 10 May 1963, CIA. Bulik sent a variant of this plan four days later, co-signed by Kisevalter.

'Anna Chisholm, an intelligence agent . . .'; 'death by shooting': 'Sentence on behalf of the Union of Soviet Socialist Republics', *Pravda*, 12 May 1963.

'a long roar of applause': 'Wynne sentenced to eight years' by Mark Frankland, *Observer*, 12 May 1963.

'not expecting a Butlin's holiday camp': 'Mr Wynne may lodge an appeal', *Guardian*, 13 May 1963.

'talk in Moscow': 'Wynne sentenced to eight years' by Mark Frankland, *Observer*, 12 May 1963.

'masquerade': 'Trial of Mr. Wynne a Masquerade?' by Victor Zorza, *Guardian*, 14 May 1963.

His hair had become increasingly grey . . . watching the procession: *Tower of Secrets* by Sheymov, pp. 390–1.

taken to Butyrskaya prison: 'Oleg Gordievsky in an interview with Andrei Shary on the 40th anniversary of the Penkovsky case', Radio Liberty, 9 May 2003. Gordievsky also claimed that Penkovsky was put in a cheap coffin and that his cremation was filmed because, in the atmosphere of the time, unless there was incontrovertible proof that Penkovsky was dead conspiracy theories would spring up and soon people would be saying they had spotted him alive.

executed at 4.17 p.m., and incinerated at 9.45 p.m. the same day: KGB memorandum shown in *Penkovsky, espion pour la paix* (Betula Productions/ France Télévisions, 2011). There have been persistent rumours that Penkovsky was cremated alive, but this document refutes it. In 2001, former KGB chairman Vladimir Semichastny also dismissed the rumour as one of numerous 'fairy tales' about the agency's activities, and said that he had simply been shot. See 'Spy vs. Counter Spy: Conversations with a Former KGB Chief' by Nikolai Dobryukha, *Moscow Times*, 16 March 2001.

'request for mercy': 'Sentence Carried Out', *Pravda*, 17 May 1963.

Part II: The Fallout
Chapter 12: In the Cold

'loss of vigilance and unworthy conduct': *Nikita Khrushchev and the Creation of a Superpower* by Sergei Khrushchev (Pennsylvania State University Press, 2001), p. 682. See also 'Penkovsky: Marshal Demoted', *Guardian*, 30 May 1963.

Some three hundred Soviet agents were also reported: '"Spy" Envoys Recalled' by James E. Warner, *Daily Express*, 20 May 1963.

'I explained that after Penkovsky was apprehended . . .': 'Memorandum for the Record by Director of Central Intelligence McCone, Washington', 26 February 1964, CIA.

Khrushchev was deposed: *One Hell of a Gamble* by Fursenko and Naftali, pp. 353–4.

The President disliked the fact: *Getting to Know the President: CIA Briefings of Presidential Candidates, 1952–1992* by John L. Helgerson, Center for the Study of Intelligence, 1996, CIA p.68. Also see 'Memorandum: Soviet MRBMs in Cuba, John A McCone', 31 October 1962, Document 4 in McAuliffe, for an idea of McCone's 'I told you so' tone after the crisis.

'sufficient strength to knock out the USA and England': 'Meeting 32', 22 September 1961, CIA.

'patiently awaiting the time when we can begin a war'; 'rain of rockets'; 'In fact, there was talk about this with Castro and possibly a few rockets are already there': 'Meeting 1', 20 April 1961, CIA.

'I would like to get a report . . .': 'Top Secret memorandum from Kennedy to McCone', 13 May 1963, CIA.

'due to a combination of circumstances . . .' . . . 'multiplied the number of possible security leaks': 'The Compromise of Oleg V. Penkovsky', CIA, quoted in Schecter and Deriabin, p. 373.

'any information he supplied us . . .' . . . '. . . hurt them for years to come': 'Memorandum for Deputy Director (Plans) – Subject: Oleg Penkovsky', 23 May 1963; and attachment, 'Bona Fides of the Penkovskiy Operation', CIA.

'more than 8,000 pages of translated reporting . . .': 'The Essential Facts of The Penkovskiy Case, memorandum from Richard Helms to the Director of Central Intelligence', 31 May 1963, CIA. For the full memo, see Appendix C.

'We think that the case was blown . . .': 'Penkovskiy Case, memo for the record', 26 June 1963, CIA. A later memorandum, the declassified version of which still contains significant redactions, stated that an unnamed Soviet source had suggested that Soviet intelligence in the United States had realised that important information was leaking and had launched a 'discreet investigation' that, by a process of elimination, had led to Penkovsky: 'Penkovskiy Case, memo for the record', 8 July 1963, CIA.

'Should the CIA amend . . .': *Newsweek*, 15 July 1963, p. 7.

'treacle-footed'; 'the chummy reluctance of one Harrovian or Etonian . . .': ibid., pp. 22–3. If this seems overly harsh, when MI5 investigated whether its deputy head Graham Mitchell was a Soviet agent fellow MI5 officer James Robertson strongly objected to the idea, partly no doubt because Mitchell happened to be his brother-in-law, but also because he felt that 'social upstarts' had no right to cast aspersions on a Wykehamist. See Bower, p. 330.

designing kitchen interiors: *The Man from Odessa* by Wynne contains an illustration of one of his designs.

According to MI5's authorised history: *The Defence of the Realm* by Andrew, pp. 499–500. Neither the identity nor precise position of the source has been revealed, making it difficult to gauge their credibility. Andrew states that they were stationed within a KGB *rezidentura*, but an FBI memorandum by J. Edgar Hoover refers to a colonel with the Soviet mission to the United Nations, suggesting it may have been Aleksei Kulak, who was codenamed FEDORA by the FBI. See 'Soviet Personnel Intelligence Activities Internal Security – Russia', Director, Secret, 18 June 1963, John Profumo (BOWTIE) dossier, Part 1, p. 41, FBI. For further context, see 'KGB did bug Profumo and Keeler pillow talk to steal nuclear secrets' by Jason Lewis, *Daily Mail*, 24 July 2010.

'suitably tailored': *The Defence of the Realm* by Andrew, p. 496.

part of his job to re-examine the Penkovsky case: Bagley, p. 53.

'"liquid affairs", sabotage and assassination': 'Record on Cable from Chief, SR Division, re Possible KGB role in Kennedy Slaying from TH Bagley', 23 November 1963, CIA.

'who have long been connected to pro-fascist and racist organizations': *The Sword and the Shield* by Andrew and Mitrokhin, p. 225.

'float' the idea of an exchange 'to see what reaction it produced': 'Letter from SG Cartledge, British Embassy, Moscow, to PG Westlake, Permanent Under-Secretary's Department, Foreign Office, London', 9 January 1964, UK National Archives, FO 181/1177.

pushed into a yellow Mercedes: 'Espionage: In from the Cold', *Time*, 1 May 1964.

told that if he spoke: *The Man from Moscow* by Wynne, p. 211.

Police on both sides . . . radio contact with British headquarters: 'Wynne Flying Home', *Evening News*, 22 April 1964; 'Mr. Greville Wynne Freed in Berlin Exchange', *The Times*, 23 April 1964.

took just twelve minutes: ibid.

In January, Yuri Nosenko . . . crucial intelligence about it: Bagley, pp. 80–7; Wise, pp. 132–4.

as Golitsyn had claimed: according to Golitsyn, the KGB had circulated a 'special secret review' of the Popov case among its staff that revealed he had been detected as a result of 'reports from agents abroad' and surveillance. Golitsyn, *New Lies for Old* (Dodd, Mead & Company, 1984), p. 71 and corresponding endnote on pp. 373–4.

Now Nosenko told . . . from General Gribanov: Mangold, p. 344; Bagley, p. 152.

George Kisevalter recalled . . . uncovered his equipment: Wise, pp. 132–4.

using a wax: this detail is from a version of the story Nosenko gave in 1989. See *The Storm Birds* by Gordon Brook-Shepherd (Henry Holt & Company, 1989), p. 191.

Bagley wasn't keen . . . bound for the United States: Bagley, p. 91, Epstein, p. 59; Mangold, p. 150; Ashley, pp. 277–8.

Chapter 13: The Iceberg War
'man who came in from the cold' . . . 'late to bed': 'Should Intelligence Imperil an Innocent Man's Life?' by Chapman Pincher; and 'So Nice to See You!', both in *Daily Express*, 23 April 1964.

'the Iceberg War': 'This Shadowy War' by Pincher, *Daily Express*, 21 October 1965.

'the only rule of espionage': 'U.S. Blunder Could Hit Britain's Spy Network' by Pincher, *Daily Express*, 12 November 1965.

Claims that the book was a CIA forgery emerged: the issue was finally settled in 1976, when the Church Committee Senate hearings concluded that by 1967 the CIA had secretly 'produced, subsidized or sponsored' well over a thousand books. The CIA admitted to the committee that one of these was *The Penkovsky Papers*, which wasn't Penkovsky's diary, as had been claimed, but had been stitched together 'for operational reasons' from the case materials. 'Final Report of the Select Committee to Study Governmental Operations with Respect to Intelligence Activities, Foreign and Military Intelligence (Book I)', United States Senate (United States Government Printing Office, 1976), pp. 192–4.

'and he never came back': 'False, false . . . that book about my husband' by Robin Stafford, *Daily Express*, 23 November 1965.

given a week to leave: 'Out, Says Moscow', *Daily Express*, 26 November 1965.

repeated problems with visas: 'No Visa', *Observer*, 20 November 1966.

travel privileges revoked: 'Kremlin Curbs Diplomats', *Daily Express*, 27 November 1965.

he had even warned: 'Meeting 14', 3 May 1961, CIA.

'evasive and inconsistent': Ashley, p. 279.

one of the CIA's most controversial decisions: there are many accounts of this, but one of the most cogent is Mangold, pp. 151–69.

'false statement': Mangold, pp. 175 and 361–2, note 16.

Bossard regularly placed classified documents: see '21 Years for Missile Spy', *Evening Times*, 10 May 1965; and '21 Years' Gaol for Selling Secrets to Russians', *The Times*, 11 May 1965.

One of Wright's claims in *Spycatcher* . . . '". . . and expect us to believe this?"': *Spycatcher* by Wright with Greengrass, pp. 263–6.

Spycatcher has sold over two million copies: Peter Wright obituary, *Daily Telegraph*, 28 April 1995.

the CIA granted two authors: Schecter is a former White House press secretary who was instrumental in the smuggling of Khrushchev's memoirs from the Soviet Union, while Deriabin was a former KGB major who had once been Stalin's bodyguard, and who had defected to the West in 1954 – he had also worked on *The Penkovsky Papers*.

'primarily on the combination of intelligence sources . . .': transcript of interview with Graybeal on 29 January 1998 for *Cold War*, episode 21:

'Spies', CNN–BBC, National Security Archive, George Washington University.

'follow the progress of Soviet missile emplacement in Cuba by the hour': *Her Majesty's Secret Service* by Andrew, p. 496.

'precise capabilities of the SS-4 MRBM . . .': *A Look Over My Shoulder* by Helms with Hood, p. 216. Helms added that because Kennedy knew how long it would take to prepare the SS-4s to fire, and that there were no nuclear warheads visible on the island, this intelligence also gave the President a much clearer indication of how much time he had to nego-tiate with Khrushchev. That claim doesn't quite seem to have been the case, though: in 2008, declassified US reconnaissance photographs revealed that the CIA had missed some crucial information – the Soviets *had* placed nuclear warheads on Cuba, housed in storage bunkers in Bejucal and Managua. See Dobbs, pp. 175 and 384–5.

Part III: Walking Back the Cat
Chapter 14: Beneath the Smoke
other Russian sources had done during and after the trial: see also *Lubyanka 2*, a glossy official history of KGB operations published in 1999 in collaboration with the Moscow City Archives, which repeat-edly refers to her as Anna and Anne Chisholm, pp. 272–3.

the KGB had placed Ruari under surveillance in 1960: There is some evidence for this. John Miller relates in his memoir that Ruari Chisholm once gave him a lift home from the British embassy club and drew his attention to heavy surveillance from KGB cars behind and in front of them. He tells me he thinks this took place in the autumn of 1960. *All Them Cornfields and Ballet in the Evening* by Miller, p. 155; and Miller to author, 22 February 2013.

'we noted for the first time that Penkovsky or someone had a meeting with Anne Chisholm': Schecter and Deriabin, p. 410.

'protecting a mole in the American or British services . . .' . . . 'Counterintelligence even now cannot disclose how Penkovsky was uncovered': ibid., pp. 410–13.

'Our officers never saw those meetings': Bower, pp. 286–7.

Penkovsky: Agent of Three Powers: 'Documentary Detective' strand, directed by Vakhtang Mikeladze, (RTS/FSB, 1997).

'a mole inside the CIA . . .': Schecter talking at the International Spy Museum, Washington, C-SPAN, 15 October 2002.

two high-profile Russian TV documentaries: *Delo temnoe: Glavnyĭ predatel' Sovet·skogo Soyuza* (*Dark Deeds: The Chief Traitor of the Soviet Union*), directed by Andrey Lazarev, NTV, first broadcast 7 June 2011; and *Chelovek bez litsa: Pen'kovskiĭ* (*The Man without a Face: Penkovsky*), directed by Alexander Dzyublo, Russia 1, first broadcast 14 July 2011.

'James Garth': Bagley, pp. 150–1.

he told me as we sat: Tennent 'Pete' Bagley to author, 24 May 2011.

debriefed Greville Wynne on his return: former CIA officer John Hart mentioned an undated debriefing of Wynne in *The CIA's Russians* (p. 73), but did not refer to the Zepp incident, so until Wynne's debriefings are declassified by either MI6 or, as they apparently have copies of them, the CIA, it is impossible to judge whether Bagley's recall of this story told to him by McCaul and the date of the conversation Wynne had with Penkovsky are accurate. It's hard to think of any good reason *not* to declassify Wynne's debriefings after half a century.

reported directly to Dickie Franks: *No Other Choice*, pp. 182–4.

as he later claimed: *The Man from Moscow* by Wynne, pp. 22–6. Wynne claimed a much longer history of cooperation with MI5, and a 'Captain James' who lunched him at the Ivy in 1955. Wynne's accounts are highly coloured and contain several errors, but it may still be that he was recruited before Blake left the department.

'retired KGB colonel' . . . 'Don't believe for a minute that old story . . .': Bagley, p. 154.

Penkovsky, espion pour la paix: directed by Nicolas Jallot (Betula Productions/France Télévisions, 2011).

made him listen to one of the CIA transmissions on his transmitter: transcript of interview with Alexander Zagvozdin, December 1997 for *Cold War*, episode 21: 'Spies', CNN–BBC, Liddell Hart Military Archives, London, COLDWAR: 28/125.

He went on to head the KGB's German department: Barron, p. 226; Murphy, Kondrashev and Bailey, pp. 312 and 493, note 19; and the biography of Sergei Kondrashev on the website of the SVR.

the KGB had decided it was time: *The Sword and the Shield* by Andrew and Mitrokhin, p. 20.

Kondrashev told him that the KGB had known ... 'they had this covered': Bagley to author, 24 May 2011.

'In each case ... sheer luck and hard work': *Spy Handler* by Cherkashin and Feifer, pp. 260–1.

'It takes a mole to catch a mole': Bagley, p. 143.

'willing to fight': 'The Soviet Missile Base Venture in Cuba', 17 February 1964, CIA, p. 86.

'known to the British intelligence organs' and worked 'with their knowledge and on their instructions': *The Crown Jewels* by West and Tsarev, p. 160.

'the BBC revealed': 'Tory MP Raymond Mawby sold information to Czech spies by Gordon Corera', BBC Online, 28 June 2012.

several different versions of the story: Faulks, pp. 267–8.

'Yuri Krutikov': I can find no mention of anyone of this name in any source other than Faulks's book, but several details point to this being Yuri Krotkov, a charming and sophisticated gay playwright and screen-writer who assisted the KGB in compromising foreigners sexually. It may be that Faulks's sources got the name slightly wrong, or that Krotkov adopted a cover name similar to his real one for the purposes of this operation, which was a common KGB technique (Gribanov did the same, calling himself Gorbunov): it seems extremely unlikely that two men with such similar names and characters were arranging honey traps for the KGB at the same time. Krotkov defected to Britain in September 1963 – there is no indication that he revealed he recruited Jeremy Wolfenden, but it may have been one of dozens of such operations, and he might not have realised it was significant, or even remembered it. It could also be that he did reveal it, but that British intelligence either ignored or suppressed the information: apart from his involvement in the operations against Maurice Dejean and Wilfred Burchett, very little has been revealed of his activities, and Krotkov was employed by the KGB for nearly two decades. For more, see 'The KGB In Action' by Krotkov, *The New Review*, 111 (June 1973), reproduced in *The Russian Century: A Hundred Years of Russian Lives*, pp. 290–305; and 'Testimony of George Karlin [Yuri Krotkov], Hearings before the Subcommittee to Investigate the Administration of the Internal Security Act and Other Internal Security Laws of the Committee on the Judiciary', United States Senate, Ninety-First Congress, 3, 4 and 5 November 1969 (US Government Printing Office, 1970).

'The nature of any entrapment . . .': Faulks, p. 234.

remembered where all the pick-up places were: ibid., p. 250.

'to go along with what the KGB asked him'; 'have a chat with MI5': ibid., p. 268.

'debriefed by the Foreign Office': ibid., p. 271.

'anything that he would not want the KGB to know': ibid., p. 269.

Wolfenden had been reading his post: ibid., p. 270.

the Russians had forced him to file it: Knightley, p. 386.

'a hastily-compiled list . . .': 'Wynne Reprisal by Russia' by Jeremy Wolfenden, *Daily Telegraph*, 26 September 1964. See Appendix E for the full article.

Wynne's relationship with them was soured: *The Man from Odessa* by Wynne, p. 267. Wynne doesn't seem to have realised that the threat of a boycott was never followed through.

'already become famous as the place . . .': 'Russians Arrest Science "Spy"' by Jeremy Wolfenden, *Daily Telegraph*, 12 December 1962.

'their own version of what Mr. Wynne said under interrogation': 'Russia delays articles on Wynne' by Jeremy Wolfenden, *Daily Telegraph*, 10 September 1964. See Appendix D for full article.

'they gambled that any information he gave . . .': Faulks, p. 269.

'Nobody in MI6 would have trusted him to that degree . . .': Miller to author, 30 August 2011.

'The truth could have been less sensational . . .': Janie Chisholm to author, 16 August 2011.

'all the bits about us'; 'You mustn't talk because we have an English girl . . .': Faulks, p. 274. Wynne had said in court that when he had delivered a package to Chisholm he had been told that a 'young English nursemaid' slept in the next room, and that she used to 'go out with Russian civilians', but the bald statement that she would leak information to the press was not made. 'Wynne: British Spy Chiefs Duped Me' by Martin Page, *Daily Express*, 9 May 1963.

SULIKO: entry on Krotkov in *A Counterintelligence Reader: American Revolution into the New Millennium* (vol. III), edited by Frank J. Rafalko, US National Counterintelligence Executive, p. 195.

the snaring of the French and Canadian ambassadors: Maurice Dejean and John Watkins. For more on those cases, see Barron, pp. 170–92.

the flat in Chapligin Street: 'Testimony of George Karlin [Yuri Krotkov], Hearings before the Subcommittee to Investigate the Administration of the Internal Security Act and Other Internal Security Laws of the Committee on the Judiciary', United States Senate, Ninety-First Congress, 3, 4 and 5 November 1969 (US Government Printing Office, 1970), p. 9.

A small room with a large oak desk: Faulks mentions in *The Fatal Englishman* that the KGB had an office in the hotel, and that Wolfenden was taken there; see p. 268.

Epilogue

a $213,700 'resettlement' package: 'Memorandum on resettlement for Greville Wynne', 17 February 1966, CIA. Cited in Schecter and Deriabin, pp. 366 and 469, note 27.

'substantial' damages: 'Mr. Wynne was questioned over libellous article', *The Times*, 14 February 1967.

Whittingham flew out: Sylvan Mason (daughter of Jack Whittingham) to author, 18 April 2011. A decade earlier, Whittingham had been one of the co-writers of *Thunderball*, the first planned James Bond film, before it had become enmeshed in a legal quagmire – see *The Battle for Bond* by Robert Sellers (Tomahawk Press, 2008).

the Chisholms moved to the Sussex countryside ... '... that was a surprise.': Janie Chisholm to author, 30 August 2011.

Janet Chisholm died in 2004: see obituaries from *The Times*, 10 August 2004; *Daily Telegraph*, 6 August 2004; and the BBC, 12 August 2004.

Shortly after the disintegration of the Soviet Union ... '... as a result of the stress': Janie Chisholm to author, 16 and 30 August 2011.

CMG Moscow: Cowell in 'The Role of the Intelligence Services in the Second World War' edited by Andrew, Aldrich, Kandiah and Staerck, Institute of Contemporary British History Witness Seminar, 9 November 1994, p. 46.

Gervase Cowell also became involved . . . chairman of the Special Forces Club Historical Sub-Committee: obituary of Cowell by Phillip Knightley, *Guardian*, 16 May 2000.

'I help the old to remember and the young to understand': see http://www.our-secret-war.org, a website inspired by his words that captures oral histories of special forces veterans.

'the only MI6 officer who had a set of verses in Japanese haiku format published in *The Jerusalem Post*': Elliott and Shukman, p. 23.

Kisevalter Center for Advanced Studies: Ashley, p. 13.

Joe Bulik retired in 1976 and became a rancher: 'Ex-CIA chief, Russian friend made spy history' by Bill Briggs, *Denver Post*, 18 August, 1992.

fell victim to James Angleton's paranoia . . . aged eighty-eight: 'CIA Cold Warrior Paul Garbler: Won Payment Over Loyalty Slur' by Adam Bernstein, *Washington Post*, 6 April 2006.

anything else wouldn't have worked: Ashley, p. 228.

SELECT BIBLIOGRAPHY

Declassified documents
All the CIA's files on Penkovsky can be found online at http://www.foia.cia.gov.

The Berlin Tunnel Operation 1952–1956, Clandestine Services History, 24 June 1968, CIA

'CIA/DI/ONE National Intelligence Estimate 11-8/1-61, Supplement to NIE 11-8-61, Strength and Deployment of Soviet Long-Range Ballistic Missile Forces', 21 September 1961

'FALLEX 62: Report by the Home Office', May 1963, UK National Archives

'Final Report of the Select Committee to Study Governmental Operations with Respect to Intelligence Activities, Supplementary Detailed Staff Reports on Foreign and Military Intelligence (Book IV)', United States Senate (United States Government Printing Office, 1976)

Government War Book, BURLINGTON Manning Orders, Appendix B, First Information Slip, Annex 4, Treasury, UK National Archives

'Minutes of Soviet party presidium meeting', 26 May 1961, edited and annotated by Timothy Naftali, translation by Olga Rivkin and Timothy Naftali, Kremlin Decision Making Project, Miller Center of Public Affairs, University of Virginia

Records of the Cabinet Office, East–West Relations, UK National Archives, CAB 129/105

Records of the Prime Minister's Office: Correspondence and Papers, 1964–1970, UK National Archives, PREM 13/1791

'Soviet Tactics in the Berlin Crisis, SNIE 11-10/1-61', 5 October 1961, CIA

'Testimony of George Karlin [Yuri Krotkov], Hearings before the Subcommittee to Investigate the Administration of the Internal Security Act and Other Internal Security Laws of the Committee on the Judiciary', United States Senate, Ninety-First Congress, 3, 4 and 5 November 1969 (US Government Printing Office, 1970)

US Department of State, Office of the Historian, Foreign Relations of the United States 1961–1963, vol. X, Cuba, January 1961–September 1962

'US Reaffirms Policy on Prevention of Aggressive Actions by Cuba: Statement by President Kennedy', 4 September 1962, Department of State Bulletin, vol. 47

Joan and John Bird (eds), CIA Analysis of the Warsaw Pact Forces: The Importance of Clandestine Reporting, 2012, CIA

William Burr (ed.), First Strike Options and the Berlin Crisis, September 1961, National Security Archive Electronic Briefing Book No. 56, 2001, National Security Archive, George Washington University

Cleveland Cram, Of Moles and Molehunters: A Review of Counterintelligence Literature, 1977–92, Center for the Study of Intelligence, October 1993, CIA

Harold P. Ford, William E. Colby as Director of Central Intelligence, 1973–1976 (CIA, 1993, declassified 2011)

John L. Helgerson, Getting to Know the President: CIA Briefings of Presidential Candidates, 1952–1992, Center for the Study of Intelligence, 1996, CIA

Thomas R. Johnson, American Cryptology during the Cold War, Book II: Centralization Wins, 1960–1972, National Security Agency

Leonard F. Parkinson and Logan H. Potter, 'Closing the Missile Gap', 28 May 1975, Center for the Study of Intelligence, CIA

Frank J. Rafalko (ed.), *A Counterintelligence Reader*, vols I–IV, US National Counterintelligence Executive

Donald P. Steury (ed.), *On the Front Lines of the Cold War: Documents on the Intelligence War in Berlin, 1946 to 1961*, Center for the Study of Intelligence, 1999, CIA

Articles and books

Christopher Andrew, *Her Majesty's Secret Service* (Penguin, 1987)

Christopher Andrew, *The Defence of the Realm: The Authorized History of MI5* (Penguin, 2009)

Christopher Andrew, Richard J. Aldrich, Michael D. Kandiah and Gillian Staerck (eds), 'The Role of the Intelligence Services in the Second World War', Institute of Contemporary British History Witness Seminar, 9 November 1994

Christopher Andrew and Oleg Gordievsky, *KGB: The Inside Story of its Foreign Operations from Lenin to Gorbachev* (Sceptre, 1991)

Christopher Andrew and Vasili Mitrokhin, *The Sword and the Shield: The Mitrokhin Archive and the Secret History of the KGB* (Basic Books, 1999)

Christopher Andrew and Vasili Mitrokhin, *The Mitrokhin Archive II: The KGB and the World* (Allen Lane, 2005)

Clarence Ashley, *CIA SpyMaster* (Pelican Publishing, 2004)

David Atlee Phillips, *The Night Watch* (Ballantine, 1977)

Tennent H. Bagley, *Spy Wars* (Yale University Press, 2007)

Tennent H. Bagley and Peter Deriabin, *The KGB: Masters of the Soviet Union* (Robson, 1990)

Gordon S. Barrass, *The Great Cold War* (Stanford University Press, 2009)

)

John Barron, *KGB: The Secret Work of Soviet Secret Agents* (Bantam, 1974)

Bruce G. Blair, *The Logic of Accidental Nuclear War* (The Brookings Institution, 1993)

George Blake, *No Other Choice* (Jonathan Cape, 1990)

James G. Blight, Bruce J. Allyn and David A. Welch, *Cuba On The Brink: Castro, The Missile Crisis and the Soviet Collapse* (Rowman & Littlefield, 2002)

Jonathan Bloch and Patrick Fitzgerald, *British Intelligence and Covert Action* (Brandon, 1984)

Genrikh Borovik, *The Philby Files: The Secret Life of the Master-Spy – KGB Archives Revealed*, ed. Phillip Knightley (Little, Brown, 1994)

Douglas Botting, *One Chilly Siberian Morning* (Travel Book Club, 1965)

Tom Bower, *The Perfect English Spy* (Mandarin, 1996)

Gordon Brook-Shepherd, *The Storm Birds: Soviet Post-war Defectors* (Henry Holt & Company, 1989)

Dino A. Brugioni, *Eyeball to Eyeball: The Inside Story of the Cuban Missile Crisis* (Random House, 1990)

William F. Buckley Jr., *Spytime: The Undoing of James Jesus Angleton* (Thomson Learning, 2001)

John Cairncross, *The Enigma Spy* (Century, 1997)

Nigel Calder, *Nuclear Nightmares: An Investigation into Possible Wars* (BBC, 1980)

John le Carré, *The Russia House* (Coronet, 1989)

Robert Cecil, *A Divided Life: A Biography of Donald Maclean* (Coronet, 1990)

Laurence Chang and Peter Kornbluh (eds), *The Cuban Missile Crisis, 1962: A National Security Archive Documents Reader* (The New Press, 1992)

Victor Cherkashin with Gregory Feifer, *Spy Handler* (Basic Books, 2005)

Nikolai Chistyakov, *Po zakonu i sovesti* (*By Law and Conscience*) (Military Publishing House, Moscow, 1979)

Bob Clarke, *The Illustrated Guide to Armageddon: Britain's Cold War* (Amberley, 2009)

Dick Combs, *Inside the Soviet Alternate Universe* (Pennsylvania State University Press, 2008)

Gordon Corera, *The Art of Betrayal: Life and Death in the British Secret Service* (Weidenfeld & Nicolson, 2011)

Richard Deacon, *'C': A Biography of Sir Maurice Oldfield* (Futura, 1985)

Michael Dobbs, *One Minute to Midnight* (Arrow, 2009)

Christopher Dobson and Ronald Payne, *The Dictionary of Espionage* (Grafton, 1986)

Stephen Dorril, *MI6: Inside the Covert World of Her Majesty's Secret Intelligence Service* (Touchstone, 2000)

Stephen Dorril and Robin Ramsay, *Smear! Wilson and the Secret State* (Grafton, 1992)

Robert Dover and Michael S. Goodman (eds), *Learning from the Secret Past: Cases in British Intelligence History* (Georgetown University Press, 2011)

Eric Downton, *Wars Without End* (Stoddart, 1987)

Geoffrey Elliott and Harold Shukman, *Secret Classrooms* (St Ermin's Press, 2002)

Edward Jay Epstein, *Deception: The Invisible War Between the KGB and the CIA* (Simon & Schuster, 1989)

Nicholas Faith, *A Very Different Country* (Sinclair-Stevenson, 2002)

Sebastian Faulks, *The Fatal Englishman* (Vintage, 1996)

Florence Fitzsimmons Garbler, *CIA Wife* (Fithian, 1994)

M. R. D. Foot (ed.), *Secret Lives* (Oxford University Press, 2002)

Mark Frankland, *Child of My Time* (Chatto & Windus, 1999)

Aleksandr Fursenko and Timothy Naftali, 'Using KGB Documents: The Scali-Feklisov Channel in the Cuban Missile Crisis', *Cold War International History Project Bulletin*, 5 (Spring 1995)

Aleksandr Fursenko and Timothy Naftali, *One Hell of a Gamble: Khrushchev, Castro, and Kennedy 1958–1964* (W. W. Norton, 1998)

Aleksandr Fursenko and Timothy Naftali, *Khrushchev's Cold War: The Inside Story of an American Adversary* (W. W. Norton, 2007)

Paul Garbler, *Wages of Treason* (Xlibris, 2004)

Raymond L. Garthoff, *Reflections on the Cuban Missile Crisis* (The Brookings Institution, 1987)

Anatoliy Golitsyn, *New Lies for Old: The Communist Strategy of Deception and Disinformation* (Dodd, Mead & Company, 1984)

'E. Grieg' (Evgeni Semenekhin), *Da, ya tam rabotal* (*Yes, I Worked There: Notes of a KGB Officer*), (Gaia, 1997)

David Halberstam, *The Best and the Brightest* (Ballantine, 1993)

John Limond Hart, *The CIA's Russians* (Naval Institute Press, US, 2003)

John Earl Haynes, Harvey Klehr and Alexander Vassiliev, *Spies: The Rise and Fall of the KGB in America* (Yale University Press, 2010)

Richard Helms with William Hood, *A Look Over My Shoulder: A Life in the Central Intelligence Agency* (Random House, 2003)

Peter Hennessy, *The Secret State: Preparing for the Worst 1945–2010* (Penguin, 2010)

Seymour Hersh, *The Dark Side of Camelot* (HarperCollins, 1998)

Max Holland, 'The "Photo Gap" that Delayed Discovery of Missiles', *Studies in Intelligence*, 49: 4 (2005), CIA

Henry Hurt, *Shadrin: The Spy Who Never Came Back* (Reader's Digest Press, 1981)

Keith Jeffery, *MI6: The History of the Secret Intelligence Service, 1909–1949* (Bloomsbury, 2010)

Oleg Kalugin, *Spymaster* (Basic Books, 2009)

Fred Kaplan, 'JFK's First-Strike Plan', *The Atlantic Monthly*, October 2001

Bruce Kent, *Undiscovered Ends* (HarperCollins 1992)

Phillip Knightley, *The Second Oldest Profession* (Penguin, 1988)

Arthur Krock, *Memoirs* (Popular Library Eagle Books, 1969)

David F. Krugler, *This Is Only a Test: How Washington DC Prepared for Nuclear War* (Palgrave Macmillan, 2006)

Richard Ned Lebow and Janice Gross Stein, *We All Lost the Cold War* (Princeton University Press, 1995)

Tom Mangold, *Cold Warrior* (Simon & Schuster, 1991)

David C. Martin, *Wilderness of Mirrors* (HarperCollins, 1980)

Vojtech Mastny and Malcolm Byrne (eds), *A Cardboard Castle? An Inside History of the Warsaw Pact, 1955–1991* (Central European University Press, 2005)

Mary S. McAuliffe (ed.) *CIA Documents on the Cuban Missile Crisis* (CIA, 1992)

Anatoli Maximov, *Glavnaya taïna GRU* (*The GRU's Greatest Mystery*), (Yauza, 2010)

David Miller, *The Cold War: A Military History* (John Murray, 1998)

John Miller, *All Them Cornfields and Ballet in the Evening* (Hodgson Press, 2010)

Malcolm Muggeridge, *Like It Was* (Collins, 1981)

David Murphy, Sergei A. Kondrashev and George Bailey, *Battleground Berlin: CIA vs KGB in the Cold War* (Yale University Press, 1997)

Robert F. Ober Jr., *Tchaikovsky 19, A Diplomatic Life Behind the Iron Curtain* (Xlibris, 2008)

Bruce Page, David Leitch and Phillip Knightley, *Philby: The Spy Who Betrayed a Generation* (Sphere, 1977)

George Pahomov and Nickolas Lupinin (eds), *The Russian Century: A Hundred Years of Russian Lives* (University Press of America, 2008)

Oleg Penkovsky, *The Penkovsky Papers* (Collins, 1965)

Kim Philby, *My Silent War* (Grafton, 1989)

Rufina Philby with Hayden Peake and Mikhail Lyubimov, *The Private Life of Kim Philby: The Moscow Years* (St Ermin's Press, 2003)

Chapman Pincher, *Inside Story* (Sidgwick & Jackson, 1978)

Chapman Pincher, *Their Trade Is Treachery* (Sidgwick & Jackson, 1981)

Chapman Pincher, *The Secret Offensive* (Sidgwick & Jackson, 1985)

Chapman Pincher, *Treachery* (Mainstream, 2011)

Francis Gary Powers with Curt Gentry, *Operation Overflight* (Holt, Rinehart and Winston, 1970)

Richard Reeves, *President Kennedy: Profile of Power* (Touchstone, 1994)

Frances Stonor Saunders, *Who Paid the Piper? The CIA and the Cultural Cold War* (Granta Books, 2000)

Jerrold L. Schecter and Peter S. Deriabin, *The Spy Who Saved the World* (Scribner, 1992)

William F. Scott, 'The Face of Moscow in the Missile Crisis', *Studies in Intelligence*, 37:5 (1994), CIA

Julian Semyonov, *TASS Is Authorized to Announce* (Avon, 1987)

Victor Sheymov, *Tower of Secrets* (Harper Spotlight, 1993)

W. Thomas Smith, Jr. (ed.), *Encyclopedia of the Central Intelligence Agency* (2003, Checkmark)

Pavel and Anatoli Sudoplatov with Jerrold L. Schecter and Leona P. Schecter, *Special Tasks* (Little, Brown, 1995)

Viktor Suvorov, *Aquarium: The Career and Defection of a Soviet Military Spy* (Hamish Hamilton, 1985)

William Taubman, *Khrushchev: The Man and His Era* (W. W. Norton, 2004)

Evan Thomas, 'A Singular Opportunity: Gaining Access to CIA's Records', Center for the Study of Intelligence, *Studies in Intelligence*, 39: 5 (1996), CIA

Richard C. S. Trahair, *Encyclopedia of Cold War Espionage, Spies and Secret Operations* (Greenwood Press, 2004)

Joseph Trento, *The Secret History of the CIA* (Prima, 2001)

Sergei Tsybov and Nikolai Chistyakov, *Front Taynov Voyny* (*Front of the Secret War*), (Military Publishing House, 1968)

Oleg Tumanov, *Tumanov: Confessions of a KGB Agent* (Edition Q, 1993)

Alex von Tunzelmann, *Red Heat: Conspiracy, Murder and the Cold War in the Caribbean* (Simon & Schuster, 2011)

Robert Wallace and H. Keith Melton with Henry Robert Schlesinger, *Spycraft* (Bantam, 2010)

Michael Warner, 'Lessons Unlearned: The CIA's Internal Probe of the Bay of Pigs Affair', Center for the Study of Intelligence, *Studies in Intelligence*, 42:5 (Winter 1998–9)

Deborah Welch Larson, *Anatomy of Mistrust: U.S.–Soviet Relations during the Cold War* (Cornell University Press, 2000)

Nigel West, *A Matter of Trust: M.I.5. 1945–72* (Coronet, 1982)

Nigel West, *The Friends* (Weidenfeld & Nicolson, 1988)

Nigel West and Oleg Tsarev, *The Crown Jewels* (HarperCollins, 1999)

Nigel West and Oleg Tsarev (eds), *Triplex* (Yale University Press, 2009)

Mark J. White (ed.), *The Kennedys and Cuba: The Declassified Documentary History* (Ivan R. Dee, 1999)

David Wise, *Molehunt* (Random House, 1992)

Peter Wright with Paul Greengrass, *Spycatcher* (Dell, 1988)

Greville Wynne, *The Man from Moscow* (Hutchinson, 1967)

Greville Wynne, *The Man from Odessa* (Granada, 1983)

INDEX